SPECIAL AGENT

Special Agent

TWENTY-FIVE YEARS WITH THE U.S. TREASURY

DEPARTMENT AND SECRET SERVICE

Frank J. Wilson & Beth Day

FREDERICK MULLER LIMITED
LONDON

First published in Great Britain 1966 by
Frederick Muller Limited
Printed in Great Britain
by Ebenezer Baylis and Son Limited
The Trinity Press, Worcester, and London
and bound by Leighton Straker Bookbinding Co. Ltd.

for
Judith

ILLUSTRATIONS

1

The terrible tragedy at Dallas, on November 22, 1963, when our President, John F. Kennedy, was assassinated by the Marxist Lee Harvey Oswald and the subsequent report and recommendations made by the Warren Commission have turned the country's attention in an unprecedented way on the duties and methods of the United States Secret Service. For it is the first and foremost job of the Service to protect the life of the President.

This was not always so. In 1865, the Secret Service was founded, originally, as a division of the Treasury Department, to deal with counterfeiting. In 1894, after President Cleveland's wife had become alarmed by threats upon her husband's life and the lives of her children, the Service was called upon to provide protection for the President and his family on an informal, part-time basis. A small detail of men was assigned to the White House, and also to accompany the President's family to their summer home in Massachusetts on vacations. Members of the opposition in Congress complained bitterly at this expense, for which there was then no appropriation. But President Cleveland held his ground and retained the White House detail during his tenure in office.

His successor, President McKinley, yielded to political pressure, however, and except for a temporary wartime detail during the Spanish American war, the White House guard was abolished. On its own authority, the Secret Service sent two or three agents along with the President when he traveled, but this small, informal detail was in no way adequate to protect the President when he made scheduled public appearances before crowds of people, such as that gathered at the Pan American Exposition, to "shake hands with the President," on that fateful day in 1901.

After McKinley's assassination, Congress awoke to the staggering fact that this country had lost three of our Presidents by assassination in a short thirty-six year period—Lincoln, Garfield, and McKinley—and in 1902 an appropriation was made and a formal White House detail established. The Secret Service was given the responsibility for the protection of the life of the President on a full-time basis.

During the following sixty-two years, which included two world wars, the Secret Service efficiently protected nine Presidents and was highly commended by them for its devoted and able protection. The Service also conducted with honor and with success many important and hazardous assignments, such as the investigation of the original Ku Klux Klan, in the late sixties and early seventies; the exposure of the Spanish spy ring, in 1898; the Western land fraud investigation; the notorious Louisiana lottery, in the first decade of this century; and the disgraceful Teapot Dome scandal, in the roaring twenties.

From 1914 to 1917, President Wilson authorized Secretary of the Treasury William Gibbs McAdoo to use Secret Service agents to investigate violations of Wilson's 1914 Neutrality Proclamation. In 1915, Frank Burke, an ace undercover agent, followed Dr. Heinrich Friedrich Albert, a high German official functioning in the United States as an undercover agent of the Kaiser, onto an elevated train in New York City, where he snatched a fat black briefcase from Dr. Albert. The "Albert Papers," as they were known, turned out to contain documentary dynamite, proving conclusively that Germany was violating the Neutrality Proclamation with extensive espionage activities in this country prior to our entry in the war. It was one of the most important single-handed accomplishments in the history of World War One and of the Secret Service, a coup which German propagandist George Sylvester Viereck stated in his memoirs was to Germany "like the loss of the battle of the Marne."

It is no empty or idle boast that the agents of the United States Secret Service and the White House Police are ready at all times to lay down their lives for the President, if the need arises. During the decade before and during World War Two, when, as Chief of the Secret Service, it was my privilege and responsibility to protect the lives of Presidents Roosevelt and Truman, I have seen our agents frantically leap high in the air to intercept a bouquet or other flying object hurled at the President from a high window or balcony along a parade route, for fear it might enclose a powerful hidden bomb timed to explode the second it hit in or near the President's auto. Lately, most of our agents were former college football players adept at intercepting forward passes. The agents realized that perhaps a bomb might suddenly explode when the flying object struck their hands, but they faithfully and efficiently performed their duty by diverting it from the President.

They stopped bullets, too. In 1950, when two Puerto Rican fanatics stormed Blair House, the temporary home of President Truman, in a fast, fierce, furious, and desperate attempt to assassinate him, the expert marksmanship on the part of the Secret Service men cut down the would-be killers. But in that battle of bullets one White House officer was killed and two were seriously wounded.

Since the members of the Secret Service—as well as the other Treasury Department agents handling federal crimes

—traditionally shun publicity, their methods of operation are often little understood by the citizens they serve. Whenever I read a lurid fictional account of the operation of so-called "government agents" or watch them blasting away with machine guns and giving the "third degree" to their victims on my television set, I don't know whether to laugh or shudder at such misrepresentation of our work. In my own more than a quarter of a century as a special agent for the government, first in the Intelligence division of the Internal Revenue Bureau and later as Chief of the Secret Service, I often ran across equally distorted views of how government investigators work.

Once, during my long fight to put racketeer Al Capone behind bars, a fellow agent, Bill Hodgins, was questioning a former prizefighter named Tony about a shipment of whiskey, which he and three Capone guerrillas had hijacked from the Bugs Moran Syndicate. This was in one corner of our office in Chicago, while I was nearby querying a recalcitrant attorney about a sizeable item of income which he claimed was not taxable. Both Tony and the attorney were shouting their answers and, to shut up my man with a legal decision, I yelled over both of them: "Bill, bring me my regulation forty-five; I'm going to settle this noise in short order!"

Poor Tony thought I was referring to him. He rushed over to me, his beefy face pale with fright. "Please, please mister! Don't get your gun. I won't say another word!"

At this point, Bill handed me what I had asked for, and I showed it to Tony. It was a two-inch thick book, titled *Regulations Forty Five, Internal Revenue Bureau.*

In point of fact, I wore the regulation .32 caliber Colt revolver in a shoulder holster under my coat for twenty-eight years without ever having occasion to use it, although there were certainly times when I was afraid I might have to. And practice as I might, my marksmanship never reached a level higher than "fair."

Government agents must "get their man," it is true; but

not with any flash of gunfire or sock in the jaw. When we get them, we must get them for good, legally and ethically, so that their menace can be permanently removed from society. As a government agent I have had to fight war profiteers, public enemies, baby snatchers, tax cheaters, would-be assassins, and corrupt public officials. But my weapon had to be the final one: an airtight case that would stand up in any court, before any jury, and by which lawbreakers would receive sentence for their crimes, either to the electric chair, Alcatraz or other federal penitentiaries, or, in the case of the mentally deranged, to the confinement of mental institutions.

The careful, step-by-step preliminary work in building a federal case is usually conducted with few—and sometimes no—interviews with the criminals themselves. The one method we use which involves any physical discomfort on the part of the person we are after is the "bench treatment." This consists of relegating forgetful, defiant, and unwilling witnesses to a bench outside the Grand Jury room for hour after hour, day after day, "waiting to be called." It's surprising how their memories can improve under such conditions —especially the most active, outdoor types.

My desire to go into law enforcement work stemmed from the example set by my father, a farm boy turned policeman in Buffalo, New York. A strong, dedicated man, he epitomized for me an honorable life, one of duty and bravery. The proudest moment of my boyhood was when my father was selected to guard President McKinley during the public parade when he came to Buffalo to speak to the annual convention of veterans of the Grand Army of the Republic in 1897.

No Knight of the Holy Grail ever seemed more heroic to my mind than my father that day, riding alongside the Presidential carriage, magnificent in his blue uniform with brass buttons and gray helmet, astride a frisky black mare. Mother and I had been waiting on Main Street more than an hour to see Papa riding in the parade, and just as the parade passed us, Papa's horse, Blackie, reared up on her hind legs. Mother screamed. But Papa just smiled down at us, calmed the horse, and rode on.

He not only rode in the parade that day, but my father also guarded the President when he appeared in the streets of Buffalo during that entire week. When the President and his party had gone, Father said: "It's been a rough, strenuous week. But it was worth it to get that cordial handshake and thanks from the President of the United States!"

I decided at that moment that one day I, too, would guard Presidents.

It was but a brief four years later, on another trip to Buffalo, that President McKinley was shot down, while standing in the receiving line at the Pan American Exposition in the Temple of Music. He was assassinated by Anarchist Leon Czolgosz, who took his place in the line of citizens waiting to greet the President, with a revolver hidden in his bandaged hand. Police, detectives, guards, and soldiers were all around, but no efforts had been made to screen the crowd who pushed up against and touched the President.

President McKinley lingered between life and death for a few days. The night that he actually died, I had a first-hand view of how an efficient local police department could handle an incendiary situation. As a thirteen-year-old kid, I was part of the rabid mob that gathered around the Buffalo police headquarters where the assassin, Czolgosz, was in custody. They were shouting.

"Lynch him!"

"Let's kill the bastard!"

"Put the fiend in a boat and send him over Niagara Falls!"

As the crowd grew in numbers—by midnight it had reached nearly two thousand—their collective fury reached fever pitch. The police, fearing they would seize Czolgosz and lynch him, sent for reinforcements.

Reinforcements of several patrol wagons filled with police arrived just as one of the mob's ringleaders was yelling:

"Let's rush the station and drag the sonofabitch out of there!"

While the extra forces got the crowd under control, I noticed that one of the patrol wagons—filled with a number of uniformed police, one of whom I recognized as my friend, Captain John Martin, who was in charge of that detail— left the station. No one questioned the wagon that was leaving. While the threatening crowd still milled around the entrance to the station, Captain Martin succeeded in quietly spiriting his prisoner, disguised in a police uniform, away from danger. This simple ruse, which deprived the furious mob of its intended prey, seemed to me the quintessence of police strategy. As a friend of Captain Martin's, I felt a vicarious thrill, as though I, too, had been a link in this chain of dramatic events. I could think of no finer career than to be numbered amongst such efficient officers of the law.

It was two in the morning before the mob realized it had been outwitted. The jail to which the assassin was moved was kept secret. The crowd had no choice but to break up and go home. Which I also did, to find my father waiting on the verandah with a definite purpose in mind, promptly carried out in the woodshed regardless of the hour!

What a contrast between the capable methods with which Captain Martin handled the Buffalo crisis and the bumbling inefficiency displayed by the Dallas police at the time of President Kennedy's assassination! Since the murder was committed in that city, the Dallas Police Department had exclusive jurisdiction to investigate the crime and apprehend the guilty person from the time the first shots were fired. When they rushed into the building where the assassin, Lee Harvey Oswald, was hiding, he was allowed to escape. Oswald was captured within two hours, but not before he had shot and fatally wounded a Dallas police officer.

With maximum publicity, Oswald was held for two days at police headquarters, while the Dallas police chief boasted on television and over the radio that they had a sure case against him. Meanwhile, threats against Oswald's life were made and the police belatedly decided they should remove him to the county jail. Instead of moving him secretly, they *publicly announced* the hour at which he was to be moved and allowed press, radio, and television representatives to be present. The removal became a melodramatic spectacle, which ended in a disgraceful and tragic event, when, in the basement of police headquarters, Jack Ruby, a man with a Dallas police record, approached Oswald, placed a revolver in his middle, and killed him, as the negligent Dallas police stood by and millions of the nation's astonished television viewers looked on.

That unjustified murder of the assassin of President Kennedy without a fair trial by a jury of his peers will be a permanent blot on the records of American justice. It gave the unfriendly press in Communist countries an opportunity to allege that the assassin was brazenly murdered, in order to hide the facts from the American public. Oswald's lips were forever sealed and the possibility of learning directly from him the background and motive for his horrendous crime vanished.

One of the difficulties facing the Secret Service charged with the protection of the President is that the degree of co-operation and the efficiency of the local police varies from city to city. In some of the larger cities, fortunately, this is extremely high, especially in New York City, Washington, D.C., and Chicago, where the President makes his most frequent public appearances. During my term as Chief, to encourage such co-operation, I made speeches before the annual conventions of the International Association of Chiefs of Police, stressing the deep appreciation of the Secret Service for the highly valuable co-operation rendered by the police of many cities, counties, and states.

Without their active assistance, every trip of the President outside the White House would be tremendously hazardous, since the manpower of the Secret Service is limited. The duties of the Service and the local police are made much more difficult because powerful politicians, political strategists, and local reception committees give only scant consideration for the safety of the President or other persons who are to be protected. They appear principally interested in garnering or getting votes for the President and for local officials running for election on his ticket. They are concerned only with staging big parades and public receptions with maximum fanfare, which turn out to have minimum security precautions.

An example of such committee disregard occurred in 1939 when the King and Queen of England were the guests of our country and visited New York City. I went to New York to confer with officials regarding the program. It was necessary for me, with the help of Police Commissioner Lewis Valentine, to force Grover Whalan, the Chairman of the Reception Committee, to cancel his plans for a slow parade up Broadway with the royal couple in an open car where they would be targets not only for the traditional ticker tape but for an assassin's bullets as well. Valentine strongly supported me in my objection to that parade when I emphatically told Whalan that we were charged with the safety of the King and Queen and that if anything happened to them it would be Valentine and me who would be responsible. Whelan bitterly protested, but we finally persuaded him to settle for a fast auto trip from the Battery up the West Side highway plus a reception at the World's Fair and a formal luncheon, where we could enforce appropriate protection measures.

President Kennedy might be living today if it had been possible to convince him and his political strategists of the wisdom of a similar procedure at Dallas. However, I do not think the tragedy should, even to the slightest degree, reflect on the Secret Service. It has limited manpower and a continuous lack of success in convincing all Presidents that they should avoid the hazards of parades in open autos and should discourage invitations to appear before large groups or assemblies where a crackpot or a potential assassin might easily gain admittance.

The route by which men enter the Secret Service is personal and varied. Some become government agents for purely altruistic reasons; others for personal prestige. The young man who chooses such a career cannot expect to accumulate even a small fortune, although upon retirement he will have earned a substantial annuity and he will enjoy the respect of his fellow Americans.

Even in the slow, detailed work of pinning an income tax evasion rap on a racketeer there is a thrill, because danger is always with you. A successful government agent must love his job—and take a measure of his pay in the gratification that comes from successfully protecting our country and its citizens.

By the time I had graduated from high school, I was big enough and strong enough for the career I sought: that of policeman or detective. But I did have a physical handicap, bad eyes. I was woefully nearsighted. When World War One came along, I faked the eye test to get accepted, but they caught up with me on the rifle range at Fort Niagara, New York. My colonel, who was watching a regular Army sergeant coaching me, happened to notice that I could not hit the broadside of a barn. He ordered me to look at a hill about half a mile away and tell him what I saw.

"Two white horses, sir," I replied promptly.

"Two white cows," corrected the colonel, dryly. "Report to the medical officer for an eye examination."

The doctor put an eye chart in front of me and said, "Read."

All I could make out was an enormous "E" at the top of the chart.

The doctor promptly ordered an honorable discharge for physical disability. I was brokenhearted. Here was the greatest epic of all the ages and I could have no part in it! The one crumb of consolation I had was a report that Canada had recently reduced the physical qualifications for her army. I took a steamer across Lake Ontario to Toronto and tried to enlist there. No luck.

I then cast about for some way to help the war effort through civilian service. When the Treasury Department advertised for men to take the Civil Service examination for criminal investigator, I took the test and passed it. The Honorable Herbert Hoover had just been appointed food administrator by President Wilson, and I applied to him for a job as investigator for the Food Administration. A telegram came ordering me to report to the United States Food Administration office in New York City. They did not give me a blue uniform with brass buttons, but they did give me a big badge and a pocket commission signed by Food Administrator Hoover and with my picture on it. My title was Special Investigator.

I was a government agent, on the first rung of the law enforcement ladder which was eventually to lead me into the Secret Service.

2

The food shortage in the countries of our European Allies was extremely acute in 1918. The Kaiser's submarines had sunk hundreds of ships with cargoes of food bound for France, Italy, and England. Our government was informed confidentially by authorities in Great Britain, France, and Italy that if the shipments of food which the United States had pledged were not maintained, the Allies might not be able to continue the war. French army rations had been curtailed once and Italian army rations had been reduced twice. These same sources reported that at one time only about two weeks' supply of food was on hand in England. As a result of Herbert Hoover's campaign, food was being saved by loyal American housewives and in public restaurants. Sugar and flour were rationed. Food processors and dealers were licensed by the Food Administration in order to prevent profiteering. Food production, especially wheat, was substantially increased by patriotic farmers. The Food Administration promoted meatless days.

"FOOD WILL WIN THE WAR"—Herbert Hoover spread that pertinent slogan to every home and hamlet across America.

A short time after I reported to the Food Administration in New York City, an office was opened in Buffalo, to which I was transferred.

James B. Stafford, a well-known and highly respected citizen, had just been appointed United States Food Administrator for Northern and Western New York State, with headquarters at Buffalo. He was seventy years old, over six feet tall, and straight as an arrow. "Don't be afraid to bring in the Big Fish if you catch any," he said grimly.

This was exactly what I needed to build up my enthusiasm. Turned down for overseas combat, I threw myself into the job of locating and exposing war profiteers as zealously as if every one of them had been conspiring against me personally.

As we began rounding up violators, Mr. Stafford quickly realized that if we followed the regular procedure with criminal cases—taking them through the United States District Attorney for presentation to the United States Commissioner, the Grand Jury, and finally for prosecution in Federal Court —the war might well be over before the majority of the cases were settled.

Besides, what we needed was immediate publicity focused on these violators to deter others. Mr. Stafford urged me to aim for the "big fish," on the sound premise that prosecution of them would in turn frighten "little fish" into obeying the food laws. The bigger and more important the firms or individuals that are prosecuted, the less chance the little fellow feels he has to get away with a similar crime.

To provide a blast of unfavorable publicity, plus loss of prestige and public patronage, which we wanted to keep potential hoarders and profiteers in line, we worked out our own system of hearings. I acted as prosecuting attorney, summarizing the case and presenting the evidence. Mr. Stafford then took over, chastising and shaming the merchants for their lack of patriotism. Although he could revoke or suspend their licenses, Mr. Stafford generally concluded our informal hearings (always well attended by the press) by offering the violators the "alternative" of making a substantial voluntary donation to the Red Cross. The prompt unfavorable publicity carried by the newspapers, and the fall away of patronage by loyal citizens, was usually sufficient punishment without the loss of a license. It also accomplished our prime purpose, which was to discourage other violators.

Mr. Stafford and I ran the office alone for a time. Later we were assigned more investigators, ending up with five agents and two stenographers. I was promoted to Chief Investigator and given full powers to prosecute any profiteer, big or little, until the war was ended.

In spite of the success of our efforts, however, we knew that we were skating on thin legal ice, since we had no real authority to force anyone to make a "voluntary" donation.

Finally we met our match, an "unco-operative" millionaire, guilty of hoarding sugar and flour (two of my investigators, acting on a tip, had found five barrels of each in his barn under layers of hay), who turned up with his lawyer and defied the Administrator, claiming that Mr. Stafford had no right to hold the hearing or force a violator to make a "voluntary" contribution.

I was feeling pretty sick about the whole thing when Mr. Stafford came up with a brilliant suggestion. "Let's see if we can get the United States Attorney to get a quick indictment and then set the case for a prompt trial."

It was my first appearance before a Federal Grand Jury, and even now I can relive the chilly, nervous tension that took possession of me, as I tugged at my tie, smoothed my hair with my palms, and pulled the creases out of my coat. But I returned to the office in a glow of excited triumph, for we got the indictment.

"Smart boy, Frank!" said Mr. Stafford. "If you ever do other than law enforcement work, you'll be a criminal yourself!"

It was an education and a privilege to work with as zealous a public servant as Mr. Stafford, but I also learned, with him, the disaster that can befall a man who dares to go after the really big fish.

Shortly after our millionaire's case was closed, I got a tip from a wholesale dealer in Chippewa that Armour & Company were selling cold-storage butter as fresh, and charging excessive prices.

Cautioning me to build up a watertight case, Mr. Stafford warned me: "A big corporation like that will fight us to the bitter end, so we must be absolutely certain that our case is sound."

In one month we found three hundred and seventy sales in which the retail dealers had received cold-storage butter when they were paying for fresh butter. It reassured me when I went to see the United States Attorney to have him tell me that the case was sound and that we had plenty of incontrovertible evidence.

The manager of the Buffalo branch of Armour & Company was notified to appear at a hearing one week later. Two days after the notice had been delivered, I was approached by a friendly reporter. "There's a top drawer man from the Armour Company in town," he told me. "He called on a political boss to ask for some help on the case coming up for a hearing. What do you think the boss told him?"

"I can't imagine."

"Armour & Company might as well take its medicine, for nobody around here can fix or influence old man Stafford."

My grin of delight was wiped out by the rest of the story. "The political boss also said, 'I'd like to help you, and here's a suggestion. See Clark, Jones and Smith. They are attorneys for the bank that has a whopper of a mortgage on old man Stafford's building. He owes some back interest on the mortgage and he's hard up for ready cash.' "

The representative of Armour & Company retained the bank's attorneys, and one of them came to see Mr. Stafford. Adopting a man-to-man attitude, he said, "Jim, you just

can't embarrass that fine old firm of Armour & Company
by a public hearing. Suppose you let me make a donation to
the Red Cross for them. I'll send it to the New York office
so that they won't get any bad publicity around here about
it."

Mr. Stafford bristled. "What I say is that the case is a serious violation extending over a long period and if there is to
be one law for the little fellow and another for such big
firms as Armour & Company what good is either the law or
the Food Administrator?"

The lawyer lost no more time, but played his trump card.
"You know our bank has been awfully easy with you."

"If your bank doesn't like the way I conduct this office,
I'm sorry," Mr. Stafford replied, "but we are at war. I require
all small stores to comply with the law and I'll require the
big ones to do so."

Three days later Mr. Stafford received a telegram from
the Legal Division of the Food Administration at Washington requesting him to appear there for a conference in relation to the Armour case. I was told to get the complete file
together and we were in Washington the following day.

We were accorded a courteous and respectful conference
with the Food Administration attorneys, but before we left,
they indicated that perhaps it might be advisable to *delay*
action on the case.

Our next call was on Mr. Herbert Hoover, Food Administrator. It was the second time I'd been in Washington and
the first time I'd been in the presence of an important person.
I felt timid when we walked in, but in a couple of minutes
my fear and nervousness vanished when confronted with
Mr. Hoover's open, friendly smile and cordial greeting. A
heavy-set, square-faced man, he had a lively sparkle in his
eyes and a deliberate, unhurried manner. Unlike other men
prominent in politics whom I was to know later, he didn't
shuffle with papers on his desk or attempt to convey the impression you were using up his precious time.

Ten years later, when Hoover was President and I had just concluded the Capone investigation, we met again at Springfield, Illinois, where he had come to dedicate a Lincoln monument. He recognized me and took time to congratulate me on the work I had been doing. "You did a fine job up in Chicago," he said heartily. And, like my father, I felt such "thanks" from a President made a tough job worth-while.

Mr. Stafford and I gave Mr. Hoover a brief outline of the Armour case and my heart leaped when Mr. Hoover raised his eyebrows at the mention of the Armour name and promptly became very interested. "I'll talk to the Legal Division about that case."

At our next conference with the Food Administration lawyers no mention was made of their previous suggestion of delay. On the contrary, they now seemed enthusiastic about the case and authorized us to proceed.

The hearing was duly held and Armour & Company was found guilty of the charges.

Mr. Stafford announced that the license of Armour & Company would be suspended or they could make a "voluntary" contribution of $5,000 to the "Free Milk Fund for the Babies of France." The Company appealed the decision of Food Administrator Stafford to the United States Food Administration at Washington. Mr. Stafford's decision was sustained by his superiors there.

The Food Administration license of Armour & Company to deal in butter and eggs at their Buffalo branch was suspended for three months. It was customary to tack a large cardboard sign announcing suspension of a dealer, which was printed in red, on the door of the licensee who was put out of business. I had the great satisfaction of performing that assignment at Armour, but instead of only using one sign, I took along five signs and nailed them securely at various prominent spots outside the Company.

The next day Mr. Stafford received formal notice from the bank demanding prompt payment of the whole amount of his mortgage plus the interest. It was impossible for him to raise another loan on the property, for mortgage money was very tight in Buffalo at that time. The bank hounded him into selling the building at a tremendous sacrifice in order to meet their payment demands, and for his equity he received only about $1,500. A local realtor estimated that the forced sale caused a loss of approximately one hundred thousand dollars to Mr. Stafford. His insistence in fulfilling his duty as United States Food Administrator for Buffalo had wiped out his lifetime savings.

Nonetheless, Mr. Stafford remained at his post until the war ended. After the armistice, when it was no longer necessary to enforce wartime food laws and our office was disbanding, Mr. Stafford said to me: "Frank, your forte is investigative work. I urge you to continue in it, and I'll guarantee you will never regret it."

My experience with the Food Administration had indeed decided the course of my life.

My next job was also investigative—as Special Agent in the Intelligence Unit of the Internal Revenue Bureau.

I had got a taste of the personal cost of bringing in the "big fish" from Mr. Stafford and the Food Administration. My next hard lesson in the pitfalls of federal law enforcement work came when I tangled with "boss justice."

Boss justice was the term used by law-enforcement agents and police to describe the deliberate miscarriage of justice in important criminal cases, where corrupt political bosses exercised direct or indirect control over investigations and over prosecutions which jointly involved corrupt public officials and big shot racketeers.

My trial by fire came during the early part of the sadly corrupt Harding administration. Political bosses Harry Daugherty, the Attorney General in Washington, leader of the Ohio gang, and Boise Penrose, United States Senator from Pennsylvania, virtually hand-picked Warren G. Harding for the presidency. A few weeks after inauguration day, in 1921, one of the first moves of Daugherty and Penrose was to make an incompetent weakling, Roy Haynes of the Ohio Gang, the director of prohibition for the United States. Haynes in turn appointed as state prohibition directors many dishonest or inefficient men. State directors appointed ward politicians, crooks, or protégés of the bosses as federal prohibition agents. None of them had civil service status.

The prohibition directors enjoyed great power and heavy responsibility. It was their special function to issue permits for the withdrawal from distilleries of whiskey for medicinal purposes and alcohol for manufacturing purposes. Soon the rumor got around that the Ohio Gang and their henchmen in Washington were selling to racketeers for fancy prices withdrawal permits for thousand-case lots of whiskey and one-hundred-barrel lots of alcohol. The shipments were promptly diverted to big-shot bootleggers.

I was on duty in Philadelphia, investigating a tax-fraud case, when a friendly tip was whispered to me by a young lady clerk whom I had taken to a movie. She told me that it would be profitable to investigate her employer, William (Boss) McConnell, a hale, moon-faced fellow who, with the blessing of Penrose and Daugherty, had recently been named federal prohibition director for Pennsylvania.

I soon found four suspicious withdrawal permits that had been issued by Director McConnell on the second day he was in office. Each was for one thousand cases of bottled-in-bond whiskey. One was issued in the name of a drug company in Scranton. I rushed up there and found it to be a one-room plant manufacturing a patent medicine and incapable of using a thousand cases of whiskey in ten years. Furthermore, the owner of the company knew nothing about the shipment, had neither ordered nor received it, and was furious because his firm name had been misused.

I also established that the other three permits had been issued to drug firms that did not know that their names had figured on the whiskey withdrawal permits. We traced the shipments from the distillery and discovered that they had been delivered to big-shot racketeers in Philadelphia, Sam Singer and Bubu Hoff, who had cut the whiskey with raw alcohol, added coloring chemicals, and sold it to bootleggers at a big price. They in turn sold it to night clubs and speakeasies. This report went straight to Washington and landed on the desk of Secretary of the Treasury Andrew Mellon. Word came back "to press the investigation full force and let the chips fly."

Instinct, plus inclination, drew me into a friendship with a Philadelphia official who seemed to be immune to the general atmosphere of bribery, graft, and deceit. He was T. Henry Walnut, Assistant United States Attorney. We often had dinner together at the famous old Greene's Restaurant, and Walnut would say to me, "Watch your step, Frank. Watch out for the Ohio Gang and the Penrose organization. They control everything."

I had some of the finest fellows and ablest investigators in the service as co-workers—Herbert Lucas, John Conwell, Ed Quigley, and John Conners. We spent six months tracing big shipments of whiskey and one-hundred-barrel lots of alcohol covered by fraudulent withdrawal permits issued by Director McConnell. Over one thousand permits for whiskey for medicinal purposes had been issued to legitimate drug companies in Pennsylvania which did not know their names were used. In this way the corrupt politicians delivered some two million gallons of liquor into the hands of racketeers.

"Frank, what did I tell you?" said Walnut, his voice a mixture of anger, frustration, and disgust when I laid that evidence before him. "I predicted that the Ohio Gang and the Penrose machine would get every drop of bonded liquor in Pennsylvania into the hands of the big-shot racketeers in six months."

Walnut and I, with the co-operation of the other agents, worked on until we finally had an iron-clad case against Director McConnell. Three of McConnell's staff, who aided

in the issuance of the illegal permits, and forty-five henchmen, racketeers, politicians, and big-shot bootleggers were
also involved in the conspiracy. The day before we were
to take this evidence to the Grand Jury, Walnut snapped,
"Something's happened, Frank."

"What?" I asked.

"Two of Attorney General Daugherty's confidential aides
have just arrived from Washington. We'll have to look for
a 'fix.' "

That afternoon Walnut and I were called into United
States Attorney George Cole's office to "review the case" for
Daugherty's aides. George Cole was a sour old gentleman,
impressed with his own importance. On the wall in back
of his fancy mahogany desk were autographed photographs
of his sponsor, Senator Penrose, and of Attorney General
Daugherty. The two extremely dignified emissaries from
Washington, Mr. Harry Smith and Mr. James Jones, listened
so attentively to our explanation of the evidence and compli-
mented me so highly on our methods in getting some racketeers, owners of night clubs and speakeasies, to admit their
part in the conspiracy that I visualized McConnell in Atlanta
penitentiary for a long term.

I was still thrilling to the thought when, flicking his handkerchief across his lips, Mr. Smith rose slowly and said, as
casually as if he were telling us the time of day, "Gentlemen,
it is the desire of the Attorney General that this case should
not be presented to the Grand Jury."

A white fury instantly shot through me and it seemed to
shoot straight through Walnut at the same moment. He
sprang forward, his chin jutting out like the bowsprit of an
old clipper ship.

"By God, this case will be presented to the Grand Jury or
I'll be fired," he shouted, and at the same time brought his
fist down on Cole's desk so hard that I thought the desk or
the fist would break into pieces.

"You keep cool, Walnut! I'm running things here." Cole

placed a placating hand on Walnut's shoulder. "We must bow to the wishes of our chief, the Attorney General."

"I felt all along that because this case involved the Penrose-Daugherty political organization it would be booted and we'd have trouble," Walnut replied bitterly. "But I won't be kicked around by the Ohio Gang. I won't see Boss Justice make a farce of law enforcement."

At nine-thirty the next morning Walnut came into my office with his overcoat over his arm. "I just wanted to say good-bye, Frank. I've been fired. But this is not the end of the McConnell case," he added.

And it was not. Vigilant reporters plastered the story of Walnut's sudden dismissal across the front pages of the Philadelphia papers. They printed a frank statement made by Walnut that United States Attorney General Daugherty had sent two confidential aides from Washington with orders that the McConnell case should not be presented to the Grand Jury, that he had objected, and that he had been fired. The press associations flashed the story to Washington, and that same afternoon alert Washington press correspondents were pounding at Daugherty's door demanding explanations.

He hotly denied interfering with the case, but the power of America's mighty press was so great that Daugherty at once telephoned United States Attorney Cole. "Get that McConnell case before the Grand Jury tomorrow."

Cole immediately telephoned me, ordering me to have my witnesses available at nine o'clock and to get together all my exhibits. He also assigned another assistant to take the place of Walnut temporarily and present the case to the Grand Jury.

We got our indictment of forty-nine defendants, including McConnell, in five days. Up to that time it looked as if I might be able to salvage my dream of having William (Boss) McConnell make that little trip to Atlanta penitentiary, but the sad facts were that once the public and the newspapers had been placated by the indictment, the case was tucked quietly away.

Walnut was replaced by a newly appointed Assistant United States Attorney sponsored by the Daugherty-Penrose organization, and whenever the case was set for trial he found new reasons for delay.

After two years we eventually got the case into court. It had been on trial for eleven days when there was a sudden hush-hush conference before the bench. The jurors were sent out. The defense lawyers had raised a technical point, charging that the indictment was faulty. I noticed that Walnut's successor argued very *feebly against* the defense charge, and he brazenly brushed off several suggestions by me and by his able young assistant. The assistant was Francis Biddle, later to become United States Attorney General in the Cabinet of President Franklin Roosevelt.

When the jury returned to court to their amazement the judge dismissed the indictment. The jurors were dumfounded. One, when he got out in the hall, exclaimed, "McConnell's guilty as hell. This is a fix." An alert reporter polled the jurors before they had a chance to leave the courthouse and every juror said he was ready to vote for McConnell's conviction!

The newspapers printed another sheaf of miscarriage-of-justice editorials. And, again to placate the public, the Daugherty-Penrose team allowed McConnell to be re-indicted, this time on a minor charge of misfeasance. That indictment was allowed to die a slow death on the calendar.

The McConnell case was one of the most discouraging I have ever handled. But it gave me a sober insight into the workings of crooked politics, which was later to stand me in good stead when I fought other cases of "boss justice" versus American justice.

The success of the illegal liquor permits graft made the big shots in Washington bold. They moved into other profitable fields, the Veterans Bureau, of which their friend

Charles R. Forbes was the director, the Office of Alien Property Custodian, of which their friend Thomas W. Miller was the director, the Department of the Interior, of which Albert Fall was Secretary, and other governmental activities over which the Treasury Department had no jurisdiction. The Gang almost took over the Internal Revenue Bureau but for the quick action of Secretary of the Treasury Andrew Mellon and Commissioner of Internal Revenue David H. Blair.

The public finally became aroused after the press—especially Pulitzer Prize-winner Paul Anderson of the St. Louis *Post Dispatch*—exposed the crooked dealings of the Ohio Gang and Senator Burton K. Wheeler, Chairman of the Senate Investigating Committee, exposed the corrupt activities of Harry Daugherty. One of Calvin Coolidge's first acts as President was to demand Daugherty's resignation as Attorney General.

One by one the Ohio Gang, the Harding Poker Cabinet, and their corrupt associates got their just deserts. Secretary Fall; Forbes, Director of the Veterans Bureau; and Miller, the Alien Property Custodian—all went to jail. Jake Harmon, Oklahoma political boss, was murdered by his sweetheart. Charles F. Cramer, General Counsel of the Veterans Bureau, committed suicide. Boss Penrose, Senator from Pennsylvania, died suddenly, and a fortune in unexplained thousand-dollar bills was found in his safe-deposit box. Attorney General Harry Daugherty died in disgrace. Jess Smith of Ohio, the "bag man" or collector for Harry Daugherty, blew out his own brains at the Wardman Park Hotel in Washington as he was about to be arrested by federal agents.

During this disgraceful period, I saw President Harding once, when a group of Treasury Department agents were invited to the White House. He was a tall, distinguished-looking man, with an amiable, handsome face that seemed on the verge of a smile or a laugh. I doubt at that time he had a clue as to the degrading depths to which his appointees were carrying the country during his administration. My predecessor in the Secret Service, Chief William H. Moran, told me that only a short time before he died, Harding indeed saw clearly the entire sordid picture, and that the shock, according to Moran, hastened his death.

3

Before prohibition racketeerism in the United States was spasmodic. With the country in the clutch of a relatively unenforceable law, however, law defiance became popular and acceptable. To satisfy the national thirst, racketeers made tremendous fortunes smuggling liquor into the United States and manufacturing and distributing illegal whiskey, beer, and wine to the thousands of speakeasies which flourished across the country. They became extremely well organized, operating as crime syndicates. Their defiance of all laws was secretly and silently abetted through political fixes. As their fortunes increased, they expanded their operations, muscling into control of gambling casinos, brothels, numbers games, slot machines, horse books, and phoney labor unions. They brazenly machine-gunned rival gangs and boldly kidnaped adults for big ransom money. Extortion was widespread, bombings of business establishments were frequent.

At the top of the crime world sat Alphonse "Scarface" Capone, King of the Racketeers. As a government agent, I had watched his rise from bouncer in a dive to head of the most powerful crime syndicate in America. In 1927, Chicago had one hundred and thirty-five unsolved murders, the majority of them attributable to Capone and his Mafia torpedoes. He had even gotten away with the murder of an assistant state district attorney, who had been so unwise as to invade Capone's crime stronghold in Cicero, the thriving Chicago suburb where some of Capone's biggest gambling dives, including the Ship and the Hawthorne Smoke Shop, were located.

One of the most brazen battles in defiance of law and order occurred when Bugs Moran, leader of a powerful competing North Side Syndicate, led a furious offensive against Capone in Cicero. At noon, Bugs descended upon a restaurant where Capone was eating, bringing with him an autocade of eight loads of his gang armed with sawed-off shotguns and tommy guns. They poured a thousand shots into the restaurant and adjoining stores. Scarface crawled on the floor to a hallway at the rear of the restaurant. The other diners jumped under the tables. No one was killed, but three innocent bystanders on the street were injured, one woman lost the sight of her left eye. No arrests were made.

The following year seven of the Moran mob were lined up against a wall and cruelly machine-gunned in a garage on North Clark Street, the murderers disguised in police uniforms. This time the echoes of citizens' protests reached to the halls of Congress and the White House. The Chicago Chamber of Commerce decided to appeal directly to our new President, Herbert Hoover. The day after the Chicago Committee called on President Hoover, he issued special instructions to Andrew Mellon, Secretary of the Treasury, who, in turn, relayed them to Commissioner Lucas of the Internal Revenue Bureau. The next day I was called to Washington.

The big boss smiled. "Frank," he said, "we have been directed to investigate the income tax returns of Scarface Al Capone and the gang of racketeers associated with him. Prohibition agents and local police are unable or afraid to get evidence against the gang. We can't let them defy our

laws any longer. Proceed to Chicago at once. You may select the agents you wish to assist you."

Although I welcomed a chance to preside at the downfall
of Public Enemy Number One, I wasn't too happy about
this Chicago assignment at this time. The previous year,
while working on a tax case in Washington, I had met,
promptly pursued, and married the loveliest, most graceful,
and animated girl it had been my privilege to know. Skeptics
to the contrary, for me it had been a case of love at first sight.
I had dropped by a dancing school after work one afternoon
to brush up on my neglected social duties, had taken one
private lesson, and had enjoyed it so much I asked for
another that same evening. No private instructor was available, but the owner of the school introduced me to a class
from the Women's City Club, who let me join them. My
first partner was a diminutive, sparkling, sassy little Wash-
ingtonian, Judith Barbaux, who worked at the Defense Department. She was the daughter of a Parisian employed in the
State Department and an American girl of Irish descent.
Judith was their only child—a spirited, lovable, and spoiled
one at that. We were married within a few months and set
up housekeeping in Baltimore, where I had just been promoted to Agent in Charge. We found a little yellow cottage
at the edge of the city and I had set out beds of roses and
azaleas, and put up feeders for the cardinals, bluejays,
thrush, and squirrels that Judith loved. Nothing could have
been further from our Baltimore idyll than the wide-open
racketeer-infested Chicago of 1928.

There are some things you can tell a woman and some
you can't. When Judith and I started out for Chicago, all I
said was, "Sweetheart, I'm after a fellow named Curly
Brown. The government says we've got to put him away."

If I had told her that "Curly Brown" was an alias of Scarface Al Capone, she probably would have urged me to take
up some respectable trade like keeping books.

We settled into an apartment in a hotel, and for nearly a

year my able associates—Arthur P. Madden, Nels Tessem,
James N. Sullivan, Michael F. Malone, Clarence L. Converse, Archie Martin, and William Hodgins—and I tussled
with the tax case against Capone, making slight headway.
We legged it to banks, trying to find some record of business
transactions involving Scarface. Not a tumble. I prowled the
crummy streets of Cicero, where a twitch of Al's little finger
had the force of an edict; but there was no clue that a dollar
from the big gambling places, the horse parlors, the brothels,
or the bootleg joints ever reached his pockets directly.

One day I called upon Colonel McCormick, publisher of
the Chicago *Tribune,* and asked his permission to see one of
his reporters, Jake Lingle, whom I heard had many underworld contacts. Colonel McCormick was co-operative and
promised me an interview with Lingle inside of forty-eight
hours. The next afternoon Lingle was shot down and murdered in the Randolph Street subway.

My first break did, however, come from the press. I went
to St. Louis to see John Rogers, a reporter I knew on the
Post Dispatch, and asked his help. We lunched at the swank
Missouri Athletic Club with a friend of his, Edward O'Hare,
who entertained us with interesting stories about his bright
twelve-year-old son, Butch. He said Butch was set on going
to the United States Naval Academy at Annapolis and that
he wanted to be an admiral when he grew up. O'Hare said:
"If I never do another thing in my life, I'm going to see that
kid's wish to get into Annapolis is granted."

Rogers phoned me later that week. "I can put you in
touch with a businessman who got sucked into the Capone
Syndicate. He's willing to help you."

"Well, that's swell," I replied. "Who is he?"

Rogers gave me one of the biggest surprises of my life.
"Eddie O'Hare, the gentleman you had lunch with. He
wanted to look you over. He's satisfied."

"I hope he doesn't have too much blood on his hands and
that we can depend on him."

"I've known him for twenty years," Rogers replied. "He never got drawn directly into any of the gang wars. He limits his activity to legitimate dog tracks and has no connection with the Capone booze and vice rackets. He has wanted for a long time to get away from Capone, but once the syndicate sucks in a businessman they just don't let him retire."

In the early twenties Eddie O'Hare had bought an interest in the patent on the mechanical rabbit the greyhounds chase at dog races. Soon he had control of a prosperous dog track near St. Louis. He wanted to expand and started a dog track in Cicero. After stealing the election in 1925 for mayor of Cicero, Capone suddenly declared himself "in" as partner in O'Hare's dog track. Eddie realized too late that Capone was so powerful in Cicero he couldn't operate the dog track without accepting this new silent partner. If he didn't accept, he might be bumped off. I sympathized with O'Hare as I realized the serious predicament into which he unconsciously had been thrown.

"How come he's willing to work with me?" I asked John Rogers.

"He's nuts about that boy Butch," Rogers explained. "He is dead set on getting him into Annapolis and he figures he must break away. But he can't do it while Capone is on the throne. I told him you were making headway and that if he helped, the big shot might be on his way to the penitentiary a little quicker."

"Does he realize that in helping me put Scarface on the spot, he is taking his life in his hands?" I asked.

"Hell, Frank," Rogers said, "if Eddie had ten lives to live he'd jeopardize every one of them for that boy Butch."

I saw my new undercover man, Eddie O'Hare, infrequently, but I was in almost constant touch with John Rogers. At the end of a year the leads and advice that Rogers passed on to me from Eddie were of such tremendous importance that I considered them the most important single factor resulting in the conviction of Al Capone.

My other undercover man on the Capone case was my "secret weapon," our own "Mysterious Mike Malone," with whom I had worked on the McConnell case and who I thought then, and still think, was the greatest natural undercover worker the Service has ever had. Five feet, eight inches tall, a barrel-chested, powerful two hundred pounds, with jet black hair, sharp brown eyes underscored with heavy dark circles, and a brilliant, friendly smile, Mike could pass easily for Italian, Jew, Greek, or whomever the occasion demanded. He was actually "black Irish" from Jersey City. During World War One he had been in an airplane crash, then married the nurse who attended him. They had one child, a little girl, who was killed by a truck at the age of three. After that, Mike and his wife drifted apart. He went into undercover work for the government. And he seemed to lose interest in everything else. It became his total life.

With leads on the Capone case so slow to materialize, I decided to try to get Mike to infiltrate into the Capone gang.

The supreme headquarters of the Capone Syndicate was in the Lexington Hotel, just outside Chicago's Loop. There, from his fourth floor suite, the King directed the widespread activities of the Syndicate, including bloody gang battles, operations of gambling joints and bawdy houses, the manufacture and sale of bootleg liquor, the manipulation of elections in Chicago and Cook County, and strong arm support by Capone guerrillas of city, county, and state officials friendly to him.

In addition to the large suite Scarface used as an office, and several others assigned to his Board of Directors—Jack (Greasy Thumb) Guzik, generalissimo of the gambling and vice business; Ralph (Bottles) Capone, brother of Scarface, in command of the bootleg liquor business; and Frank Nitti, the Enforcer—around one hundred other gangsters, gamblers, and strong arm Mafia guerrillas occupied choice rooms on three floors of the hotel.

Mike Malone smiled widely when I suggested that he

move into the Lexington. An old hand at undercover work, Mike checked in under the name of a Philadelphia gangster who was wanted for a stickup. All his suits, shirts, and neckties bore labels from Wanamaker's in Philadelphia. Mike worked slowly, didn't try to push himself at any of the boys; they soon warmed up to him and began inviting him to sit in on their crap games. I began getting regular phone reports and, occasionally, when he could shake the mob, Mike turned up at our apartment for a midnight meal.

One night, while Mike was playing cards with some of the gang, word came around that Scarface was feeling expansive and had decided to throw a birthday party for Frank Nitti. Mike was included among the guests. It was the first look he had had at the "inner sanctum." Capone shook hands with all the boys, including Mike, with the graciousness befitting a king. His lavishly furnished suite—for which he paid $18,000 a year—was adorned with a striking oil of George Washington and one of Big Bill Thompson, notorious political boss and Mayor of Chicago, who had threatened to punch King George of England in the nose if he ever set foot in Chicago; also with photographs of Fatty Arbuckle and Theda Bara, popular stars of the movies in the roaring twenties.

One day Mike phoned me to say that there was an unusual tenseness around the hotel and that the gang was to have a party that night on the second floor of the New Florence Restaurant, a spaghetti house near the hotel. He had become friendly with one of the gang, Mike Kelly, who said, "You'd better go along with us." Mike said, "Sure, I'll be there," and then asked my advice as to whether he should show up at the party.

I said, "Go ahead, let me know the names of the politicians who show up and any of the gangsters from out of town." But as soon as I hung up I started worrying.

I rounded up Agents Converse, Tessem, and Sullivan, and, with a young lady stenographer from our office for a decoy, we drove down to the Florence to watch. We saw Mike go in with some of the gang, but although we were still around when the party broke up, none of us saw him leave. Back at my apartment, I was sweating bullets when my phone finally rang around two A.M. I grabbed it, heard a nickle drop, and knew it was Mike. "Saw you across the street," he said. "Anything up?"

"No," I grunted, "but I'm glad you're alive."

"I did have one bad scare tonight," Mike admitted. "The waiter set a big steak in front of me. I was starved by then, so I cut off a big hunk. It nearly gagged me. I thought I'd have a convulsion and I was sure they were poisoning me. I coughed and spat it out. My friend, Kelly, was laughing. 'Didn't you ever eat spiced, peppered steak before?' he asked me. 'It's the Big Feller's favorite dish, and they always serve it at his parties.' "

My boys were always talking about how cool and calculating I was. "He sweats ice water," they said. But as a matter of record, I was getting a little "nervy" as the Capone case dragged on without any appreciable break. I was very aware of the potential danger that surrounded all of us: Mike, the other agents, myself—and Judith. Once, when I was trying to subpoena an elusive associate of Scarface's named O'Dwyer, I found he played golf weekends at a certain club and Judith and I drove out and parked near the entrance to see if I might spot him. Judith took some needlepoint and I had a book. We waited all Saturday afternoon with no luck. Early Sunday morning we came back. About eleven o'clock a big sport Cadillac drove up with four of the toughest-looking characters I ever saw. I experienced a throb of long overdue excitement as I said to Judith, "I'll bet that tall one is our baby." A few minutes later I drifted in to look at the register and felt like yelling "hip-hip-hurrah" when I saw the name I wanted.

I told Judith my man was out on the links. Pulling my little De Soto over, I parked it next to his big Cadillac. About one o'clock Judith announced dramatically that she was starving to death. This was just the opening I needed to get her out of the way until after the serving of the subpoena. Using all the persuasive power I was supposed to possess, I coaxed, "Honey, I know you must be hungry. Why don't you take the bus down to that little hotel where we had dinner last night, get your lunch, and wait for me." Judith promptly banished all thought of hunger and said flatly, "Those four gangsters might try to beat you up. I'm sticking right here with you."

I laughed, wondering what my sweet little half-pint of a wife figured she might do in a mix-up with four gangsters.

When I saw the four thugs leaving the clubhouse, I approached them and called out, "O'Dwyer!" When my man turned with a surly epithet, I thrust the subpoena at him. "I'm Special Agent Wilson. I have this subpoena for you."

To my surprise he snatched it, then turned on me. "I'm gonna break your goddammed . . ."

Judith had been taking it all in. When he got as far as "break your goddammed"—she pressed her hand on our auto horn and held it there. The blast was terrific. Men came running out of the club. O'Dwyer stopped, startled. Two of his men had drawn revolvers. Seeing the others coming, O'Dwyer motioned quickly to his men. "Let's get going." They piled in their car and drove off. I took a deep breath. I'd never laugh at Judith's offer of help again!

After almost two years on the Capone case I was in a real sweat. We had leads—some fairly good ones—but nothing big enough to make a case, and no witnesses who counted. One night I sent the boys home, called Judith to say I'd be late, and spread out the stuff we had over our little office to review it once more and see if there was something I might have missed. By one o'clock in the morning I had found nothing of value and I was so bleary-eyed I couldn't see. I was gathering up the stuff when I accidentally bumped the filing cabinet and it clicked closed. I didn't have the key.

"Now, where'll I put this?" I thought disgustedly. Just outside the glorified phone booth we used for an office was a storeroom. I found an old filing cabinet there, opened it, and pulled out several bundles tied with string. In the back was a heavy package covered in brown paper. Something prompted me to examine it, so I snipped the string and found myself holding three ledgers, black ones with red corners. The first one didn't mean much. The second one I recognized as a "special column cash book." My eye leaped over the column headings: "Bird cage," "21," "Craps," "Faro," "Roullette," "Horse bets." You didn't have to be a detective to see that here was the financial record of a big gambling operation. The take ran from $20,000 to $30,000 a day. Net profits for fourteen months were $590,000.

"Who could have run a joint that size?" I asked myself. The answer was easy—Scarface Capone. I was jubilant.

The next day I found out that the ledgers had been seized by police in a raid on the Hawthorne Smoke Shop in Cicero, where diamond-studded crowds from Chicago laid down $3,000,000 a year in wagers. If I could hang that income around the neck of Capone, we'd have a case.

But first I had to identify the handwriting in the ledger. I think we must have collected handwriting samples from every hoodlum in Chicago. We got them from the voting registers in the wards, from savings accounts of banks, from police courts, and from the bonds the hoods signed when they were pinched.

The long process finally left me with a character named Lew Shumway, whose writing on a deposit slip in a little bank in Cicero was a dead twin to that in the books. All I had to go on was this description: "Shumway is a perfect little gentleman, refined, slight, harmless—not like a racketeer at all."

I figured that Shumway might have followed the Capone gang to Florida for the winter to work in a gambling joint or at one of the race tracks. I needed a little sunshine myself, so I decided to go to Florida to search for him.

I went out to the Hialeah race track and was standing by the rail looking into the boxes, when I found myself staring directly into the face of the man I had been stalking for over two years. The King of Racketeers sat with a jeweled moll on either side of him, smoking a long Havana cigar, occasionally raising huge binoculars to his eyes and greeting a parade of fawning sycophants who came to shake his hand. Four tough-looking Sicilian bodyguards were alongside his box.

I looked upon his pudgy olive face, his thick pursed lips, the rolls of fat descending from his chin—and the scar, like a heavy pencil line across his left cheek—and clenched my fists in frustration. "Good God," I thought, "when a country cop wants a man he just walks up and says, 'You're pinched.' Here I am, with the whole United States government behind me, as powerless as a canary." I turned my back upon the King in the box seat with his seventy-five-cent Havana cigar, bit off the end of one of my own nickel stogies, and continued my search for Shumway.

Gentleman Lew was not at Hialeah. I went on with the hunt at the dog track of the Miami Beach Kennel Club. The second night I was there I thought I spotted my man back of the betting windows in the cashier's department. I tailed him home, then called on him the next morning while he was having breakfast with his wife, and invited him to come over to my office with me. On arriving at the office I told him, "I am investigating the income tax liability of Alphonse Capone."

Gentleman Lew didn't merely shake. He rattled. I gave him a glass of water. "I've got something stronger across the hall if you'd like a shot, Lew," I offered.

With a little "medicine" in him he pulled himself together. "Oh, you're mistaken, Mr. Wilson. I don't know Al Capone."

"Lew," I said, "I know you're in a helluva spot. You have

two choices. If you refuse to play ball with me, I'll have to
send a deputy marshal looking for you at the dog track. I'll
have him ask for you by name and serve a subpoena on you.
As soon as the gang knows the government has located you,
they will pass the word to Scarface. Knowing your reputation as a gentleman and a truthful man, Scarface will probably decide to have you bumped off at once so you can't
testify."

I paused to let him think it over. "If you don't like that
idea, Lew, take choice number two. Come clean with the
United States government and tell me the truth about this
cash book and this ledger. You were bookkeeper at the Hawthorne Smoke Shop. You can identify every entry in these
books—and you can tell who your boss was. I'll guarantee
to keep it secret until the day of the trial. I'll send you away
to a safe place where the Mafia can't locate you. Play ball,
Lew, and I'll guarantee that Mrs. Shumway will not become
a widow."

Gentleman Lew quivered like a harp string, but I had
persuaded him. He gave a complete and honest statement to
Agent Joe Brown of Miami, Florida, and me, detailing the
operation of the Smoke Shop, the entries in the books, the
names of the partners, and who was employed in the joint.
He said that Scarface Capone was the big shot from whom
he took orders, that the set of books not only showed
the profits credited to Scarface but it also showed the big
amounts paid out weekly for protection to police and local
politicians.

That night I spirited Shumway out of Miami so that even
his wife thought he was going to see a sick relative in Oklahoma. For safe-keeping, I hid him in a quiet spot with an
agent-bodyguard until we'd need him again.

Convincing people to testify against Scarface took all our
ingenuity. They were all terrified—with good reason. One
important Chicagoan said bluntly, "Why, Mr. Wilson, if I
tell you about my deals with Capone, he'll have me taken for

D

a one-way ride." Another described to me, with a shudder at the memory, an occasion when Capone invited to a banquet three powerful gangland leaders whom he found had plotted to kill him. After the meal was finished, Scarface got up and announced, "This is what we do to traitors." He then brutally beat the brains out of them with a baseball bat, and their bodies were found in a roadside dump two days later.

Another witness, a broad-shouldered, six-foot Italian, about seventy years old, went into hysterics when we tapped him. He showed up at the hearing, accompanied by his wife, sobbing, shaking, and pale. "For God's sake, let me alone," he begged. "They kill me if I talk. . . ."

"Who do you mean by they?" I asked him.

He moved close to me and in a whisper said, "They—the Mafia! The Black Hand torpedoes murder anyone who squeals on him. Thirty years ago they cut the throat of my wife's brother in New York. To get away from the Black Hand we moved to Cleveland and then to Chicago. Most of my countrymen say that the Black Hand disgraces our loyal American Italians. We pray that they don't hurt us or our children. Our padres in church beg us to pray that the Mafia will not keep disgracing us and our country. And Mr. Wilson, please, you watch out, because Capone might get them after you."

I decided it was now time to start closing in on some of the big shots surrounding Capone. If we could pin an income tax violation on one of them and send him to the penitentiary, it would be evidence to terrified witnesses that Scarface would be our next victim. After a meeting we decided to concentrate on Frank Nitti, the Capone Enforcer, a title Nitti had earned because whenever Capone wanted an enemy "rubbed out" he passed the word to Nitti.

In a few months of intensive digging, principally by Agents Tessem, Sullivan, and Hodgins, we had what we considered sufficient evidence to sustain an indictment and court conviction for tax evasion against Nitti. Most of it came from Nitti's cut from the profits of alcohol stills and gambling joints. We took the evidence to United States Attorney George E. Q. Johnson and his able assistants, Dwight Green (Green later became Governor of Illinois) and Jake Grossman. They expressed astonishment over the fact that we had dug up so much evidence. "Let's go, we'll get the Grand Jury without delay."

The Chicago newspapers spread big banner headlines announcing the indictment of Nitti. In accordance with usual procedure, a warrant for the arrest of Nitti was issued and turned over to the United States marshal. The marshal reported to the United States Attorney that he was unable to locate Nitti.

Attorney Johnson asked me to find him. "I know it's not your duty, but somebody's got to uphold the reputation of the government."

That night my agents and I set out in different directions looking for Nitti. I stopped at some night clubs in Cicero. No luck. Then I contacted a friendly source and was pleasantly surprised when he whispered, "Watch for Nitti in a black Ford with Wisconsin license number ———. Don't look for him in the Loop. Watch Cicero, Berwyn, Burnam, and Stickney." After a four-day search, a sharp-eyed agent spotted the auto in Cicero driven by a woman. He tailed the car to an apartment house in Berwyn. About midnight, a detail of agents saw a man who looked like Nitti enter the building and they followed.

Close up, the man didn't look like the wanted Nitti. He looked like Hitler. He had dyed his hair and raised a mustache. He handed the agents his business card: "Frank J. Belmont, Sales Manager, Continental Co., 101 Wall Street, New York City."

"Get your duds on and come along."

In a few minutes Frank Nitti was locked in a cell at the Cook County jail. We had found an account in a Cicero bank which I thought was Nitti's. One of the checks for twenty-five dollars was in favor of the Salvation Army. So I said to him, "You're not such a bad guy. You gave the Salvation Army twenty-five bucks last month."

"How in hell did you know about that?"

"Well," I replied, "here's your cancelled check covering that generous donation."

He took a good look at the check and volunteered, "They came around every month begging for money and I helped them out. That time I didn't have anything smaller than a grand in my pocket, so I gave them the check."

The bank account showed deposits of over $200,000 in six months. The money was Nitti's cut from the profits of alcohol stills operating in Cicero, in Little Sicily, and the West Side of Chicago, and from The Ship. In a week Nitti was in court, had pleaded guilty, and was given one and one-half years; and next day he was on his way to Leavenworth penitentiary.

After the Chicago papers spread feature stories that Nitti was safely resting in Leavenworth, it threw a big scare into a lot of the big shots around Chicago. Three days after Nitti's conviction, I was called to the office of the Collector of Internal Revenue and shown thirty-seven amended tax returns with big checks attached, which had just been filed by worried Chicago racketeers. These checks totaled $836,000.

A few months later we indicted Greasy Thumb Jack Guzik, the financial manager of the syndicate. He was convicted, and the judge sent him off to Leavenworth for five years. Ralph Capone, brother of Al, was convicted; he drew a three-year sentence. Then we picked out Sam Big Belly Guzik, the 350-pound brother of Jack, and he was presented with a three-year sentence.

Each time we obtained a conviction of one of the syndicate principals, the papers spread the news in big headlines. As a result, our potential witnesses became aware of the important fact that the United States government meant business.

It was time to close in on Capone.

Capone hired a Washington lawyer who was supposed to have a lot of pull. The lawyer bounced into our Washington office and indicated that Capone would pay $700,000 to settle the tax case without a prosecution. He was directed to contact me in Chicago. When he appeared, I respectfully listened, and then told him to bring his client to our office. Capone left his burly bodyguards outside the federal building. He sullenly acknowledged the introduction by his lawyer. "This is my client, Mr. Alphonse James Capone." He was about six feet tall, 240 pounds, powerful shoulders and arms, shifty, dark eyes, a fine set of white teeth and a protruding stomach. The vicious-looking scar on the left side of his face extended for about six inches. He was dressed immaculately in a stylish dark blue double-breasted suit with a neat white linen handkerchief, its four sharp points protruding about one inch from the upper pocket. He wore a ring set with a big diamond and a heavy gold-and-diamond-studded watch chain, which he fingered nervously. He had on black sport shoes with white tips, blue silk socks with white clocks, and a snappy blue necktie with large white polka dots. He had a big flabby paw and dainty manicured nails. When he pulled out a silk handkerchief, I got a strong whiff of lily-of-the-valley.

We got down to business quickly. Scarface's sullen smile turned to an angry scowl when I threw him some pertinent questions about his income. He stalled, evaded direct answers, and never looked me straight in the eye.

When the stenographer was dismissed, Scarface stuck his big paw in his pocket, pulled out six Corona cigars, and shoved them at me. "Smoke?"

"No," I said shortly.

He scowled. "Somebody's trying to push me around. You better take good care of yourself, Wilson."

"You bet I will," I told him.

There were no handshakes as is usual when we close an

interview with a taxpayer. I didn't intend to soil my hands with his blood-stained paw.

Two weeks later Eddie O'Hare called up on my unlisted phone. "I've got to see you."

I hustled out to our meeting place. Eddie's first excited words were, "Frank, you've got to move right away—this afternoon, I mean. Scarface has four Mafia Sicilian killers from Brooklyn in town to bump you off and has put a price of twenty-five grand on your head. They know you and your wife are living in Room 307 at the Sheridan Plaza Hotel, and they have the garage spotted where you keep your car. They know you take it to the garage around midnight and walk alone down the dark alley for a half-block to your hotel. They have two machine guns. The Sicilians also have orders to get Art Madden, United States Attorney Johnson, and Pat Roche."

"That lousy s.o.b.," I muttered. "Thanks, Eddie, for tipping me off. Someday I'll try to do a good turn for your boy."

I hurried over to the Sheridan Plaza and told Judith, "I've got to work in the office for several nights. We can have dinner together every night if I am at a Loop hotel near the office, so we are moving downtown to the Palmer House."

Judith was trained not to ask too many questions, and she packed our bags quickly. In checking out of the Sheridan Plaza I said, "I'm leaving unexpectedly. Have to run over to Kansas City."

I went to the Palmer House where I knew the house dick, who helped me get a room on the top floor. I registered there under another name.

I left Judith and immediately got in touch with the other three potential victims. Within a few hours the Chicago *Tribune* had received a tip from an underworld source, and they in turn relayed it to me. It confirmed the exact details Eddie O'Hare had given me. I called the state attorney's office, but before his posse of sheriffs could locate Capone, an investigator working in the state attorney's office had tipped off Scarface that they were out for him. He got scared, sent the Sicilians back to Brooklyn, and hopped a plane for Florida.

I had known all along that it was only a matter of time until Judith found out who the "Curly Brown" I was chasing actually was. In a series of articles for the Chicago *Tribune* on the Jake Lingle case, John Boettiger (whom I later knew at the White House when he married Anna Roosevelt) disclosed the anonymous tip the *Tribune* had received, that Capone had imported four Mafia Sicilians to assassinate United States Attorney Johnson, Art Madden, Pat Roche, and me. Judith was with Agent Jim Sullivan's wife, Alice, when she happened to see the article. Alice called me at the office to tell me that Judith was crying and she urged me to come home and pacify her.

"No," I told Alice. "It's best she fights it out alone."

That night when I got home Judith had an extra fine dinner prepared and all was serene. She said nothing about her discovery till after we'd done the dishes and gone for a little drive in the country.

"Frank, I'm worried," she finally said, her voice quiet and in control. "I read about your assignment in the paper. And I've been thinking about it all day. I know you wouldn't want to quit in the middle of a case and it wouldn't be fair to ask you to . . ." She sighed, but didn't break down. "From now on, we'll just have to pray harder for your safety and harder for your success than we ever did before. But remember," and her eyes shot sparks, "you have to agree to take me with you whenever you can, so I can help you!" Judith—all of five feet—Judith, who loved tiny, helpless things—babies, puppies, birds fallen from their nests—was going to protect me from the Capone mob!

I gathered her in my arms, thanking my luck again for having found such a brave and generous girl. Like Winston Churchill, whom I was later to have the opportunity to guard, when he visited President Roosevelt, I was numbered among those fortunate men who "get married and live happily ever after."

The terror and fear of a "one-way ride" strongly instilled in potential witnesses by Capone was not entirely eliminated by the convictions of such Capone Syndicate men as Frank Nitti, Ralph Capone, or Jack and Sam Guzik. There was continued balking of our endeavors to establish the amount of income actually received by Scarface Al.

For example, Agents Tessem and Hodgins went to the Pinkert State Bank in Cicero to see if it had conducted any business with Capone or his gang. When they showed the cashier their credentials, he said the bank would be happy to help. But when Agent Hodgins asked specific questions about the bank's possible transactions, directly or indirectly, with the mob or its gambling establishments, the cashier denied any such dealings.

Then Hodgins asked if any tellers could remember business dealings of this kind, just to be sure, since a former bank employee had reported frequent transactions of this kind. The cashier was agreeable, and after a half-hour wait, he came back to report no progress.

But we didn't give up so easily, and the next day Hodgins and Tessem began to analyze the bank records for 1926–1929. They found several entries covering cashier's checks purchased by and payable to J. C. Dunbar, always in round figures, usually $10,000, $20,000, and so on; the total came to $450,000. But the bank cashier didn't know any J. C. Dunbar. Again he was asked to check with the tellers.

Only one teller came forward, who told Agent Tessem, "Oh, Dunbar was a speculator, came in with cash and bought cashier's checks. He wasn't introduced to the bank. He just drifted in."

"What kind of speculator was he?"

"I don't know, maybe grain speculator or stock market. I never asked him."

But when asked what Mr. Dunbar looked like, the teller

could remember nothing unusual or distinctive about him.

It wasn't easy, yet the Agents persisted. Requesting all cancelled cashier's checks issued by the bank from 1926–1928, they found that almost half the cancelled checks had been endorsed by Capone's financial man, Jack Guzik. When they were brought before a Grand Jury, the cashier and the tellers were unable to remember anything about their good customer, Mr. Dunbar.

When a former teller at the bank was shown Dunbar's checks, he remembered him very well as the cashier of The Ship. He was known as Mr. Dunbar to the cashiers and officers of the bank and as Fred to the tellers. This man gave us a fine description of Fred, and told us, "He was a little fussy and would request brand-new bills." He also told us that Fred was a tough guy, but that he once saw him turn pale when a little cockroach showed up on a bundle of hundred-dollar bills. "He got so excited," the man recalled, "that I didn't get the usual five-dollar tip from him that day." I remembered that fear of little bugs on the part of Fred.

We found out that his real name was Fred Reis and that he had been working in a big Syndicate gambling joint just outside of Miami, and that he was now supposed to be lying low in St. Louis.

Agent Tessem and I left Chicago and drove all night to get to St. Louis so as to grab Fred Reis, alias J. C. Dunbar, before he slipped completely out of sight. Post office inspectors were helpful enough to inform us that a special delivery letter was about to be delivered to Reis from Louis Lipschultz, Al Capone's lieutenant. We simply tailed the mailman. When Reis saw Tessem and me, he tried to slam the door, but I had my big foot in the way. I handed him a subpoena to appear at the Federal Building, but he refused to accept it and threw it on the floor. We then insisted Reis come along with us, but as we drove over the long Mississippi River bridge toward East St. Louis, it must have suddenly dawned on Reis that we could be Capone torpedoes taking him for a ride.

"Is this a snatch? Who are you? If you're government men, show me your badges," Reis snarled.

Because we were in traffic and I couldn't get at my badge then, I told him to sit still and stop asking questions. This made him certain he was being taken for a ride.

"I never squawked or squealed on Capone in my life. This ain't fair. I don't want to die. I've got a wife and family. Please let me go."

But he became very defiant once we arrived at the East St. Louis Federal Building and he denied ever having seen the cashier's checks or the Pinkert Bank. Once again he was the tough guy, fearing nothing in this world—except maybe tiny insects, and so we guided ourselves accordingly.

Committed as a material witness to an ancient jail in Dansville, Illinois, where none of the Syndicate shysters were likely to find him, we put Reis in a specially-designed third floor cell.

He took one look at it and gasped, "This ain't fit for a dog!"

Cockroaches and other wild life were virtually holding a convention on the premises. I told him I'd give him a nice, clean hotel room if he'd be interested in "playing ball with Uncle Sam."

"Nuts to you, copper!" Reis hissed.

While we waited the four days it took Reis to come around to our point of view, we learned that forty-eight hours after we'd picked him up, Capone was offering a one-thousand-dollar reward for information about Reis's whereabouts after Reis's landlord had sent word to Scarface that two very tough-looking gangsters had rushed him out of his apartment.

Reis figured his old friends had let him down, and he was going to make them regret it. He admitted to being the cashier of The Ship in Cicero, that the boss was Al Capone, and that the cashier's checks represented *net* profits. In order not to keep a lot of currency on hand, Reis bought cashier's checks payable to himself, which he would cash whenever currency was demanded.

We spirited Reis back to Chicago and sneaked him into the Grand Jury chambers in the middle of the night. There, he gave the ten-carat testimony I had been waiting for, which put the lush profits of The Ship squarely into the pockets of Capone. We packed our scowling little treasure off to South America in the hands of able agents until his case was called.

During this waiting period, the Secret Six of the Chicago Chamber of Commerce furnished me with money for Reis's wife and daughter, living in California, for Reis's trip to South America, and for various purposes for which the government had no appropriation. Their financial and other help was an extremely important factor in the case.

Our long grind against Capone at last showed good results. We secured proof that Scarface lived like a millionaire, throwing big, expensive parties at his winter mansion in Miami Beach, where he entertained racketeer leaders and boss politicians from New York, Detroit, Philadelphia. We dug up evidence of the purchase of armored autos and yachts. His weekly bill for meat alone at Miami exceeded a thousand dollars. He used a gold-plated dinner service when entertaining local and national politicians. He bought seven-dollar silk ties by the dozen, glove silk underwear at fifteen dollars a suit, fifty-dollar French pajamas, fifteen custom-made suits at a time, and sixteen-cylinder limousines—and diamond belt buckles for his friends at Christmas.

We indicted Capone, showing unreported net income of $1,038,654. He entered a plea of "guilty," expecting to make a deal for a light sentence.

When Capone was called to court, the judge advised him that if he had pleaded guilty with the expectation that he could make a deal for a short sentence, the judge would allow him to withdraw his plea. Capone quickly changed his plea to "not guilty."

One week before the trial was to begin, Eddie O'Hare called. He wanted to see me, and named a place on the far north side of Chicago. I was there in half an hour.

"The big shot is going to outsmart you yet," Eddie said.

"Don't be silly, Eddie. We won't let Capone outsmart us —not now!"

"Oh, no? Well, the fix is in already!" Eddie blurted. "Capone has a complete list of the prospective jurors. They're fixing them one by one. They're passing out thousand-dollar bills. They're promising political jobs. They're giving out tickets to prize fights. They're giving donations to churches. They're using threats and muscle, too, Frank!"

"Eddie, you've been reading detective stories," I scoffed. "The judge and the United States attorney don't even have the jury list yet."

"Oh, yeah!" he asserted. "Well, take a look at this!" He handed me a list of ten names and addresses. "There you are," he said. "Right off that jury list, names thirty to thirty-nine!"

I think my heart stopped for a couple of seconds. I knew we had a winning hand—we had worked on it long enough —but Capone was going to beat us with an ace in the hole. I rushed back to my office and broke the news to United States Attorney Johnson.

Johnson slammed his fist on the desk hard enough to crack the wood. He roared, "So Capone's even got the court employees under his thumb! My confidence in government employees is shot to hell. Some skunk probably got a few thousand dollars for selling Capone that list."

We hustled to the chambers of Federal Judge James H. Wilkerson, who was to conduct the Capone trial. There was some reassurance in just looking at the strong-faced, heavy-set Judge. Somehow he seemed like a match for Scarface Al. Without moving a muscle he gazed at the ten names Eddie had given me. Then he said, rationing his words as if they were precious jewels, "I do not have my jury list yet. I do not believe it wise for me to ask for it, lest I engender suspicion. We will sit tight and wait for it to come to me in due course. I shall call you gentlemen when I get it."

The next morning Judge Wilkerson sent for United States Attorney Johnson, Art Madden, and me. He had the jury list on his desk. The ten names on the list Eddie had given me tallied exactly with names thirty to thirty-nine on the panel. But the Judge did not appear ruffled. He simply said, "Bring your case into court as planned, gentlemen. Leave the rest to me."

The day the trial started, Judith fixed me my favorite dish, baked pears, for breakfast. I had on a rather loud necktie and she made me change it for a plain blue one, saying I should dress more conservatively when going to court.

It was a bright October day in Chicago—Indian summer. The ancient, frowning Chicago courthouse looked as if Ringling Brothers had pitched their circus on its grimy, gray stone doorstep. I had to fight my way through crowds of clawing, clamoring reporters, photographers, and sob sisters; climb around tripods; and crunch over a carpet of flash bulbs. This was the largest group of press and radio correspondents that had covered a criminal trial.

Scarface came into the courtroom in a mustard-colored suit and yellow tie, smiled expansively, and sat down with his lawyers at the counsel table just a few feet from me. I thought of that day, two years before, at the Hialeah race track when I first set eyes on him. Phil d'Andrea, Al's favorite bodyguard, sat beside him—Phil, with his greased, flat hair, looking like a croupier at a crap game, fawning over Al, adjusting Al's chair, carefully plucking a thread from Al's mighty shoulders.

Judge Wilkerson entered in his black robe and called his bailiff to the bench. He said in crisp, stern tones, "Judge Woodward has another trial commencing today. Go to his courtroom and bring me his entire panel of jurors. Take my entire panel to Judge Woodward."

The switch was so easy, so smooth, so simple. Capone's face clouded, but he did not bat an eyelash. In the black cloud was the despair of a gambler who had made his final raise—and lost. American justice had made a touchdown and the most powerful public enemy of the roaring twenties was toppling from his throne.

The trial marched on. My gems, Gentleman Lew Shumway and bug-bedeviled Fred Reis, stood their ground on the witness stand, though Capone and Phil d'Andrea were staring holes through them the entire time.

I was suspicious of D'Andrea and voiced my feelings to Mike Malone. He said, "D'Andrea is treacherous; he'll do anything Al suggests, and he is fearless. Watch all your evidence or he will steal some of your exhibits."

We were pushing the trial to a close so court was being held on Saturday. That day D'Andrea sat down at the counsel table with his back to me. He was only about four feet away. I noticed a bulge around his hip pocket. I sent out word to Agents Tessem and Sullivan to watch me and watch Phil. As soon as Judge Wilkerson declared a recess, I tapped Phil on the shoulder and whispered, "Come outside for a minute."

The first door in the hall led into the Judge's chambers. When we got to that door I grabbed Phil and ordered, "Come in here for a minute!"

Agent Sullivan opened the door and Agent Tessem gave him a shove. Just inside the door D'Andrea was relieved of a .38 caliber revolver which he had in his hip pocket. He scowled and stuttered something. In his vest pocket we found some extra cartridges.

"D'Andrea, you're under arrest."

We notified Judge Wilkerson and D'Andrea was charged with contempt of court. He got a sentence of six months in jail. A few years later he got a sentence of seven years on a federal charge of extorting $5,000,000 from motion picture officials for not calling strikes of Hollywood studio employees.

The Capone trial wound up in mid-October. As the jury went to its deliberations, about five o'clock, I felt sure we had won. I went to dinner with United States Attorney Johnson and his assistants and Art Madden. Later we were joined by Agents Nels Tessem, Jim Sullivan, Bill Hodgins, Mike Malone, and Clarence Converse.

They were the most efficient group of agents with whom I ever had the pleasure of working, tackling the toughest assignments I could dig up with great willingness. It was their initiative, keenness, fearlessness, and stubborness that finally brought the successful results—and much of my praise goes to their demonstration of remarkable teamwork during our three-year investigation.

We expected any moment to be called back for the verdict. Three hours passed. We were back in Johnson's office, rather silent now, none of us willing to admit he was worried. It was a veritable wake. I telephoned Judith. She was crying from sheer nervous exhaustion, but she cheered me up, saying, "Don't worry, you're going to win the case."

At midnight word came that the jury was filing in. We ran downstairs two steps at a time and fought our way into the crowded courtroom. I studied the jurors' faces and was sure that I saw a friendly glimmer in the eyes of the foreman.

"Gentlemen," intoned Judge Wilkerson, "have you reached a verdict?"

"Yes, sir."

"What is your verdict?"

"Guilty."

The sentence was eleven years and a fine of $50,000.

The crowd in the courtroom broke up the way a circus does after the last performance. Reporters ran out of court. Lawyers ran. Mobsters ran. Everybody seemed to be running. Everybody but Scarface Al Capone. He bumped for-

ward as if a blackjack had hit him noiselessly on the back of
the head.

Two husky United States marshals slipped handcuffs on
the King of Racketeers and hurried him to a cell. One of the
marshals said, "From now on, your highness will have a
royal throne in Alcatraz."

United States Attorney Johnson thanked Judge Wilkerson and the members of the jury and stated, "The conviction
of this powerful law-defiant racketeer king and public enemy
number one is a victory of an aroused public that demanded
American justice." He also commended the special agents,
whose mutual team work with attorneys had done so much
to help bring the case to a successful conclusion.

Scarface served his full prison term, and upon his discharge in 1942, his family hurried him to his home on Palm
Island. His physical condition was serious. He was spurned
and ridiculed by his former associates in the underworld who
had once bowed to his every wish. He died at Palm Island on
January 25, 1947.

Scarface was buried in Chicago by six professional pall-
bearers during a driving snowstorm. About a dozen mourn-
ers and a few reporters were present—a startling contrast to
those spectacular funerals of murdered leaders of Chicago
racketeer gangs, which were attended by powerful politicians and officials and tremendous crowds in the days when
Scarface was king.

Once the big shot—who was thought to have had more
power than the law—was actually convicted, tax violators
began to kick in, right and left. Floods of amended and de-
linquent returns, with checks attached, showed up not only
in Chicago but at other Internal Revenue offices all across
the country from scared tax cheaters. A Supervisor of Col-
lectors' Offices reported to me that the estimate of the
amount of income taxes collected through these returns was
over $4,500,000.

While we were concentrating our efforts on the tax cheating of Scarface, other special Internal Revenue agents were on the trail of tax dodgers around the country, especially men and women who were prominent in the business world, in the entertainment world, and in the underworld. It was found that Charlie Chaplin had deliberately neglected to report a big slice of his profits. He was forced to pay additional taxes and penalties of $1,174,627. Miss Marjorie Berger, a public accountant in Hollywood, who had developed a fraudulent scheme to reduce the income tax of a group of movie stars, was hit with a two-and-one-half year sentence in a federal penitentiary. Twenty-two of the group, including Tom Mix, entered pleas of guilty. As a result of these cases the government collected close to another $2,000,000 in taxes and penalties. Some of those caught in the net spread by the special agents were Waxey Gordon of New York, Johnnie Torrio of Brooklyn, Jimmie Fontaine of Washington, Larry Fay of New York, James McCormick, marriage license commissioner of New York, Boss Nucky Johnson of New Jersey, and Boss Tom Pendergast of Kansas City.

After the Capone case was closed, Judith and I went back to our neglected little house in Baltimore. Mysterious Mike Malone checked out of the Lexington and "disappeared" once more, to turn up again on the next case where we needed him. The St. Louis *Post Dispatch* had kept its word, and not one bit of our evidence was published until it was disclosed at the trial of Capone. The co-operation given me by John Rogers, with the permission of his editors, was a tremendous factor in the successful outcome of the case.

Luck ran out for Eddie O'Hare in 1939. He was driving his auto in a suburb of Chicago when another car suddenly pulled alongside of him and he was blasted with bullets from a sawed-off shotgun. He died instantly. The murderers made a safe getaway. But Eddie's big dream was realized. His boy Butch did receive an appointment to Annapolis Naval Academy, from which he graduated with high honors.

E

Butch became a Navy pilot in World War Two; single-handedly he downed seven Japanese planes in a bloody battle over the Pacific and was awarded the Congressional Medal of Honor by President Roosevelt, who said, "Your action was one of the most daring single combat flights in the history of American aviation." Butch later gave his life for his country in a fierce air fight with the Japanese over the Pacific. Chicago's International Airport was named O'Hare Airport in his honor on September 18, 1949, and rededicated in March of 1963 by President John F. Kennedy.

4

Our temporary calm in Baltimore did not last long. Capone was still in Cook County jail, awaiting transference to Alcatraz, when the kidnaping of the Lindbergh baby rocked the world. In a desperate play Scarface Al Capone then made a cock-and-bull offer to find the baby within forty-eight hours if he were given his freedom. Equally desperate for very different reasons, Colonel Lindbergh telephoned the Secretary of the Treasury, Ogden Mills, and asked assistance from agents who were familiar with Capone and his gang. I was assigned to the case along with Art Madden of Chicago.

I had already, unofficially, offered my services to Colonel Lindbergh on the long shot that the kidnaping might be the work of organized racketeers. As strongly as Judith had opposed, in her heart, my work with Capone, she equally strongly insisted I "do something" on the Lindbergh case. Like the rest of America, we were shocked and stunned— and somehow felt vaguely guilty—about this cruel crime. It was a blot on the face of America—just as the Kennedy assassination was to be later—which none of us could ignore or forget.

By the time I was officially called in, I knew, through my own underworld sources, that Capone had nothing to do with the Lindbergh kidnaping and could shed no light on the real culprit.

When I went to see Colonel Lindbergh and his wife at their home in Hopewell, New Jersey, they both fully expected to recover their child quickly. I was impressed with Colonel Lindbergh's simple, direct manner, his deliberate, thoughtful way of speaking. In five minutes I felt as though I'd known him five years. Mrs. Lindbergh was a little bit of a thing, terribly distraught, but making a tremendous effort to control herself. She had a dainty, shy quality that I found charming, and her rare, fleeting smile was beautiful. Colonel Henry Breckenridge, Lindbergh's friend and attorney, was present, as he was devoting all his time to helping the Colonel during this tense period. I liked his serious eyes and warmed up to him right away.

We advised Colonel Lindbergh to disregard Capone's bluff. He then showed us the letter which the kidnaper had left in the nursery when the child was taken. It proved that this criminal was calculating and clever. In his request for $50,000 ransom he stipulated that $25,000 must be in twenty-dollar bills, 15,000 in ten-dollar bills and 10,000 in five-dollar bills. Obviously, he was well aware that it was much harder to trace bills of lower denominations.

It was almost impossible to carry on a connected conversation with Colonel Lindbergh, since he was called to the telephone every three or four minutes. Offers of every kind of assistance—serious to ridiculous—flooded in. Messengers were going and coming; state police guards were being relieved and posted; telegrams were being received or answered; and thousands of letters were being opened and sorted by New Jersey State Police officers. Looking about the big garage which had been hastily converted into a general office, I noticed that the whole length of one side was stacked waist-high from the floor with bundles of mail.

After two weeks of frenzied waiting for a reliable lead, a phone message came in from an hysterical woman, who swore that she had just discovered that the baby searched for by all Americans was in the apartment next to hers, where a new tenant had just moved in. She gave an address in the Bronx. Four agents rushed to the address, breaking all speed regulations.

When they got to the apartment, the woman was outside, and led them to the suite in which the child was being held. The agents walked in and there in a high chair was a beautiful child with golden locks. An agent quickly grabbed the child, who was just as described in the pictures and circulars spread all over the country and abroad.

One agent said, "It's the kid all right."

Another exclaimed, "My God, we've got him."

The child seemed unafraid and smiled at the agents.

Another agent gasped, "At last—we've found him."

The fourth agent, father of four children, hollered, "Oh, I'm so happy."

And then . . .

He quickly lifted the child and, on a hunch, unpinned the infant's diaper. "What do you know? It's a girl!"

Agent Art Madden and I were in continuous contact with Colonel Lindbergh, his lawyer and friend Colonel Breckinridge, and Colonel Schwarzkopf, superintendent of the New Jersey State Police. We headquartered in the Phi Gamma Delta fraternity house in New York City, so as to avoid reporters. In all phone conversations we used the code name "The College Boys." Lindbergh's code name was "Axle." Colonel Breckinridge's name was "Professor Brandon." Colonel Schwarzkopf became "Mr. Blackburn."

Dr. John F. Condon—"Jafsie"—entered the case of his own accord. A seventy-two-year-old retired principal of a New York City school, Dr. Condon, like so many other Americans, had become incensed over the crime, and he had written a letter published in his local paper, *The Bronx*

Home News, offering an extra $1,000 to anyone who would restore the baby to its parents, and also offering to serve as a "go-between" for the kidnaper and Colonel Lindbergh. To our amazement, this offer was accepted.

Two days after his letter appeared, Dr. Condon received a note saying the kidnaper trusted him to act as intermediary and enclosing a letter addressed to Colonel Lindbergh to see if he, too, would accept Jafsie (Condon's initials, J.F.C.) as a go-between. These notes were signed with the same secret symbol that appeared on the note the kidnaper had left in the nursery: two intersecting circles with red filling in the center and three holes about 1/16 of an inch in diameter. To the right and left of the center holes were two small vertical wavy lines.

Colonel Breckinridge prepared an ad which was put in the special notices of the New York *American:*

MONEY IS READY, JAFSIE.

Dr. Condon received several more letters from the kidnaper, and finally met him at Woodlawn Cemetery, where he told the man, who said his name was "John," that a ransom payment would not be made unless the kidnaper produced evidence that he had the baby.

"John" replied: "I'll send you his sleeping suit as evidence."

Three days later, a brown parcel came by mail to the home of Dr. Condon. It contained a baby's sleeping suit.

Mrs. Lindbergh was able positively to identify the sleeping suit. In accordance with the instructions in the letter which came with the package, they placed an ad in the New York paper reading: I ACCEPT. MONEY IS READY. JAFSIE.

That night, Madden and I were called for a conference with Colonel Lindbergh at the New York apartment of Colonel Breckinridge, the Lindbergh lawyer. On a previous occasion we had strongly urged that we be allowed to list the serial numbers of the bills which were to be used in the ransom payment. But Colonel Lindbergh feared that such action might possibly jeopardize the life of his baby.

"Colonel, I'm all against the idea of a blind trade," I told him. "You know if that baby isn't turned over to you the moment the ransom is paid, we haven't any protection. It's bad business."

"What can we do?" he asked.

"We've got to take the serial numbers of the ransom bills so that if you are double-crossed we can trace the money to the guilty man when he spends it." Art Madden supported me strongly in this appeal.

I explained to Colonel Lindbergh that we could give all banks in this country and abroad a list of the numbers, and could put the tellers on the alert so they could spot the bills. Sooner or later the money was bound to be spent.

We left Breckinridge's apartment about 2:30 A.M. and Lindbergh drove me to my hotel. His last words were, "All right, take the serial numbers. I'll phone Harry Davison at the office of J. P. Morgan & Company first thing in the morning and arrange with him for you to go down to their office to do the job."

We made up the ransom package in twenties, tens, and fives in accordance with the specifications in the kidnap note. A dozen of Morgan Company's bookkeepers stayed up most of the night recording and witnessing (so that the records could be used in court) the serial numbers of each bill. We purposely included $25,000 in gold certificates, because there were fewer of these bills in circulation and they could be spotted by bank tellers much more easily than other types of bills.

On the next evening a taxi driver came to Dr. Condon's house about eight o'clock with a note. He said that a man at 188th Street and Madison Avenue gave it to him. It instructed Dr. Condon to go to Bergen's Flower store, Tremont Avenue, which is located very nearly opposite St. Raymond's Cemetery. Colonel Lindbergh went along with him. The two put the ransom money in a box and proceeded to Bergen's Flower store in an automobile operated by Colonel Lindbergh. There, Dr. Condon found a second note on a table with a stone on it, with the following directions: "Cross the street and walk to Widdemere Avenue and I'll meet you." He went to the corner and waited about five minutes, leaving Colonel Lindbergh in the car parked about fifty yards from the corner.

He started to walk away when someone yelled from the cemetery, "Hey, Doc, here I am."

Dr. Condon said, "All right," and walked toward the sound until he came to a hedge fence partly around the cemetery.

"Here I am," said a man's voice, which the Doctor recognized to be the same "John's" that he had heard at Woodlawn Cemetery on the previous occasion. "Have you got the money?"

"No," said Dr. Condon, "but it is in the automobile. I can't give you the money unless you show something for it."

"I sent you the sleeping suit," "John" said, "and I will give you directions where the baby is."

Dr. Condon went back to the car, got the box, and carried it to the hedge. "John" gave him a sealed note, which he said should not be opened for two hours.

The note stated that the baby would be found between Gay Head and Horse Neck Beach near Elizabeth Island on the boat *Nellie*.

With Colonel Breckinridge, Jafsie, and Chief Elmer Irey of the Treasury Department in Washington, Lindbergh drove along the Boston Post Road and crossed into Connecticut to a point on Long Island Sound where the party boarded a plane which Lindbergh had arranged for. He headed the plane to their rendezvous, arriving there about dawn; then he skillfully guided the plane, swooping low over all inlets, bays, and anchorages along the shore. With dogged persistence, Lindbergh continued the search, covering miles and miles of water front along Long Island Sound. He landed at Cuttyhunk and made inquiries of the natives as to whether they knew of any yacht bearing the name of *Nellie*. The group became discouraged, except for Lindbergh. He wanted his baby. He wouldn't give up hope. The plane rose from its berth at Cuttyhunk and the anxious father again guided it from port to port and bay to bay, swooping down close to all small craft to see if the much sought after boat *Nellie* might be spotted. While Lindbergh searched from the air, the Coast Guard searched up and down the Sound. At nightfall, crushed with bitter disappointment, Lindbergh finally landed the plane, and the group headed back to New York.

Lindbergh returned with dead, vacant eyes from that flight. His abortive search for the boat *Nellie,* aboard which the kidnaper said he would find his son, was the most bitter disappointment of his life. Anger blanched his face as he exclaimed through clenched teeth, "We've been double-crossed."

A few days later a big, bluff backslapper, John Hughes Curtis, a boat builder from Norfolk, got Lindbergh's ear and high-pressured him into believing the baby was with a gang on a schooner off Cape May, New Jersey. Curtis was introduced and vouched for by a Norfolk minister. I was not favorably impressed. However, he persuaded Colonel Lindbergh to go to sea with him several times in search for the schooner. The last time was a day I will never forget—May 11th.

I was at the fraternity club, mulling over some transcripts of wire taps we had put on two suspects, when Colonel Breckinridge telephoned. "Be downstairs in ten minutes. Go to Hopewell immediately. Report baby's body found."

A truck driver who had to make a comfort stop along the road had found the baby's body in the woods just a few miles from the Lindbergh home. Later, during the trial, the circumstantial evidence indicated that the kidnaper, Hauptmann, had killed the child the moment he took it from the crib, then left the body in the woods. He had made no preparations to care for the infant, since he did not wish to run the risk of secreting the baby.

We were all gathered at the Lindbergh home talking about the discovery of the body when Lindy's car came crunching up the gravel driveway. He walked in. His gray suit was unpressed. He had spent a strenuous day on a rough sea with Curtis, looking for the schooner.

Colonel Schwarzkopf spoke quietly to Colonel Lindbergh. "Better come into the study. We've got some bad news."

Lindbergh simply stood rooted and said, "Thanks." He started to walk away, then pivoted, looked at me and said in words frosted with disgust, "Curtis is out in my car."

I pumped Curtis until three o'clock in the morning—and marveled at the stubborn way he clung to his tissue of bunk about the baby being on the schooner. He finally broke down, confessed to Lieutenant Keaten of the New Jersey State Police, Inspector Walsh of the Jersey City Police, and me that he had gone publicity crazy and made up the lies about the schooner off Cape May. He cried and said he was ashamed of his inhuman hoax that had so cruelly misled the mother and father of the baby. We swore out a warrant for his arrest for obstructing justice. I helped prepare the case for trial and testified at the trial. Curtis was sentenced to a year in jail.

On May 12th, the day after the body of the baby was found, President Herbert Hoover issued instructions to the Secretary of the Treasury and other government agencies to continue the investigation.

The realization that her baby was dead, after those ten weeks of vacillating hope, brought tremendous pressure upon Anne Morrow Lindbergh, which it took all her resources to withstand. One day I had lunch with the Lindberghs at Hopewell. Mrs. Lindbergh toyed with her food and seemed intent only on telling me more and more details that might help solve the crime, I asked about the nursery window. Was it locked? No. Just how much was it open? When I had finished my lunch, Mrs. Lindbergh said, "Come up to the nursery. I will show you exactly how the window was."

We followed her into the nursery. The crib, which Colonel Lindbergh had shown me on my first visit to the home, was gone. All the baby's toys were gone. As she walked toward the window, I saw Mrs. Lindbergh's eye dart for a swift moment to the corner where the crib had stood. Then she set the window just as it had been set the night of March 1st.

We walked through an adjoining room. My eyes roved over the walls and I stopped short. Mrs. Lindbergh paused at the door and watched me as I studied the flowered wallpaper. There was something strange about it. I couldn't tell just what it was at first. Then I noticed that on one side of the room the wallpaper had flowers with brightly colored centers; on the remainder of the wallpaper the centers of the flowers were plain.

"Oh, that," said Mrs. Lindbergh. "I've been touching up the centers of the flowers—I haven't finished yet. It's comforting to have something to do."

I think that, more than anything else, made me realize the battle she was putting up.

The possibility that perhaps the kidnaping had been an "inside job," involving servants or employees in the Lindbergh home at Hopewell or the Morrow home at Englewood, was explored. In due time all of the employees were cleared completely, except one. She was Violet Sharpe, a twenty-year-old girl, retiring and unattractive, who had recently arrived from England. She was a maid in the Morrow home. Violet was a timid, excitable, and nervous little lady who was terrified when she was questioned by three Jersey City detectives. She said that she had been at a movie in Englewood the night of the kidnaping, but they promptly estab-

lished that the movie she named was not showing there at
the time. On the basis of that, some of the boys were quite
willing to hang the murder on Violet.

I was requested by Colonel Schwarzkopf to take over the
questioning and he assigned Lieutenant Keaten to co-operate with me—from that time, Keaten worked with me; he
was one of the best investigators with whom I had ever been
teamed up. We arranged to interview Violet at a police
station near Englewood and to have a police matron present.
We sent a state trooper to the Morrow house to drive her to
the station. While he waited for Violet to get her hat and
coat, she slipped upstairs to her room and drank enough
silver polish (cyanide potassium) to kill an ox. She was
dead in about three minutes.

Violet Sharpe did not have the slightest connection with
the kidnaping. We found that she told the lie about the
movie because she had a "pick-up" date with a young fellow
in Englewood and she was ashamed to admit it. She was a
weak girl emotionally, and the blunt questions put to her by
the Jersey City detectives were too much for her. She developed a fear that the kidnaping was being pinned on her,
that she was being framed, and suicide seemed the only way
out.

Meanwhile I became interested in the nails in the crude
wooden ladder the kidnaper had left behind at the Hopewell home. I located the steel mill at which they had been
manufactured in Pittsburgh. Under the microscope, these
nails showed a slight imperfection, the very twin to an imperfection we found in one of the nail dies at the mill. Records showed just when that die had been used. We turned to
sales ledgers for that period, and, sure enough, one shipment of nails from this die had gone to a hardware store in
the Bronx. There the trail ended.

In the fall a new baby arrived in the Lindbergh family—
another boy. From that time on the Lindberghs lived at the
Morrow home in Englewood, New Jersey. Colonel Lind-

bergh got a big German shepherd police dog, Thor, to help guard the baby.

The Morrow mansion was about a hundred yards back from the street. I would drive through the front gate of the estate and to the front door of the mansion. Thor would run right to the door of my car, put his front feet on the running board, show his big sharp teeth, and growl. I would put up the window on my side, blow my horn, and wait for Banks, the butler, to rescue me. When Banks arrived, he would calm Thor and usher me into the house, saying, "Don't ever step out of that car or Thor will eat you alive."

When my business with Colonel Lindbergh was completed, Mrs. Lindbergh or Mrs. Morrow would appear and extend a cordial invitation to remain for lunch or for dinner. If it was not close to mealtime they would send in cookies and a pot of coffee or some ice cream in the warm weather, and frequently they would join us. Their friendly, gracious, but simple hospitality was a bright spot in those tedious, disappointing days when it appeared that we were making no headway on the investigation. Sometimes the nursemaid would bring in the new baby so we could see how fast he was growing or if he had a new tooth. The Colonel was proud of Thor and would bring him in to show some of his tricks.

On one occasion we had a long conference with the Colonel, with seven agents and the police present. I knew that the Colonel got a kick out of showing off Thor, so after the conference was over I suggested that he bring the dog in.

The Colonel seemed tickled and soon had Thor doing some difficult tricks. We moved outside. Two wire-haired terriers on leashes, puppies, were brought up by Mrs. Lindbergh. She said, "Thor, take the babies for a walk." He took the leashes in his mouth and led the puppies around the yard. Then the Colonel said, "Thor, take the babies for a little swim." With the leashes still in his mouth, Thor proceeded to the swimming pool and pulled the puppies in with him.

They were about halfway across the pool when one puppy went under and stayed under. Quick as a wink the Colonel dived in and rescued the pup. That climax ended the animal show for the day.

When months dragged by without a break in the case, I was sent out on other assignments. I was in St. Louis in the *Post Dispatch* office when the teletype clicked out the arrest in New York City of Bruno Richard Hauptmann, who had been identified as the passer of one of the Lindbergh ransom bills. I phoned my office in Washington and was directed to proceed to New York.

In the Bronx jail I set my eyes upon this square-faced German. He looked, even then, more like a rock than a man —utterly cold, seemingly inanimate. How simply he had been caught! He paid for a gasoline purchase with a ten-dollar bill, and the gas station man, Ernest Lyons, worried about counterfeit ten-dollar bills which were then flooding New York, had jotted Hauptmann's car license number on the face of the bill. When the bill was deposited at a branch of the Corn Exchange bank it was spotted as Lindbergh ransom money, with Hauptmann's car license number on the face of the bill. The bank reported it and Hauptmann, a carpenter, was picked up the next day. He had one of the twenty-dollar ransom bills in his pocket; and $14,600 in ransom money was found buried under the floor of his garage and in a secret panel in the wall.

"How did you happen to have that money in your garage?" I asked the stolid carpenter, as he stared at me from his cell.

"Never had it," he muttered.

"Have you ever been out to Hopewell?"

"Don't know where it is."

"Aren't you the man Dr. Condon met in the cemetery?"

"No."

After Hauptmann was indicted, I tried to question him again. "How come you had all that money in your garage?"

"Leave me alone," Bruno said morosely. "My lawyers told me not to talk to nobody."

"Yes, but for the sake of your wife and that little boy of yours, you should explain things. Maybe we can help you," I persisted.

Hauptmann looked up through his lifeless eyes, which resembled a pair of onyx marbles. "I don't talk to you."

In the weeks preceding the trial, we went to work on Hauptmann's financial history, starting at the day he collected the ransom. If Hauptmann had received $50,000 ransom on April 2, 1932, and $14,600 had been recovered on his premises, there still was $35,400 to account for. Hauptmann had been a meticulous record-keeper. We studied his methodical accounts in the diaries found in his home, with his day-by-day disbursements and receipts, and easily established that in March, 1932, he had not been worth a penny more than $4,942, including a used car.

But in the month of the kidnaping, the diary stopped. There simply were no more entries. We checked banks, brokerage houses, travel agencies, auto companies, stores —anywhere Hauptmann could have spent or deposited any money. By January, 1935, when the trial opened, we had a financial statement fully explaining the $35,000 he had spent between the night he collected the $50,000 ransom and the day he was arrested. Hauptmann had opened several brokerage accounts and had lost $9,132 gambling on the stock market. He had sent his wife vacationing to Germany. He had bought a car. He had gone to Florida. Yet, in all this time he had been unemployed, without a dollar of income.

Hauptmann was indicted by the Hunterdon County Grand Jury at Flemington, New Jersey. Flemington was a smug, somnolent town whose inhabitants wanted nothing more than to be left alone, a desire that was dashed one hundred percent when the Hauptmann trial descended upon it. Over six hundred reporters, photographers, radio technicians, and such famous journalists as Damon Runyon, Walter Winchell, Dorothy Kilgallen, and Adela Rogers St. Johns were in Flemington to report the details of the trial daily. The streets were choked with sound trucks and automobiles with tripods on their roofs; the small hotels were aflame with lights all night.

The trial opened January 2, 1935. After witnesses had established the discovery of the body of the baby, Anne Morrow Lindbergh was called as a witness. She made a pathetic picture as she nervously faced the morbid crowd, but her testimony was cool, calm, and without bitterness. She reiterated the events at her home on March 1st and definitely identified the sleeping garment which had been delivered to Jafsie.

Colonel Lindbergh was called and testified fully, regarding the night of the kidnaping, the notes written by the kidnaper, the negotiations, and finally the ransom payment by Jafsie to a man at St. Raymond's Cemetery. The climax of his testimony was when he stated that he heard a voice in the cemetery call to Jafsie, "Hey, Doctor, over here, Doctor."

Attorney General Wilentz then asked Colonel Lindbergh, "Have you heard that voice since?"

The avid crowd in the courtroom leaned forward in their seats.

In a calm voice Colonel Lindbergh replied, "I have."

"Whose voice was it?"

"It was the voice of Bruno Richard Hauptmann."

The "Bull of Brooklyn," as Chief Defense Counsel Reilly was known in legal circles, then went to work to tear Colonel Lindbergh's testimony to pieces. He had a great reputation as a cross examiner, but he was completely unsuccessful in his efforts to confuse Colonel Lindbergh or to have him change or modify his testimony.

Dr. Condon's testimony paralleled that of Colonel Lindbergh. Again the "Bull of Brooklyn" exerted tremendous efforts to confuse Dr. Condon. Again he was unsuccessful.

Attorney General Wilentz, the chief prosecuting attorney, then directed me to take the witness stand. I identified 493 twenty-dollar United States Gold Certificates and 474 ten-dollar United States Gold Certificates, the $14,600 found hidden in Hauptmann's garage, as bills with serial numbers identical to the serial numbers of the ransom bills which we had recorded carefully that night in the office of J. P. Morgan & Company.

I observed Adela Rogers St. Johns in the front row of the press section making notes while I was testifying. The next day, newspapers across the country carried her description of me:

> Courthouse, Flemington, New Jersey
> January 11

The Federal boys moved into the Hauptmann trial today and with awe we saw the United States Government, cold, relentless, infinitely patient, following the trail of the Lindbergh kidnapper. . . .

Frank J. Wilson, a big, slow-moving, slow-speaking man, with a round, kindly face, and round, moonlike glasses and a slow smile. A Special Agent of the United States Treasury Department. He wasn't a movie conception of the part—he didn't measure up to any fiction detective. But before he was through with his slow, thorough answers, I felt I would rather have Philo Vance or Anthony Abbott after me—oh, a whole lot rather.

They might get tired. Mr. Wilson never would. A year—ten years—twenty years—you would never be safe, never be out of reach of that relentless glacier. . . .

Mr. Lloyd Fischer did a fine job of cross-examining. But Agent Wilson was not moved . . . He knew his job. He did it. You could no more shake him nor reflect upon his honesty or his sureness of his facts than you could melt a glacier with a blow torch.

F

After I left the witness stand, Attorney General Wilentz placed handwriting experts on the stand to prove that the handwriting in the note left in the nursery when the baby was stolen, and in the series of notes or letters written to Jafsie, was that of Bruno Richard Hauptmann.

The next witness, Arthur Koehler, from the Forest Products Laboratory of the Department of Agriculture, who had made a study of the homemade ladder used by the kidnaper, established that it had been constructed in part from a floorboard in the attic of the Hauptmann home.

Bruno Richard Hauptmann was the first defense witness. He swore that on March 1st, the night of the kidnaping, he was at a bake shop and restaurant in the Bronx, where his wife, Anna, was employed; that he had called to take her home as was his custom every Tuesday. His wife corroborated his story.

Bruno also swore that on the night of April 2nd, at the time the ransom was paid, he was at home with several friends, enjoying their regular Saturday "music evening." Anna corroborated his statement. Their friend, Hans Kloppenberg, swore that Bruno was home on the night of April 2nd. None of the other persons present at the "music evening" were called as witnesses.

Hauptmann proclaimed that the $14,600 found hidden in his garage was brought to his home by Isadore Fisch, a friend whom he had known for a long time, and left with him for safe-keeping as he was about to go to Europe. Bruno alleged that they had gone into the fur business and investment business early in 1932. Fisch was in poor health, and in 1933, he had decided to return to his former home in Germany. Our investigation had established that Fisch died in a German sanitarium of tuberculosis early in 1934, friendless and destitute.

The jury retired to study the evidence at 11:23 A.M. on February 13, 1935. At 10:44 P.M., the jury entered the court-room to announce its verdict. Colonel Lindbergh was not present.

Justice Trenchard: "Ladies and Gentlemen of the jury, have you arrived at a verdict?"

Foreman Walton speaking calmly: "We, the jury, find the defendant, Bruno Richard Hauptmann, guilty of murder in the first degree."

Aside from the possession and use of the ransom money and the testimony of the handwriting experts, the evidence which I believe was the *final* weight that swung the jury to a verdict of guilty was given by Colonel Lindbergh himself. It was the unhappy father's unhesitating statement that the voice of Hauptmann was that of the man whom he had heard speak on that April night in 1932, when Jafsie paid the kidnaper $50,000 at St. Raymond's Cemetery. Each of the twelve jurors knew that Colonel Lindbergh was a man who had frequently bet his life on the sound of a motor in the days when most planes had only one engine. There was no question of his keen and highly sensitive hearing, and the voice he heard in the cemetery on that April night, when the ransom to obtain the return of his baby was paid, was one that would remain in the memory of Charles Lindbergh for as long as he was able to remember anything. When he had given his testimony, the Hunterdon County jury remembered, too.

Hauptmann's lawyers appeared before New Jersey's Court of Errors and Appeals on June 20, 1935. After an extremely serious study of 2,500 pages of testimony, of legal briefs, and careful consideration of all phases of the evidence and the trial at Flemington, the judges (nine lawyers and four laymen) voted unanimously to uphold the decision and verdict of the lower court.

Shortly after the New Jersey Court of Errors and Appeals sustained the verdict of the lower court, a Jersey businessman, wise to the slick ways of politicians, warned me, "Watch out for the Governor, Frank. He'll throw a monkey wrench in the Lindbergh case. He's dead set on getting Colonel Schwarzkopf out."

Colonel Schwarzkopf had been appointed as Superintendent of the New Jersey State Police back in 1921, and because of his efficiency, he had been reappointed by succeeding governors, both Republican and Democrat. Governor Hoffman wanted his own man in this key position, and he intended to get rid of Schwarzkopf. However, prominent New Jersey businessmen recognized the efficient and nonpolitical operation of the police department all during the fourteen years Colonel Schwarzkopf, a West Point graduate with a fine war record, had served in the Superintendent's job, and they urged that he be continued.

"What can Governor Hoffman do?" I replied. "The case is closed, the jury has rendered a verdict of guilty, and the upper court has sustained the verdict."

"Oh," answered the businessman, "don't you know the Governor is a publicity hound? He'll stall the execution of Hauptmann. He'll find some way to embarrass Colonel Schwarzkopf and the State Police."

Late in October, the Governor made a secret midnight visit to Hauptmann in his state prison cell, where he was awaiting execution in the electric chair. The visit was in direct violation of prison regulations. News of that visit leaked out and was published in papers across the country. Citizens were astounded. State Assemblyman Crawford Jamieson characterized the illegal visit to the death house cell at midnight in order to interview the condemned man as "nothing but the exploitation of the celebrated Lindbergh crime for the purpose of providing our Governor with national publicity." At that time Hoffman was being publicized as the most likely candidate for vice-president on the Republican ticket in 1936.

The Governor was irked at the published statement of Assemblyman Jamieson. He issued a public bulletin: "Rumors allege the existence of evidence not presented by the police at the trial. Some of them allege other conditions disadvantageous to the defense. All these rumors must be set at rest. The case of Hauptmann is one with which the dimensions of American justice will be measured by all Americans and by the world."

The Governor's strong statement spread far and wide and created serious doubt about the case in the minds of many Americans. It became evident that my smart Jersey businessman friend had correctly sized up the situation.

Governor Hoffman summarily ordered the State Police to reopen the investigation and to call upon Federal authorities and the New York City Police for co-operation, but Police Commissioner Lew Valentine of New York City and Attorney General Homer Cummings declined to do so.

The Governor then proceeded to set up a court in his capitol office, which reporters termed a "cracker-barrel court." Colonel Schwarzkopf resigned, and the Governor appointed Warden Kimberling to succeed him. Hauptmann was granted a thirty-day reprieve.

By the time Governor Hoffman had ordered a three-day stay of execution for Hauptmann, which set the execution for April 3rd in the New Jersey State prison, members of the state legislature were considering impeachment proceedings against the Governor. But on April 3rd, still vigorously maintaining his innocence, Hauptmann paid the penalty of death in the electric chair for the murder of the Lindbergh baby.

Because of Governor Hoffman's exploitation of the Lindbergh case, using it as a political football, there unfortunately has been some cloud of doubt as to the guilt of Bruno Richard Hauptmann. There is no doubt in my mind. He was guilty—one hundred percent. The facts were there. He had a previous criminal record in Germany and was, without doubt, as cold, hard, and vicious a criminal as I ever ran into—a real villain with ice for a heart.

His death did leave one curious question unanswered.

How could he have spent $35,000 of the ransom money gambling in the stock market and sending his wife to Germany, without some of it being traced to him at an earlier date? That's the heartbreak of being a detective. Able bank tellers became tired of meticulously inspecting every bill deposited in a bank after the first flush of excitement had worn off. A year after the kidnaping I was still going around to banks giving pep talks and strongly urging them to search for the ransom bills. I always got the answer, "Oh, yes, we're keeping an eye open. You bet." But when I slyly asked, "Have you got your list of serial numbers handy?" they'd get nervous. Sometimes they couldn't find that list at all.

Because of that big gap between good intentions and performance, Hauptmann almost got away with murder.

5

During the long wait between the news of the death of the Lindbergh baby and Hauptmann's arrest, I was sent to New Orleans to take a look into the unreported income of Kingfish Huey Long. Early in 1932, following an allegation by the former Governor of Louisiana, John Parker, agents of the Internal Revenue Bureau had gone to Louisiana to start gathering evidence against Long, who had been governor from 1926 to 1930 and was at this time United States Senator from Louisiana. He was known as Dictator Long.

Agent Arch Burford had made a sizeable collection of evidence incriminating Long, when he got a call from a high level in Washington asking him if he could present the case within a month. When Burford said he could not work that fast, his orders were, "Then drop it!"

It was another instance of boss justice. Long was simply too powerful in Washington. The investigation lay dormant for a year. Then, during the new Roosevelt administration, the "go" whistle was blown once more, and I was put on the case. I had, as helpers, some of the agents who had worked in Louisiana earlier, plus some of my men who had been in Chicago with me, including undercover man Mike Malone.

Long, like Capone, held sway over his empire from a hotel suite in the Roosevelt Hotel in New Orleans, when he was not in Washington. Posing as a promoter seeking backing for a radio station, Mike checked into the Roosevelt, spread his charm around, and pretty soon he was lunching with local businessmen and laughing at jokes about the Kingfish's shady deals—information which he promptly passed along to me. He also became very friendly with a rich widow living at the Roosevelt, a gossip-loving busybody who seemed to know everybody in Louisiana—especially if there was any scandal to be told about them. She gave Mike a rundown on some big state road contracts involving the Kingfish and the owner of the Roosevelt Hotel. She also told how they forced an insurance company to pay them twenty percent commission on all policies covering state business and bond premiums of contractors performing work for the state, information which we later developed into evidence that helped land the hotel owner in the Atlanta penitentiary.

While drawing out the widow and her stories, Mike had one close call. He was coming down in the elevator with her, to go to lunch, when the elevator stopped for a trio of ladies on the third floor. One looked at Mike and exclaimed, "Why, it's my cousin Mike from New Jersey! Mike, I haven't seen you in twenty years!"

Mike gave her a glassy stare and said, "Oh, I'm sorry, but you are mistaken. I'm not your cousin. I never lived in Jersey."

The lady stared at him, puzzled. "Why, you look enough like Mike to be his twin!"

Mike watched his widow uneasily. But she only smiled and murmured something about people looking alike. He bolted his lunch, excused himself with a tall story about an important appointment, and called me. "I may have fooled my cousin," he told me, "but I'm not going back into that hotel till she's checked out."

I found out she was leaving that same afternoon, and

Mike returned to the Roosevelt. He was reassured that his plump little widow had no suspicions when she agreed that evening to put up the money for his radio station. From then on, his problem was to stall her off.

By the time I reopened the Long case, two very important witnesses, unearthed by the earlier investigation, had died, and some evidence had "disappeared." Getting people to agree to testify against the all-powerful Kingfish was about as difficult as getting them to give evidence against Scarface and his gang. Senator Long passed out the word to all who had been involved in dealing with him: "Keep your mouths shut—or you'll regret it." To the world at large, he bragged, "Those damn Washington agents can't touch me!"

For a while I almost believed he was right. Through the bayous and the canebrake, from the sweltering delta of the Mississippi to the oil fields in western Louisiana, dictator Long had spread the fear that seals lips. One word against the regime of the Kingfish or his corrupt pals and an honest citizen might find the tax on his house doubled, his son being flunked out of college or his scalp massaged with a baseball bat.

"We've heard all about you, Wilson," sneered a New Orleans contractor who had a big state road contract. "I don't know a thing about a deal the Kingfish made to give Frank Costello of New York and Phil Kastell of New Jersey a monopoly on the slot machine racket in Louisiana."

When I urged him to co-operate with me, he said, "I won't talk until hell freezes over. The Kingfish would immediately call a special session of the state legislature and pass a bill wrecking my business."

I spent a few Sundays driving around the state with Judith, to get the grass-roots sentiment of the local folks about the Kingfish. I would drive up to a gas station to get my tank filled, get out and buy a cigar so as to start a conversation with the boss. To my question, "How do you folks like Senator Long?" the usual answer was, "Oh, mister, we

sure do like him. Why he's giving our children free text-
books. He's giving us wonderful state roads. Besides, mister,
we had better like him and vote for him or we'll soon have
our tax assessment boosted."

One keen retired businessman told me how the Kingfish
operated. "In 1928, at age thirty-four, Huey was elected
governor. His campaign slogan was 'Every Man a King But
No Man Wears a Crown.' He promised paved roads all over
the state and free books for school children—all without a
penny's cost to the poor people. He entirely disregarded
routine procedure in transacting state business, and he made
unholy alliances with racketeers. He awarded big state contracts in his private office and when a suggestion was made
that the Louisiana highway department be consulted, he
roared, 'Hell, I *am* the highway department.' "

The Kingfish continuously stormed at the Roosevelt administration in Washington, and he even threatened to have
Louisiana secede from the Union. He was elected United
States Senator in 1930, and he quickly became the most
filibustering, rip-snorting, brazen, insulting, and contro-
versial member ever to join that conservative and dignified
body.

Because of the devastating financial panic and widespread
unemployment, millions of Americans were ready to grasp
at any straw which would seem to help them. The Kingfish,
an astute student of human nature, grasped the opportunity
to parade as a friend of the common people.

He proposed to commandeer many fortunes by levying a
capital tax on the rich. He promised to forbid anyone to in-
herit more than five million dollars. Finally he promised to
forbid any of the mighty, greedy fortune builders to make
more than one million a year, and any sum in excess was
to be taken by the government and given to poor people.

That the Kingfish fully expected eventually to be elected
president was established by his book, published after his
death, *My First Days in the White House.*

Because of the antagonistic and defiant attitude of witnesses in Louisiana, I decided to try to get some evidence outside of the state. I discovered that all of the surety bonds to insure the performance on state contracts went to a single outfit, the Hartwig-Moss Insurance Agency of which Mike Moss, an original sponsor of the Kingfish in his campaign for governor, was vice-president. Moss had lost a lot of money in the 1929 depression, and in 1931 had moved out to a nice cow ranch in Arizona.

I had fleshy, potbellied Moss subpoenaed to appear before the federal Grand Jury at New Orleans. To our astonishment, he showed up in cowboy boots, a big sombrero, and a red bandanna around his neck. He waddled on his high heels with the shaky uncertain ankles of a beginner on ice skates. I had intended to keep his presence in New Orleans a secret, but Moss's exhibitionism not only made this impossible but suggested an entirely new strategy.

I took him to Kolb's Restaurant, a fine old eating house specializing in German dishes, not far from the Roosevelt Hotel. We sat at a table in prominent view and when Huey's boys swarmed around to give Mike a handshake and look over his cowboy outfit, I'd seize every possible chance to say, "Oh, yes, Mike is all right. He's giving us lots of *cooperation.*" Mike was too busy cramming himself with sauerbraten to realize that I was baiting a trap. He gorged himself for a good hour, pausing only to remove his glass eye and fondly polish it. By the time dinner was over, half a dozen of the dictator's henchmen were already speeding over to the Roosevelt Hotel to tip off the Kingfish that Mike Moss was having lunch with me and was helping the government.

To keep Mike from close contact with the Long mob, I hid him with an agent bodyguard in a family hotel in Gulfport, Mississippi, about forty miles away. I was with Moss when Huey Long, who often took to the radio to spellbind the Cajuns and the trappers of Louisiana, came on the air with a scathing attack on him. Moss listened with an incredulous expression. His old buddy, the Kingfish, was referring to him with icy derision as "Potbelly Moss" and "Moss the double-crosser."

Moss fumed. He took out his glass eye and gave it a hard polishing. He barked at me, "The nerve of that skunk! If it hadn't been for me he'd of never been governor! That's the gratitude I get!"

When he was feeling good and sore, I gently changed the subject to the commissions on the state bonding business. "Sure," Moss bragged, "the only reason Huey ever promised me all the state bonding business was because I went and made him governor in 1928. Without my help he never woulda won.

"Promise, hell!" he went on. "Soon as the election was over, Huey told me, 'Yes, you'll get all the state bond business, Mike; you just give me the twenty percent commission.' I said, 'You never mentioned that before, Huey.' He said, 'Maybe, Mike, you just weren't listening.' "

"Still, I guess he never made you pony up that dough," I suggested.

"Oh," shouted Moss, "you can bet your bottom dollar the Kingfish got that dough. He went after it like a bear goin' for honey. He'd get me on the phone and say, 'I've got some big expenses to meet, Mike. Get those bond commissions down here fast.' Sometimes he'd say, 'I wantcha to step on it, Mike. We need that dough this afternoon.' Many's the time I took that dough down to the Roosevelt Hotel myself and handed it to Huey."

My next hot lead came from undercover man Mike Malone. He showed up at our apartment quite late one night. Holding forth at the Roosevelt Hotel bar, he had poured enough Ramos Gin fizzes (for which the bar was famous) into his rich widow and three of Long's henchmen to encourage a good gossip session. They had just told him that Long collected huge graft from dealings with the Standard

Dredging Company of New York. This firm had the state's contracts for the tremendous land fills required at the new New Orleans airport, which had been built on the marshy shores of Lake Ponchartrain.

I promptly lit out for New York, accompanied by Special Agents Paul Anderson and Ed Funk. In the petrified jungle of lower Broadway we found the Standard Dredging Company and went straight to work on its mountains of ledgers, under the guise of a routine tax check-up. Nothing jarred me until I noticed recurrent large disbursements to the company's president, Robert F. Perry, who had died just a few weeks before. The disbursements were headed, "Perry—Personal Expense Account" and ranged from $10,000 to $25,-000. I counted enough of them to total half-a-million dollars.

From then on I seized every opportunity to look into the affairs of the late Mr. Perry. "Let's open this safe," I said, pointing to an old vault about seven feet high. The auditor reluctantly opened it, disclosing shelves of yellowed papers. At the bottom was a locked drawer. I insisted that it be opened. The drawer was crammed with bills from Perry's tailor, bills for flowers for his wife.

Then I spied a Manila envelope in the bottom of that drawer: "R.F.P.—*Personal*."

From that Manila envelope I drew five small, black leather books, Perry's personal diaries for five years, 1928 to 1932. I took the diaries back to my hotel. Most of the entries were about routine matters, but I found some items I didn't understand. "H. in town," "3,600,000 yards—18,000," "Saw H. again," "4,900,000 yards—24,500"; and later in the diaries: "S. arrived in town," "4,150,000 yards—20,750," "Talked to S.," "2,900,000 yards—14,500." The thing that struck me was the constant ratio of two hundred to one between the figures labeled "yards" and the unlabeled figures which followed. I had a hunch that the smaller figures might represent payments at the rate of one-half cent per cubic yard. I again combed the company ledgers. Sure enough, I found disbursements to Perry's "personal account" on the exact days and in the exact amounts as those in the cryptic items in Perry's diaries.

But who were "H" and "S"?

Elementary. If one-half percent per cubic yard was paid to someone, who would be most likely to get it? Joe Haspel was chairman of the New Orleans Levee Board in charge of all airport contracts prior to 1929. During that period the diary items read "H." Abe Shushan, appointed by Governor Long, was the chairman of the board after 1929. During that period the diary items read "S."

Perry had arranged many of the pay-offs by buying government bonds and turning these over to Haspel and Shushan on their regular trips to New York. I found that one consignment of bonds—$10,000 worth—was shipped directly to Haspel in New Orleans. It was shipped by registered mail, leaving the beautiful scrawl of Haspel's signature on the receipt to prove he had received it.

Back in New Orleans, we called on Joe Haspel at his big seersucker suit factory. I found him in an office decked with silver-framed pictures, with an expensive Chinese rug on the floor. At first he tried to be "co-operative" with Agent Harvey Bauer and me. But when I touched on the matter of airport graft, Joe Haspel was a reluctant clam. Not until I played my ace, the $10,000 consignment of bonds sent by registered mail, did he show any signs of cracking. Then he cracked all at once.

He jerked open a bottom drawer of his desk, pulled out a bottle, and poured himself four fingers of whiskey. As he shrugged it down he gasped, "I'm a sick man, Wilson. I can't stand any more of your questions today."

Two days later the scared Haspel came to our office with his lawyer, and in order to get a break for himself he squawked on Long. He reluctantly admitted that he had collected $70,000 in graft payments in 1928 from Perry, most of which he passed on to Long for alleged campaign expenses.

By July, 1935, our tax case against Kingfish Huey Long was browned to a turn. In tax evasion cases it is customary to invite the taxpayer to explain income which we found had not been reported. The Kingfish was no exception. Some of his racketeer pals had stalled for six months after we had invited them in to explain their failure to report income. I saw by the papers that the Kingfish was in New Orleans, home from the Senate, so I decided to pay him a visit.

Fully expecting a run-around before we could get a conference with the Kingfish, I telephoned the Roosevelt Hotel and told Huey's secretary, "We've been going over his tax returns and there are a few minor items we'd like to discuss."

To my surprise, the telephone rang within five minutes.

"This is Senator Long," said a high-pitched voice, which could be heard ten feet from the receiver. "My secretary says you have some tax items to discuss with me."

"That's correct, Senator," I replied. "We'd like to see you at your convenience."

"Come right on over this afternoon," he bellowed.

When Agent Burford and I walked into Room 908 at the Roosevelt, I got my first look at Huey P. Long. He stood there in his bare feet, his face darkened with a heavy growth of stubbly beard, his hair looking as if he'd been in the wake of a tornado, his limbs gangling, his head askew, his eyes peering out like gun muzzles from an ambush. The entire apparition was swathed in silk pajamas of dainty robin's egg blue, embroidered with the monogram H. P. L.

"I've heard aboutcha, Wilson. Been down here a helluva long time, haven'tcha?" said the Kingfish. "Makin' any headway?"

"Oh, yes, we're making a lot of headway," I replied.

"Say, I hear you're the guy who sent Al Capone to jail. Is that why they sentcha down here to get me and my boys?"

"Oh, I don't know, Senator. It's a pleasant assignment."

"Pleasant, I'll say it's pleasant! Why, you're in N'awlins, man, the best town on the map!"

Huey plopped himself full length on the bed, feet at the head of the bed, stomach down, and remained that way all afternoon. His mouthy, high-pitched voice filled the room, punctuated now and then by thunderclaps of laughter. When he laughed, the oscillating rolls of flesh on his body seemed to inflate his blue pajamas like a blimp.

Burford and I went over his tax returns, asking routine questions about perfectly legitimate items. The Kingfish had a remarkably long memory. He could fill in dates, places, and amounts down to the last penny on items five and six years old. It was part of our strategy to lay down a barrage of questions on completely unsuspicious items, just to establish what a fine memory for details the Kingfish had. Whenever we mentioned a town in Louisiana, he told us all about his old pals up there, about election campaigns going back ten years, about the local judges and legislators and how he'd spellbound them all with his speeches. He dragged in countless yarns, parables, racy jokes.

At the mention of one little town near Hammond, he said, "Man, they raise the best strawberries in the You-nited States up there. Say, you want to make some real money? Just come down here and I'll help you get a strawberry farm. People are gettin' richer. We'll make you rich. By jiminy, everybody's going to eat strawberries someday! Why, we'll be trucking refrigerated strawberries to every part of the country!"

This was a clear invitation to say to hell with the Treasury and let Huey set me up on a lush strawberry ranch in Louisiana. He seemed to be disappointed when we let it pass.

As we talked, a phone call came through and Huey bellowed into the instrument, "There's two of those smart fellows from Washington here right now. Checking my income tax! But they're good fellows; I'm not worried about them one bit!"

After two hours Burford and I abandoned the blank cartridges and began shooting with live ammunition.

"What about the mortgage on that house of yours, Senator?" I asked, informing him that we had evidence that $25,000 of it had been paid off by Seymour Weiss, the Long gang's treasurer, who had laid down twenty-five one-thousand-dollar bills.

The Kingfish was still on his belly. He dropped his forehead into his hands and said, "I don't remember anything about that. Man, that's none of my business. That's my wife's house."

I mentioned the expensive Wagner & Wagner suits the Kingfish had been getting—$1,320 worth in two months—all of them also paid for by Treasurer Weiss.

"I've been getting suits there for years," he said. "Any time you want a good suit of clothes, go to Wagner & Wagner. They're better'n anything in New York or Washington."

We mentioned several other disbursements, including $73 that Treasurer Weiss had paid to A. Sulka & Company in New York for two pairs of blue silk pajamas monogrammed H. P. L.

"Oh, I don't remember anything about that," the pajama-clad Kingfish said. "Most of the time I don't even wear pajamas."

At six o'clock Huey apologized for cutting us off, but he had an engagement. Then he added, "Come back again sometime. I want to help you boys all I can."

He had already helped us immeasurably. By going into his long-winded yarns, he had established his prodigious memory for details. Why, then, should his memory have been so fuzzy on much more recent matters pertaining to his tax return, such as the source of the $25,000 payment he used to pay off his mortgage?

We made another date for the next afternoon. This time we decided to take a stenographer, a pretty young girl, Miss Eleanor Mauderer. I cringed at the thought of taking her into the presence of the blubbery, pajama-clad Kingfish. So I telephoned him.

"Senator," I said, "I'm going to have a stenographer with me today."

"By jiminy," he roared, "if you have a stenographer, I'll have a stenographer. We'll both have stenographers!"

"That's okay, Senator. Then we'll just bring our *young lady* along with us."

"Say, are you telling me your stenographer is a *lady* just so I'll have to get dressed?"

"That's the idea, Senator."

"Man, I won't only be dressed! I'll get that gal of yours a swell box of candy!"

He did, too. It was on the dresser when we arrived. Our stenographer was a demure little blonde, very smartly and neatly dressed in an attractive white linen tailored suit and white pumps. She blushed when I introduced her to the Senator and he presented her with the candy. Huey was turned out in a new double-breasted white serge suit, a silk shirt, a violet tie, violet pocket hankie, and black-and-white sport shoes. He was clean-shaven, combed, shining.

It was a long session. Huey again took us on detours all over the state of Louisiana. But on pertinent matters, such as $75,000 in commissions on auto trucks bought at Corning by the state, he'd make remarks like, "I can't remember. You'd have to ask Sam Beasley about that." Beasley, purchasing agent for the Louisiana Highway Commission, had been dead for two years. Neither could Long remember anything about the disposition of $500,000 in graft paid by the Standard Dredging Company of New York in the guise of campaign contributions.

At the very end I mentioned the name of Mike Moss. Huey had been a gentleman up to then, carefully guarding his language with bows and nods to Miss Mauderer.

"Why, that potbellied ——!" he exploded. "I saved that —— from bankruptcy in 1929 and that's the thanks I get!

Everything he told you is just a damned cock-and-bull story, just ——. That one-eyed double-crosser, trying to make the public believe he's a cowboy! Why that —— couldn't even ride a pony across the street!"

The Kingfish yanked his violet hankie savagely out of his pocket and said aside to Miss Mauderer, "Excuse me, miss."

The next day we reported to our chief in Washington, Elmer Irey, that the case against Huey Long was ready for the Grand Jury. We had a clear case of tax evasion.

Irey summoned me immediately to Washington. At the Bureau of Internal Revenue I laid out our evidence before Commissioner Guy T. Helvering and Chief Irey. They beamed. Helvering said, "We will call a lawyer from the criminal division to sit in with us." In came Bob Jackson, general counsel to the Bureau, destined to be heard from later on as Supreme Court Justice and United States prosecutor at Nuremberg. We arranged for Dan Moody, former Governor of Texas, to be the special prosecutor. Burford and I were to get together with Moody in New Orleans as soon as the September primary was over, in about two weeks. We'd go straight to the Grand Jury.

I wangled a breather to "go home and tend my lawn" in Baltimore before going back for the mop-up. Judith and I had an idyllic ten days in that little yellow house, which was still our honeymoon cottage. I got the blue jays, cardinals, and squirrels back on a regular diet at the feeding stations, and turned some good, fresh earth mixed with peat moss around the roots of the azaleas.

On Monday, September 9th, I stepped out on the front verandah and picked up the morning paper. The headline smashed into my consciousness: HUEY LONG SHOT.

Then, the line below: Not Expected to Live.

I ran into the kitchen where Judith was preparing breakfast and held the newspaper in front of her eyes. All I could say was, "Look at this!"

Senator Long died the next day.

Whether the dictator was killed by a bullet from the revolver of Dr. Carl Weiss* or from the revolver of a bodyguard was a question I heard hotly debated. Dr. Weiss was the son-in-law of a state judge who had the independence and imprudence to openly oppose the Kingfish. The dictator, in retaliation, forced the state legislature to gerrymander the judge out of office. On Sunday night, September 8th, after a special session of the state legislature, Long was proceeding through a corridor to the office of the governor. At close range Dr. Weiss fired one shot at the Kingfish. Six bodyguards opened fire on the Doctor and in seconds had riddled him with sixty-eight bullets. Dr. Weiss died instantly.

Huey was hustled to a nearby hospital. He lingered for two days. One of his last orders on his dying bed was, "Don't make any public statements." To the surprise of many, no autopsy was performed.

In June, 1936, our indictments against Seymour Weiss and other henchmen of the organization were quietly dismissed—on the eve of the National Democratic Convention. Nationwide publicity was given to that political deal. Democratic papers as well as Republican ones strongly condemned the tax case dismissals by the government, resulting in the "Second Louisiana Purchase."

The Treasury Department decided to take the cases of the Louisiana politicians, who had their criminal prosecutions dismissed, into civil trials in the United States Court of Tax Appeals, as the Attorney General and the Department of Justice had no authority to dismiss cases in that court. Before we finished, the Treasury Department collected over $2,000,000 in taxes from Long's men. If we had been allowed to take the cases into criminal court we could have, without doubt, sent most of the grafters and corrupt politicians to the federal penitentiary.

Three years later the government team was again sent into

---

* Not to be confused with Long's henchman Seymour Weiss.

action in Louisiana. Efficient post office inspectors and agents of the Federal Bureau of Investigation and of the Intelligence Unit picked up the "weak evidence" and gathered some additional evidence. Then Seymour Weiss, Abe Shushan, and several big shots of the Long organization were finally convicted for fraudulent use of the mails and income tax evasion, receiving heavy penitentiary sentences.

By then I could only applaud their success from the sidelines, as I had been promoted to the Secret Service.

6

The two main responsibilities of the Secret Service division of the Treasury Department are to protect the currency and protect the life of the President. In 1936, I was brought in as Chief of the Secret Service, primarily because of the alarming rise in counterfeiting.

Wherever money has been the medium of exchange, there have always been efforts made to duplicate it. Nero is supposed to have been one of the first well-known counterfeiters. Napoleon used counterfeit Austrian and Russian currency to purchase food and supplies for his advancing armies.

Counterfeiting has always been a highly effective war weapon, since it demoralizes and cripples a nation's economy. During the Revolutionary War, when our government issued "Continental" currency, the British promptly counterfeited it—so successfully, in fact, that it became worthless ("not worth a Continental"). After this disastrous experience, our government did not again issue paper money until the Civil War. Meanwhile, banks, chartered by individual states were authorized to issue currency, for which the federal government assumed no responsibility. With no federal

92

protection for the private banks, counterfeiting became so rampant that private publishing companies regularly printed and sold "counterfeit detectors," which listed the false bills in circulation.

Toward the end of the Civil War the situation was so acute that banks and merchants begged the Secretary of the Treasury to have the government take action. The Secretary reported the matter to President Andrew Johnson, who ordered that prompt steps be taken. As a result, the United States Secret Service was formally established as a part of the Treasury Department on July 5, 1865. From 1884— the first year for which statistics are available—to 1929, the counterfeit money confiscated never exceeded $533,000 in any one year. However, the next few years brought substantial increases. In 1933, this total jumped to nearly a million dollars. By 1935, it had climbed to $1,493,310. It was clearly evident that the enforcement procedures had to be changed, not only to protect the public from big losses but also to maintain public confidence in the money which is the life blood of the nation's economic structure.

Secretary of the Treasury Henry Morgenthau became so seriously concerned that he ordered Chief William H. Moran, who had been Chief of the Secret Service since 1917, to get the situation under control. When losses continued to increase, Secretary Morgenthau directed me in the fall of 1935 to survey investigative and administrative procedures of the Service and recommend methods to bring the counterfeit situation under control. With the able assistance of Agent Bill McElveen, I submitted eighty recommendations to modernize and improve the procedures. The Secretary directed Chief Moran to put them into immediate effect. But the big losses from counterfeiting continued. When Chief Moran retired, in September of 1936, Secretary Morgenthau appointed me as his successor. My orders were: "See that counterfeiting is reduced—promptly!"

My first day as Chief found me nervous and excited.

Judith dressed me up in my newest suit, a double-breasted blue serge, and a new plain blue silk necktie. She tucked a white handkerchief neatly in my upper coat pocket and said, "Don't muss up the kerchief by crowding a lot of cigars in that pocket." She was crying when I left for the office and pleaded, "Please phone and let me know how you get along." Actually, Judith was delighted, not only with the promotion but the fact that, at long last, we could settle down in one spot like normal folks. We bought a house in Washington and I moved into my new office in the Treasury Building.

I was impressed by the dignity of the spacious, private office of the Chief. It was about twenty-five by thirty feet and covered with a Persian Sarouk rug which had been seized from a smuggler. The ceiling was fifteen feet high, and four massive windows gave me a clear view of the White House and the East Gate through which President Roosevelt passed on all auto trips. The windows were trimmed with heavy velvet rose-colored draperies and a life-sized oil of Salmon P. Chase, a distinguished Secretary of the Treasury under President Lincoln, looked down on me. My desk was the largest I had ever seen. It was of solid mahogany and had been made for former Secretary of the Treasury William Gibbs McAdoo, a son-in-law of President Woodrow Wilson. The chairs were leather upholstered, and at one end of the room there stood an oval mahogany conference table.

Since the appearance of the office was a little too sober to suit my taste, I put up some action pictures of sailing vessels. I moved in a model of the schooner, *Albatross,* the boat on which I had many thrilling times on Lake Erie as a boy, and one of the famous American sloop, *Ranger,* which I had seen win the International Cup Race off Newport. I found that the ship models served an excellent purpose when conferences in my office were becoming too heated. I would invite the excited participants to look over the yachts, and cool them down with a story about the only race we ever won sailing the *Albatross.*

I was still very new at my job when I was faced with an unexpected emergency. The wife of a Treasury Department employee, who had been sent on a special mission to China, had had a nervous breakdown during his absence, and she blamed Secretary Morgenthau for sending her husband so far away. She went to the Secretary's home, insisting she be allowed to see him. When the maid informed her that he was not at home and shut the door, the woman cried and hollered in front of the house and said she would force old man Morgenthau to bring home her husband without delay or he would be sorry. Mrs. Morgenthau heard her and, concerned about the safety of the Secretary, asked me what could be done about the situation. In an hour the woman was back at the Secretary's home again, creating a scene. In another hour she was at the Secretary's entrance to the Treasury Building, loudly demanding that she be let in to see Mr. Morgenthau. A Secret Service agent calmed her down and took her home.

The Secretary seemed worried that the woman might sneak by the receptionist in his outer office and attack him. We ordered the guards at the entrances of the Treasury Building to be on the lookout for her. I told the Secretary that I would install a push button on the floor under his desk, so he could step on it if any intruder appeared and a bell in the Secret Service field office on the floor below and also in my office would then ring. I said, "Don't worry. We'll be with you in a few seconds if the bell rings."

Two days later the alarm sounded. I sprinted to Mr. Morgenthau's office. Three agents joined me. We rushed into the office and he exclaimed, "What's the matter—are you fellows crazy?"

I cried, "Your alarm rang!"

"Get out of here!" he yelled disgustedly. "There must be a short circuit in the alarm wires."

With Secretary Morgenthau were three diplomats from China impressively dressed in Prince Albert coats and striped trousers. Not knowing what the excitement was about, they were alarmed and started to leave. I hustled over to look at the push button underneath the desk and to my great disgust I discovered Dano, Mr. Morgenthau's German shepherd, lying on the alarm button. Dano was a sleepy, fat, friendly old fellow who wouldn't hurt a flea. I gave him a quick shove and apologized to the diplomats and the Secretary for our intrusion.

The survey I had made for Secretary Morgenthau revealed the shocking fact that in certain respects the Secret Service was still back in the horse-and-buggy era. Our agents, for example, were equipped with a pocket commission book to identify them, which had not been revised in thirty years. It stated, among other things, that the agent's function was to investigate violations relating to "pay and bounty." This puzzling phrase was a relic of Civil War days in regard to pensions to veterans of that war. Many of these pocket commissions, which were being carried by agents, had been signed by Secretaries of the Treasury who had been out of office twenty and twenty-five years. The identification books had no photographs or signatures of the agents. The book of rules and regulations governing investigative procedure of agents had been issued in 1906. One section covered instructions relating to reimbursement for the hire of horse and wagon!

Nor had the Service modernized to use the advantages of electronics. With the co-operation of the United States Army and the Coast Guard, we installed our own radio system, so that in larger metropolitan areas, the home of F.D.R. at Hyde Park, and his retreat at Shangri-la, our autos were in constant communication with the central office.

We also equipped many of our field offices with teletypes. My first winter as Chief, one of the incoming teletype messages reported the destruction by fire of a Service automobile. A detail of agents were in an auto on a cold winter night in New York, keeping a counterfeit suspect under surveillance. As there was no heater in the car, the agents had placed a small kerosene stove in the back. The suspect came out of the building suddenly, got into his own car, and drove off. The agents followed but, due to icy streets, their car skidded, the stove turned over—and I had another long report on my desk. Following that incident, I directed that heaters be installed in all cars, together with radios which could be tuned in on the local police networks.

Our offices were also liberally supplied with both still and motion picture cameras for use in collecting evidence. In order to make analyses of counterfeit money and to examine evidence, a laboratory was established at the Bureau of Engraving and Printing. Certain field offices were furnished with polygraphs (lie detectors) and agents were sent to a special school in Chicago to perfect the technique of using them. We secured armored automobiles equipped with radios to be used in conveying large sums of new money sent several times a day from the Bureau of Engraving and Printing to the Treasury Department.

I required agents to attend the Treasury Department school which taught modern and improved techniques in criminal investigation. It was the first time many of them had ever enjoyed the privilege of such class instruction. For our own use, I published a weekly "house organ" for the members of the Service, so that all agents had an up-to-date running report of every major case being investigated across the country.

While studying the problem of counterfeiting, my own attitude about investigative work underwent something of a change. To begin with, so many of those involved in counterfeit cases—especially as "passers" of phoney bills—and in stealing and forging government checks, were juveniles. Rather than approach counterfeiting on the level of the number of arrests and convictions that we could make— which had been my standard in the past when I worked on cases of income tax evasion—I decided what we needed now was a crime prevention program, which would lessen counterfeiting and lessen the number of arrests necessary.

My predecessor as Chief of the Service had avoided any publicity about the work of the Service at all costs. Reporters so bold as to hang around this office of the Treasury Department were automatically kicked out. My past experience in crime investigation convinced me the greatest deterrent to certain crimes was publicity. When you show what can be done with big fish, the little fish take fright and back off. My policy, as Chief, was to woo the co-operation of all the news and publicity media: magazines, newspapers, radio and motion pictures. Counterfeiting was a national problem; it needed to be fought on a national scale. Our job was to make America "counterfeit conscious," which would have a twofold effect: help people protect themselves against counterfeiters and discourage the young from going into a racket that had so little future. Our case reports showed that the career of a counterfeiter or check forger is quite brief and none amass great wealth. Most live a hunted life and face up to fifteen years in prison for a single conviction.

To educate the public, I called in reporters and writers and launched a "Know Your Money" campaign. Since information on how to detect a counterfeit had previously been a government secret, the press ate it up alive. I have never found anyone who wasn't fascinated by the subject. Later, when it was my responsibility to go before Congress and request appropriations for my division, I always remembered to carry a few counterfeit bills in my pocket. At the point when the Congressmen began cutting down the amount I had requested, I got out my counterfeit money and showed it to them. Usually they became so interested, they forgot about any further slashing and I managed pretty much to get what I asked for.

Both *Colliers* and *Life* magazines published double-page spreads featuring enlargements of counterfeit bills and contrasting them with real money, as did many newspapers.

(The rule of thumb is that bad money usually "looks bad"; *i.e.,* the quality of paper is not as good, the engraving not as refined, the portrait in the center is less clear.)

We also got up our own booklet, *Know Your Money,* which we persuaded schools throughout the country to use as a unit of study. Through this program, we not only got the word home to the parents but we also, to our immense gratification, developed some ardent "second line" agents, schoolboys who became alert to counterfeit money and helped put us on to several gangs.

Agents on the "Know Your Money" detail took on the enormous task of alerting the 105,000 retail stores in New York City. They also lectured to business people and before school groups, and distributed warning notices which could be used by money handlers in all businesses. As soon as a new counterfeit bill came out, we circularized stores and businesses so that cashiers had the information in front of them and could identify the phoney money as soon as it was passed. When the cashiers began giving bills tendered to them a close second look, it scared the passers, and many of the smalltime operators began backing out of the game.

With the services of a professional Hollywood photographer, and using Secret Service personnel for the cast, we produced our own short motion picture *Know Your Money,* which was written and directed by Alonzo Rice, a talented agent from Boston. I persuaded Lowell Thomas to act as narrator. Within a five-year period this picture was exhibited to over twelve million persons. It was so successful that Paramount Pictures eventually took it over, retitled it *Dangerous Money,* and gave it a commercial release, so that it was shown to another twenty million persons. Columbia Pictures also produced a short on the subject, called *Making Money,* which was filmed at the Bureau of Engraving and Printing in Washington. And, at our suggestion, M-G-M filmed a dramatic picture covering a counterfeit case, which had a sequence on the detection of counterfeits. The Aetna

Life Insurance Company also co-operated with us by producing two movie shorts on counterfeiting.

The reduced cost to the government because of fewer prosecutions in the federal courts and the savings effected because of not having to house, feed, and guard so many convicted violators in Leavenworth, Atlanta, and Alcatraz offset many times the financial cost of this program. Within six years the annual losses to merchants and others through the acceptance of counterfeits dropped from amounts in excess of one million dollars to a low of $30,000.

During World War Two, my great concern was the possibility that enemy nations would successfully counterfeit our money. I had reason to be worried. In 1939 we had discovered to our considerable consternation that back in 1929 Russia had counterfeited United States hundred-dollar bills with spectacular success. First circulated widely in Berlin, the bills later showed up in China and Cuba. Then, a week before Christmas, 1932, large quantities appeared in circulation in Chicago. The counterfeit was such a perfect imitation that $60,000 was accepted by four big banks that week. The bankers refused to believe they had been swindled until agent Tom Callaghan pointed out a slight imperfection in the bill, which showed up only under a microscope. The money had come to the banks from Chicago racketeers who had "innocently" put it in circulation. They had bought it, at a nice discount, from a "count" who claimed it was "hot" money that he was selling for a mobster in New York City.

The duped bankers had cashed the phoney hundred-dollar bills, changing them with genuine fifties. When they found the money was counterfeit, they demanded restitution from the racketeers. The racketeers went after the "count" who had sold it to them, Enrique Dechow von Buelow. "We'll give you forty-eight hours to get our dough back."

Von Buelow, who had gotten the money from Dr. Valentine Gregory Burtan, a Communist in New York, was terrified. He went to Burtan and begged on his knees that the Doctor comply with the racketeers' demands. Dr. Burtan stalled and instructed the "count" to leave that night for Montreal and to register at the Mount Royal Hotel where they would meet. In Montreal a strange man walked into his hotel room and insisted that Von Buelow go to Halifax and take immediate passage for Europe.

However, Von Buelow decided that instead of becoming further involved, he would fly back to New York immediately. As he left the airplane at the Newark airport he was grabbed by Secret Service agents. He disclosed the details of his deal with Dr. Burtan, who was promptly placed under arrest. Burtan was true to the Communist code and refused to divulge the source of the counterfeits. It was established that Burtan had flown to Mexico City, where he had Communist contacts, shortly before he delivered the money to Von Buelow. No further information regarding the source of the counterfeits could be obtained. Burtan was convicted in federal court and the judge gave him the maximum sentence, fifteen years in the Lewisberg penitentiary.

In 1942, I received startling information from Scotland Yard that the Germans had already successfully counterfeited notes of the Bank of England. The first evidence came from the Banque Nationale Suisse in Zurich, Switzerland. A shipment of notes from that bank reached the Bank of England where, because of their extremely close approximation to genuine notes, the counterfeits shocked the conservative directors of the Bank. Excitement was at a high pitch and the chief cashier frantically cried for the best Scotland Yard agents to make a prompt investigation.

The counterfeits were classified as "excellent and very dangerous." One Swiss bank had accepted over $100,000 worth of the phoney money and officials of the Bank of England became so concerned over this serious threat to the stability of the English pound that they utilized the provisions of wartime censorship to prevent any report of the counterfeits from reaching the public.

I was certain that if Germany had succeeded in counterfeiting the British pound, counterfeits of American money were only a matter of time. We set up a national educational program on the theme of "The Silent Saboteur," which opened with an exhibition at Rockefeller Center in New York City and a nation-wide broadcast participated in by Winthrop Aldrich, President of the Chase National Bank, Lowell Thomas, and myself.

As the months passed, I watched for signs that enemy submarines or airplanes might be sneaking bogus United States currency onto our shores. When a group of Nazi saboteurs sneaked ashore on Long Island from a submarine and were captured twenty-five miles from New York City, I sighed with relief when it was established that the $175,000 in American money they carried was genuine.

But my fears were verified. We discovered, after V-J Day, when one of our ace counterfeit investigators, Colonel George McNally, who was attached to Supreme Headquarters of the AEF, was able to piece the facts together, that the German counterfeit operation was actually the most successful on record.

Beginning with counterfeit experiments in Berlin in 1939, the object of the German government was to counterfeit English pound notes and American dollars on a tremendous scale. Hitler ordered Himmler, by the use of counterfeits, to do everything possible to disrupt and debase the currencies of enemy nations and, at the same time, to increase the assets of Germany. A complete secret counterfeit plant was set up in an ancient castle near Friedenthal, employing a large force of engravers, printers, and other experts. Later, another pretentious plant known as "Sonderkommando" was set up in an intensively guarded section of the Sachsenhausen Concentration Camp at Oranienberg.

Professional counterfeiters were drafted. To secure the necessary technical help, Himmler issued a special appeal:

Engravers, artists, paper specialists, printers . . . are wanted for special work and will be well rewarded. The living conditions will be most excellent, and the food the finest. Now, how many would like to come and try for a pleasant job?

The trap could not have been more attractively baited, for inmates of the various camps were virtually starving. Many volunteered. A large group was selected and put to work in Block 19 of the Concentration Camp at Sachsenhausen. Block 19 differed from other blocks because it had high, barbed-wire fences charged with high-voltage electricity. The prisoner-workers soon learned that because the Nazis intended to keep the work strictly secret, they probably would never leave the camp alive. Neither would they be permitted to communicate with anybody outside the Block under threat of immediate death, and, finally, they found out that they were going to counterfeit English and American money.

These terror-stricken workers were further horrified when Block officials informed them that when the counterfeit operation was completed, all were to be put to death *at one time* in the gas chambers so as to keep the counterfeit activity strictly secret forever. In rush periods some of the workers were forced to slave eighteen hours a day. But, with the realization that they were to be gassed as soon as the work was completed, they delayed the operations in every possible way.

Ten modern printing presses were in use and an auxiliary Diesel motor was provided in the event that the electric power failed. Each worker assigned to inspection of the printed notes was furnished with a transparent plate on which he placed the counterfeits, examining each one carefully and comparing it with a genuine note. Many of these notes were intentionally soiled to give the impression of

H

having been in circulation for a considerable time. Others were punched with a small pin, supposedly to imitate the English custom of pinning together small bunches of notes in banks and the still older custom, long fallen into disuse, of Englishwomen pinning notes to the inside of their dresses and petticoats!

After considerable experimental work, the distinctive paper for the Bank of England notes was perfected. But the Germans ran into difficulties in printing the money. However, some of it came out in perfect shape, and the inspectors placed it in what they called Class I. Other, less-perfect notes were placed in Classes II and III. Hitler and his military and financial advisors decided to use three methods in placing the counterfeits in circulation. A portion of Class I was to be sent to Nazi embassies in neutral countries to be used for espionage purposes. Big amounts were unloaded in Switzerland, Spain, and Portugal. Class II was to go out through more devious channels, and Class III was to disrupt the British currency completely by being showered over London by an armada of Nazi planes. Production records we seized after the war established that in the period of about two years close to $600,000,000 had come from these printing presses in five-, ten-, twenty-, fifty-, and hundred-pound notes, and estimates place the total production over the entire period as approaching one billion dollars.

The situation became so serious that the directors of the Bank of England, in order to protect the British currency, were forced suddenly to withdraw all ten-, twenty-, fifty-, and hundred-pound notes from circulation, and to declare that after thirty days the notes would no longer be accepted as legal tender. All persons and banks holding the notes were required to surrender them to the Bank of England in exchange for new notes. The new issue had a very fine metallic thread imbedded in the paper by a new secret process and bank officials were confident that the Nazis would be unable to counterfeit them. Through this unprecedented and intelligent action, the officials of the Bank of England averted demoralization of the British currency and their people.

The Germans had a more difficult time counterfeiting American money. Their first difficulty was the special quality of our distinctive paper, which contains silk fibers, and which they were unable to duplicate. Experts from I. G. Farben were called upon for assistance. Finally, in the summer of 1944, the paper was declared satisfactory. Himmler ordered his prison camp experts to rush large quantities of American counterfeits. Part of the plant was immediately converted into a workshop for the exclusive manufacture of dollars, and a Dutchman, Abe Jacobsohn, a political prisoner who was an expert photographer and technician, was made foreman of the "photo-type" section.

Soon thereafter the workers were introduced to a tall, pale, skinny, ugly-tempered, sunken-eyed individual whose function was to instruct them in practical "photochromic" methods and other important techniques. His name and title resolved themselves into a couple of colorless words, Professor Smith. Under the expert guidance of the "Professor," the American counterfeit plates were finally perfected in December, 1944.

Early in January, 1945, some specimens were turned over to Himmler and they were so perfect that he was unable to distinguish the counterfeits from the genuine bills. However, at that time the Allied armies were approaching, and it was necessary to dismantle the Sachsenhausen plant and hurriedly move it to a camp at Mathausen near Lenz, Austria. The machinery was not set up because that camp was not considered safe from bombing and it was again moved to a site at Redl-Zipf.

The Redl-Zipf Camp adjoined a large brewery at the foot of a high hill. At the start of the war the Germans had taken possession of the brewery and had tunneled from it into the lower part of the hill and built an excellent subterranean factory about a mile underground. Here, they were making parts for a secret weapon of another sort, the V bombs which occasioned such wild excitement, great damage, and loss of life when they were dropped on London. Himmler thought that the counterfeit plant would be safe from air raids in this underground factory. However, it failed to get into heavy production, as the Allied armies were rushing into Germany.

On May 1, 1945, because the Allied troops were so near Redl-Zipf, British counterfeits amounting to sixty million pounds were destroyed by burning. Other counterfeits, plates, and equipment, including those for American money, were packed in large boxes and were rushed away in trucks and dumped in Lake Gmiendensee near the town of Rind-bach at Ebensee and in Toplitz See. The boxes had been hastily built and were not very strong, and the swift currents of the lakes carried them against sharp rocks where they burst open and the pound notes floated down the stream. Soon dozens of farmers, their wives, and children were busy fishing.

The boxes from Redl-Zipf were loaded on trucks and taken to be dumped in the lake. Of the £61,000,000, £25,-000,000 was later seized by investigators and about £31,-000,000 was dumped. One truck, in control of Robert Mathis, an Austrian Captain in the German Army, was surrendered to the approaching Americans. Its valuable load of twenty-seven boxes was turned over by Mathis and opened by Colonel George McNally, an ace Secret Service Agent on military leave serving with our Army in Europe, Inspector J. Rudkin of Scotland Yard, and Philip Reeves of the Bank of England. Besides the English pounds, the boxes contained equipment, plates, records, and counterfeit passports.

Because of the depth of the water and the swift currents, only a small portion of the notes was recovered. United States Navy divers, brought in by Colonel McNally to attempt to recover the plates, were unsuccessful.

When the investigating agents saw this tremendous treasure in apparently perfect pound notes, they could hardly believe their eyes. It was the largest counterfeit seizure ever made. After placing them under a heavy guard, Mr. Reeves had them trucked to Frankfort and flown from there to London with an escort of fighter planes.

But the facts proved that my worst fears had been justified. America was only a matter of days away from finding itself in the same critical financial plight as the one England had been in.

7

One of the first changes I made when I became Chief was in the selection and training of agents assigned to the White House Detail. There, in the most critical area of our work, that of guarding the life of the President and his family, I found that "seniority" ruled. I felt that White House agents should be young, quick, strong, and alert. Transferring those whom I considered too old and too fat for White House duty to other, slower jobs, we began picking young men—preferably with a background in athletics—and gave them intensive training in judo, fire fighting, first aid, and marksmanship.

While all Secret Service agents were equipped with revolvers, I found that many of them were not trained in the proper use of firearms and few were expert shots. A program of firearms training and practice was started and first-class instructors were obtained from the United States Coast Guard. Pistol ranges were constructed in the Treasury Building and in the Bureau of Engraving and Printing in Washington and arrangements were made for agents to use Army and National Guard ranges in the various field offices. All agents on the White House Detail and the White House police were required to prove periodically that they were expert in the use of a pistol and other weapons. As a result we developed one of the best pistol teams in the United States and our sharpshooters won many trophies. We also built up the morale of the White House police by giving them snappy new uniforms, with Sam Brown belts, which were to replace at this time the sloppy Keystone-Cop type of outfits they were wearing.

The Supervisor of the White House Detail, which numbers from fifteen to thirty agents, has an office in the West Wing. He answers to the Chief, who is also commanding officer of the White House police, which, during my tenure, grew from sixty-five in 1936 to one hundred and thirty-five during the war. The police are not Secret Service agents, but men who have requested White House duty. They are, however, almost on a par with the agents since they share the responsibility of protecting the President and the White House grounds. When the President sleeps, for example, there is an agent on guard in the hall outside his second-floor bedroom and a White House police officer on duty on the grounds below his window. Both cover entrances and gates. When the President is in his office, there is an agent in the Rose Garden outside the French doors, another at his door, and his appointment clerk is a former Secret Service agent. At dinner parties agents are stationed at all entrances; some are assigned to circulate in the dining room. A close check is kept on the automobiles in which guests arrive and depart. Since formal invitations are not transferable, the Service does not have to worry when they have been provided with a complete guest list in advance. It's the times we did not get a complete list that we worried.

No one gets into the White House without a security pass. The regular staff—which during the Roosevelt administration ran around forty domestics, one hundred office help, and thirty maintenance men—retain permanent passes.

There were also about one hundred press and radio passes issued for the reporters who covered the White House.

The guards at the entrances have unannounced inspection by their supervisors. And novelists notwithstanding, I think it would be highly unlikely that any outsider could infiltrate the White House. Every time I saw the President's car leave the East Gate from my office window in the Treasury Building across the street, I was concerned. But when I saw him return safely home, and heard those iron gates close, I breathed a sigh of relief. He was safe—for one more night.

Unlike some Presidents or distinguished persons who must be protected from assassins, President Franklin Roosevelt was never resentful of either the necessity or the methods used by the Secret Service. He seemed to realize fully the importance of having expert pistol shots or sharpshooters on the White House Detail and commended me for the intensive marksmanship program I had started. He also expressed deep satisfaction over the new protective precautions we especially worked out for him at the White House and on long trips across the country and abroad. He frequently told me that he appreciated the personal interest which I took in his welfare and security.

To begin with, President Roosevelt was realistically aware of the "sitting duck" target he presented, immobilized in his wheelchair. He was as concerned as I with the fact that he could not fight off an assailant nor run out of firing range. His physical safety completely depended on the agents around him.

Also, F.D.R. had already had several close calls with would-be assassins. He had seen his wife's uncle, Teddy Roosevelt, narrowly miss death in Milwaukee in 1912, when a crank shot at him as he was delivering a speech. The bullet went through his folded manuscript and the glasses case which he had in his breast pocket and entered his body, stopping just short of a major artery. T.R., true to type, insisted on completing his speech before he went to the hospital. But it had been a narrow escape.

When F.D.R. was assistant Secretary of the Navy, the family lived on R Street in Georgetown, across the street from Attorney General A. Mitchell Palmer. One night two anarchists attacked Palmer's house with homemade bombs, which exploded prematurely, blowing the would-be assassins to bits. The next morning, after this awful spectacle, F.D.R. was eating breakfast when his son Jimmy, then a boy of ten, ran in. "Look what I found! What is it?"

F.D.R. identified it as a piece of collarbone from one of the dead bombers and promptly lost his appetite.

F.D.R. was also made acutely "assassination conscious" by his own very narrow escape from death in Miami in 1933, when, as President-elect, one of the five bullets aimed at him by Guiseppi Zangara killed Mayor Anton Cermak of Chicago. If Zangara had been as good a shot as Lee Harvey Oswald, Roosevelt would never have been President.

I had been in Florida at that time on an income tax case, and was asked to interview the unrepentant assassin because of a rumor that Cermak's death might in some way have been connected to the Capone syndicate in Chicago. It was a theory that proved groundless, as have been most efforts to relate the lone, publicity-seeking assassin with an organized group.

The first time I met F.D.R. was in Albany in 1912, when he was a Senator in the state legislature. I was introduced to him by State Senator George Burd of my own district. Six years later, when I saw F.D.R. again in Washington, he was Assistant Secretary of the Navy. He looked at me and said quickly, "Oh, I know. Didn't Senator Burd introduce you to me in Albany?"

I had followed F.D.R.'s political rise in New York State with close personal interest, from the time he made his first big political fight bucking and defeating the Tammany machine by opposing the election of a United States Senator endorsed by Tammany; the candidate he opposed was my cousin, Billy Sheehan. Soon after I was appointed Chief, I was in the White House with Herbert Gaston, Assistant Secretary of the Treasury, when Mr. Gaston mentioned to F.D.R. that I was from Buffalo. F.D.R. promptly asked me my opinion of several Buffalo folks and I was pleased that I could advise him that the ones he mentioned were highly regarded.

"Well, there're a lot of fine folks from Buffalo," he observed, "and I liked all of them—except Billy Sheehan."

"You sure did a great job leading the fight to keep Sheehan out of the Senate," I told him, and added with a chuckle, "Billy is my cousin."

Just then the President's valet, Prettyman, said, "Mr. President, you've got to get to the press conference," and he rolled his chair toward the private office, the Oval Room, in which the President regularly greeted the newspaper boys.

As a parting shot the President remarked, "Give my regards to the fellows we were talking about when you get to Buffalo." Then he said with a big grin, "So, Chief, Billy Sheehan is your cousin! Well, we'll have to watch out for you!" and he gave a hearty chuckle.

General "Pa" Watson, Roosevelt's Military Aide, who was nearby at the time, observed, "That's the best laugh the Boss has had for days."

A week later I was not far from the President when he was conversing with some Congressmen. In a stage whisper, especially for my benefit, he said, ". . . and you know, gentlemen, it's too bad but he's a cousin of Billy Sheehan."

One of the Congressmen realized that F.D.R. was kidding me and came to my rescue, saying, "Well, don't blame the Chief. We can pick our friends but we can't pick our relatives."

The President's teasing wit, his political independence, and his great personal magnetism all attracted me. He was the sort of man to whom no one could be indifferent. You reacted by either loving or hating him. I was glad to be numbered among the devoted, which included everyone else who was close to him at the White House. They all adored "The Boss," and he ran a taut ship. Everyone knew his responsibilities and put all he had into them. F.D.R. was the kind of man who inspired service.

Mrs. Roosevelt was grand to me and all the White House Detail, but she personally insisted on being left on her own. "I don't want anything to do with agents," she said firmly. And she meant it. They were not allowed to tag her or travel with her. Occasionally, without her knowledge, when I felt the situation warranted it, I stationed agents where she was speaking, "just in case." To my knowledge she never found out. I'm sure if she had, she would have let me know she was angry.

She did highly approve of the protection we provided for her grandchildren, the "Diaper Detail" as we called it. Actually, the Roosevelt grandchildren posed an extensive problem for us. There were eleven of them, scattered in Los Angeles, Seattle, Boston, and Richmond, who had to be covered twenty-four hours a day, seven days a week. This required the fulltime service of thirty agents. Some of the mothers were, like the grandmother, grateful for the protection and highly co-operative. Others resented it. From my own standpoint, the most pleasant member of the family to deal with was Anna, F.D.R.'s pet. One of the most difficult was the President's mother. At Hyde Park, where the family —and the agents assigned to them—assembled for holidays, old Mrs. Roosevelt absolutely ruled the roost. As far as she was concerned, F.D.R. was not the President. He was her baby boy. And the agents were an unfortunate nuisance. The President's own sons and daughters, on the other hand, were thoughtful of the agents, and saw to it that they shared the holiday dinner and had a present under the Christmas tree, knowing that they were separated from their own homes and families.

Because of the assassination of President Lincoln while attending the theater, the Secret Service is always especially concerned when a President attends a theatrical performance. Intensive checks are made with reference to the character of the actors, the employees of the theater, the structure of the building, the exits, and the fire hazards. The distribution of tickets for attendance is fully controlled, with the co-operation of the theater management. An extra large force of agents is stationed throughout the auditorium.

During the war, F.D.R. attended a performance of *Watch on the Rhine* at the National Theatre in Washington. In one scene the script called for Paul Lukas, the leading man, to draw a revolver quickly and shoot a man who was madly rushing at him with a dagger. Of course, the gat was loaded with blank cartridges. We had arranged for an agent to have custody of the revolver until two minutes before Lukas was to use it, and to be sure it was loaded with blanks. However, Lukas was highly nervous, thoroughly scared, and exclaimed, "Suppose one of those alert Secret Service agents in the box near the stage doesn't realize it is in the show and he sees me pull out the gat. He may think I'm about to shoot the President and I'll get a bullet in my head. Let's cut it out." As a result, the revolver was discarded and Lukas was given a long dagger (rubber) with which he cleverly stabbed the attacker.

In contrast to the tight protection procedures in effect when we took the President to the theater was the annual banquets attended by him at the National Press Club, the White House Correspondents Association, and the Gridiron Club. We didn't have any fears that the newspaper correspondents and their guests would attempt to kill the President. We did check and double check on the professional entertainers, waiters, and other employees. F.D.R. enjoyed these affairs and he got a tremendous kick when my old friend, George O'Connor, President of the Title Insurance Company of Washington, sang a song which regularly brought down the house. Famous actors from Broadway and Hollywood were always on the program, and the President showed only slight interest in their excellent acts. Then he would whisper to the master of ceremonies that he saw George O'Connor at one of the tables and suggest that he be invited to sing. Of course, George didn't need any urging. When George started to sing, F.D.R. smiled widely and his eyes sparkled with delight. George's song revived in my memory, and the memories of the older newspaper correspondents, the happy times and sometimes wild times we had enjoyed in saloons before saloons were put out of business by the Prohibition Act. F.D.R. knew the chorus of George's song, "Saloon, Saloon, Saloon," and lustily joined in it:

> Saloon, saloon, saloon. . . . It runs through my brain like a
>   tune. I don't like café, and I hate cabaret,
> But just mention saloon and my cares fade away.
> For it brings back a fond recollection of a little old low-
>   ceiling room, with a bar and a rail,
> And a dime and a pail; Saloon, saloon, saloon.

At the sixteenth annual dinner of the White House Correspondents Association, after George had sung "Saloon, Saloon, Saloon," F.D.R. sent a penciled note to him written on the President's place card: "Dear George: Like special vintage wine you improve with age. More power to you. F.D.R."

That night, after we arrived back at the White House, F.D.R. was humming "Saloon, Saloon, Saloon." General Watson kidded him, saying, "Why probably you never saw the inside of a saloon. You come from Harvard where the fellows were all perfect gentlemen."

"Is that so?" F.D.R. observed. "Well, there was a smelly saloon 'off bounds' about a mile from Harvard where I had some good times with the boys. It had a free lunch counter loaded with cheese, onions, pickles, popcorn, and pretzels.

Also remember, General, I campaigned for state senator in 1911, and in those days a candidate didn't have a show to get elected unless he visited practically every saloon in his district. And then," he added with a mischievous twinkle, "there was a stinky saloon near the Ten Eych Hotel in Albany where we regularly met in a back room to plan our fight against Tammany, when we upstaters defeated their candidate Billy Sheehan for United States senator."

He never failed to needle me about my cousin if he had the chance.

My major objective, as I saw it, was to provide the President and his family with the maximum protection in an unostentatious manner, with the minimum interference to their normal activities. On short unannounced trips around Washington, I ruled out the motorcycle police escort which attracts special attention to the President's car.

F.D.R. was as concerned with the safety of his associates and guests as he was with that of himself and his family. Although it was not yet official for the Vice-president to be provided with protection, and we did not provide any for Vice-president Garner, F.D.R. personally requested that I supply a small informal detail to look after Vice-president Henry Wallace, when war-clouds were on the horizon, and later he requested the same for Mr. Truman. When Wallace was planning his good-will trip to South America, I had a call from F.D.R. asking that the protection we were giving to him include his traveling as well. "Send a detail with Wallace, Frank. He's going down to South America and there are some tough characters down there." We had no appropriation to cover this expense, but we managed it anyway, sending six men along. Pan American Airways also sent a vice-president of their company. I "deputized" him to take good care of my agents. I knew Wallace would get good care, but sometimes people forget about the agents, that they need food and sleep and rest, like other men. Wallace was always every inch a gentleman, yet so gracious and friendly you couldn't be in his presence five minutes without warming to him.

People who actually had appointments with the President came in at the Pennsylvania Avenue entrance. Tourists gathered at the East Gate, where they were met and then taken through on tour by White House police who served as guides and who watched them.

Uninvited guests and cranks might turn up at any entrance any hour of the day or night, although we did notice that most of the out-of-towners chose the Pennsylvania Avenue gate, since it looks most like a main entrance.

In addition to the White House police, we had agents posted at all entrances, around the clock, who were especially trained to handle uninvited visitors with a minimum of distress. We picked these men very carefully from the ranks of the Secret Service for their own personal knack with people; and then I instigated a special training program, in co-operation with St. Elizabeths Hospital in Washington, to further equip them to handle the mentally ill.

I recall one "visitor," a lanky, wild-eyed, six-foot-two individual who marched up to the Pennsylvania Avenue entrance demanding to see President Roosevelt "and no one else." Turned over to Agent Jim Sloan, the fellow confessed that he wanted the President to have people's names changed, and that he had come all the way from Chicago to urge the President to issue an order.

When Sloan gently urged him on, the visitor explained his scheme. "Every man in the undertaking business should be named Coffin. Every man in the wood business should be named Wood. All grocers ought to be named Butter or Lard or called by the name of goods sold in their stores. Dry-goods dealers ought to bear names like Thread, Buttons, Cambric, Calico. It is a shame the way this thing is done now."

"It surely is," agreed Jim.

The caller then got excited and jumped from his seat,

pacing swiftly around the narrow office where the conversation was being held.

"The wrong naming of people leads to trouble and business confusion, and there is only one safe thing, that is, to change the name. You see that steam roller standing near the White House grounds? Well, that roller ought to furnish the name of the man who runs it. He ought to be named Roller. The man who is putting down those asphalt pavements in the ground ought to be named Asphalt."

"Well, I'll certainly see that all these points are taken up in the right quarter, sir. And just so that you get back to your hotel safely, since you are a stranger in Washington, I'll send you back in a car."

The poor crank was escorted back to his hotel and arrangements were made to place him under observation in the Municipal Hospital. Agents then established that he had recently escaped from a hospital for the insane, where he had been confined for five years, and he was ordered returned to that hospital.

Then there was a tall, beautiful, slender nurse from Kansas City, Missouri. Her first name was Doris. She made an exquisite picture, in her severely cut costume, with her large, luminous brown eyes, and red-gold hair, which escaped in little tendrils around her ears. Doris had a voice to match the rest of her, like music.

"I must see the President on immediate, urgent business. If not him, the First Lady would do. She is kind and would understand."

"Tell me about it, Doris," Maurice Allen, to whom she had been referred, obligingly offered.

"My lover is not writing to me any more. I cannot sleep or eat or work. He has not written since joining the Army. Do you think that he is dead?"

With the hidden feeling that any man so neglectful of such an attractive girl deserved to be dead, Agent Allen probed a little further with the remark, "They'll do it every time,

Frank Wilson was instrumental in making America "counterfeit conscious"

The successful White House Police pistol team of 1937–38. *Left to right:* H. W. Francis, R. P. Hallion, J. J. Cash, E. L. Warden, E. Reynolds and R. G. Ford

The explosion-proof carrier built by Agent John White for the safe transportation of bombs left at the White House

Madame Chiang Kai-shek was guarded during her stay in America for part of the Second World War by a detail of Special Agents

once the Army get them. What does he do in private life,
Doris?"

"He's a doctor. He was an intern at the hospital where I
worked. Do you think that the President could find him for
me?"

"Well, one never knows," murmured Allen brightly, if a
little vaguely.

"I'm going to be interviewed at the Walter Reed Hospital
tomorrow morning for the Army Nurse Corps," offered
Doris. She seemed considerably cheered by her chat with
the courteous Allen.

"Say, that's a swell idea! As an Army nurse you might
bump into him any minute."

And on that note, smiling her way out of the office, Doris
left, and some of the beauty of the September morning
seemed to depart with her.

We reported her call to the Walter Reed Hospital and requested the result of the examination of the young woman.
Doris, it turned out, was indeed a nurse, as she had professed,
and while, according to the medical staff, currently "nervous and distraught," she was not seriously ill. After a rest
which restored her nerves, she was able to go on with her
work in an Army hospital. As to the whereabouts of her
feckless lover, we never heard.

One fellow appeared on Christmas Day on the White
House lawn, astride a white horse, wrapped in a white sheet
with blood-red letters on the back: I. C. Peace, while a
dinner dance was going on in the Treasury Department. He
pretended to the agents who surrounded him that he could
not talk, and insisted on conducting the lengthy interview
with pencil and paper. When they led him through the basement of the Treasury, some of the party guests saw this
strange apparition, but marked him off as one of the paid
performers and gave him a nice holiday-spirited round of
applause.

Often people appeared at the gates requesting personal

I

help. We had one repeat visitor, a sixty-nine-year-old Austrian American pensioner named Pearl, who came from Brooklyn where she said that she lived in a rat-infested cellar and furthermore had been unhappy ever since she had been in this country.

"I want either the President or Mrs. Roosevelt to give me a nice little house to live in and I want it right away," she insisted in a loud voice. Agent John FitzGerald, another able veteran at the White House, tried to soothe her.

"But neither the President nor Mrs. Roosevelt has a house to give you, Pearl," the poor old woman was gently told.

"$31.70 a month doesn't go very far," was Pearl's sad comment.

She seemingly was content when she left, after having unburdened herself. But she was back the next day with further demands, loudly screeching and shouting vile names, and this time she was committed to St. Elizabeths Hospital for observation. A daughter of Pearl's was located, who arranged for her to be given treatment in a mental hospital near her home to which she had formerly been confined.

Not all of the threats to the life and limb or the time of the President and his family come from personal callers. Many people use the telephone.

A Secret Service agent held a most illuminating conversation with an excited caller from Wisconsin, who demanded an interview with the President and announced that she was Mrs. Stanley K——, a Polish-American citizen of forty-two who had twenty-five children.

"That surely is a wonderful family, Mrs. K.," commended the agent warmly, as he made rapid notes of the details. "Are they all alive?" he continued pleasantly.

"Nineteen of them," was the proud and prompt reply.

"What did you want to ask the President, Mrs. K.?" the agent probed.

"Well, you see, I just love publicity and never get enough of it. So I've made a crocheted American flag, all by hand,

and it has taken me two years of hard work. And you know that a mother of nineteen does not have a lot of spare time."

"She surely doesn't," came the hearty response from the White House end of the line.

"So I'm calling tomorrow at the White House to give it to the President myself, and do you think he'll let me be taken in a picture with him and me and the flag all together? And could I bring a few of the children? About eight, say. I'll dress them up real nice," she offered.

When she hung up, the agent thought that he had talked her out of the idea. But when she arrived next day with the flag and four children she had picked up on the streets of Washington, she was escorted off the White House grounds and sent back to Wisconsin.

8

I doubt that any public figure engendered as great devotion on the one hand and as violent and irrational hate on the other as Franklin Roosevelt. Any man who sits in the chair of the President and makes decisions about the governing of the country is, at times, subject to attack in the form of vicious and threatening letters. John Quincy Adams drew a great deal of "crank" mail, as did Andrew Jackson—who made a habit of signing his name to them and sending them to Washington newspapers for publication! Cleveland also received threats on his life through the mail. But it is the Presidents who have been publicly identified with racial or religious issues who have drawn the heaviest assaults. Lincoln was so deluged with threatening mail that his occupancy of the White House was clouded by a sense of constant, imminent danger to his person. F.D.R. was the next President to be so harassed. After him, the volume of threatening letters lessened until President Kennedy took office, when it once more reached a staggering and frightening high.

Anonymous, obscene, vicious, and threatening poison-pen letters to the President, arriving by the thousands each year, seemed to me the work of neurotic men and women, and were warnings from hands guided by dangerously disordered minds. Upon study of hundreds of these letters, I found that the authors ran the social scale: a prominent lawyer, a vicious hobo, a well-known clubwoman, and a sex-crazed maniac, to cite a few examples; but they had one thing in common—irrational, paranoiac hate for our President. Such persons often make uncannily logical, vicious, and at the same time intelligent plans, and always try to execute them suddenly at an unexpected moment.

If anyone engaged in protective work ever grew indifferent to the threats surrounding the presidency, all he need do would be to spend a few hours sampling such letters. They are often shocking beyond belief. Many are utterly unprintable, since the attacks are framed in the most obscene as well as abusive language. Some of these records of verbal violence were even directed at the President's young grandchildren.

As a result of these alarming findings I conducted a series of conferences to develop a modern system for locating the anonymous writers of threatening letters to the White House. Up to that time, only a small percentage of writers had been found. But it was impossible for me to accept the theory that past Secret Service methods were above reproach and, like the laws of the Medes and Persians, unalterable simply because for thirty-five years (1901 to 1936) no President had been assassinated. Therefore, in matters of Presidential protection, my office became a conference room for developing improved procedures.

A system which I considered excellent finally was developed by two brilliant agents, John J. FitzGerald and Leonard P. Hutchinson, and I established the Protective Research Section of the Secret Service to put it into operation.

Prior to 1940–1941, when we instituted new techniques for handling the President's mail, it had all come into the mail room in the Executive wing of the White House. Deciding that this was too dangerous, we set up a Secret Service inspection mail room in the White House garage. An employee from the post office was in charge, and he was sent to the New York Police Academy of Bombs and Explosives to learn techniques for handling dangerous packages. The mail room was outfitted with a small X-ray machine and a time-bomb detector. All packages addressed to the White House were opened there, inspected, and catalogued, before being sent in to the executive mansion. Gifts addressed to the President or his wife were turned over to their personal secretaries. At Christmastime hundreds of gifts come in from all over the world, and it takes two or three weeks of overtime work for the White House mail-room employees to handle them.

Routine mail is separated and sent to the proper secretary, who will handle it.

All crank and poison-pen letters are sent to the Protective Research Section, where a scientific analysis is made of all threatening, obscene, suspicious, and questionable communications to or about the President and members of his family. Here, too, letters addressed to other officials, which might be associated with threats to the President, are carefully examined.

Just as thousands of fingerprints can be classified and identified, we developed a system for cataloguing crank letters. They are ranked under major and related classifications which provide an index to traits and habits of the writers, characteristics in vocabulary, identifying features of stationery and envelopes, obsessions, geographical locations, and standards of handwriting, typing, or printing. Often, writers of anonymous letters are identified through association with other questionable letters received in the past, which the writer had signed and which had been put on file. Some relatively nasty letters represent no more than the ideas of fairly normal people who have gotten worked up over something happening in the country and want to let off steam; they choose the head of state as their target. Others are obviously the work of deranged minds. In a breakdown of over twelve thousand items which came into the Protective Research Section in the year of 1943, we classified seventy-five percent as paranoid, nineteen percent as abusive and obscene, five percent as threatening, and one percent as suicidal.

When a letter shows an "intent to harm" the President, a case file is compiled on the writer and the case is investigated. Many letter-writers are kept under regular surveillance by Secret Service agents in their area and checked every six months. For example, there were four hundred people being checked on in the United States at the time of President Kennedy's assassination, a year when thirty-two thousand items had reached the Protective Research Section (the same amount we received against F.D.R. in 1944).

The Protective Research Section also reviews all reports from field agents concerning the investigation of anonymous and threatening letters, maintains a file of photographs and fingerprints of offenders and suspects, and a file showing the periodic checkups of potentially dangerous cranks and letter-writers in order that their whereabouts may be known to the Secret Service at all times. Files of the Section are checked for names of all waiters, clerks, laborers, or other persons being considered for employment at the White House or employed at hotels visited by the President or at points where the security of the President is involved.

This new system prevented many potentially dangerous cranks and fanatics coming from the various states to the White House to demand an interview with the President or to sneak up on him with the intention of harming him. It effected prompt and tactful handling of many who succeeded in reaching Washington. Of course, such persons could not gain access to the President, but while in Washington they were potentially dangerous to him when he left the White House. Thus, the new Section worked hand-in-hand with the Secret Service White House Detail and the White House police to prevent the assassination of, or injury to, the President, and to prevent serious situations instigated by the actions of the mentally ill or of antagonistic persons who hated the President.

The efforts of the Section were effectively directed toward the prevention of crime, in preference to having to conduct an investigation after a fatal or serious incident had occurred. When an author of a dangerous letter was tracked down and found to be mentally ill, it was our policy to appeal to the local police to have him institutionalized, or to make a direct appeal to his family. Often, we found the members of a family delighted to have the case brought to a head, and the onus of "doing something about it" transferred from them to the federal government. How often we heard the sigh of relief: "Oh, we knew he should have been institutionalized years ago, but we hated to do it!" In many instances, such hospitalization rendered a great service to the family of the patient. Numerous patients recovered and were no further cause for concern to their families or to the Secret Service.

In the course of my career as Chief, the brightest spots and the most warmly welcome letters were ones like the letter that came from the husband of a woman who had written some extremely vicious anonymous threats to the President. As a result of medical reports on her condition, we were forced to have her confined to a hospital, both for her safety and that of her husband and her small children. We arranged to have the children well cared for during her absence. She eventually recovered and was able to return to normal home life. Her husband wrote me:

. . . I want to express my gratitude for the sympathetic understanding and the kindly consideration extended to me in my recent difficulty. It involved the placement of my wife in a mental institution because of her activities in respect to certain letters to the President, and the settling of my youngsters in suitable homes.

To some people Secret Service may seem hard and inflexible, but I shall always think of your organization as a friendly cooperative group ready and eager to help, instead of always being on the alert to punish. . . .

We never knew where and when our "President haters" would next appear. One morning in 1943, I had just arrived at my desk when my secretary, Mrs. Lucille Weir, pushed a teletype message from our New York office under my nose.

"Chief, you will want to read this at once," she advised, her voice taut with controlled alarm.

The message shocked me into instant activity. It reported that a desperate Army deserter had a powerful nitroglycerine bomb with which he intended to blow President Roosevelt to bits. A local police officer in Bellmore, Long Island, had notified our New York office that the information had been phoned to him by a Mrs. Seibert of Bellmore. He said that Mrs. Seibert might be one of the many cranks who had visions about the President and wanted publicity. Agents Bill Morris and Harry Welsh rushed out to interview her. Bill had successfully handled such assignments for about twenty-five years and had an extremely good technique in handling demented persons.

Mrs. Seibert turned out to be a very sensible, patriotic, and intelligent lady. The information she had was so hot that Bill Morris quickly had several agents in on the case. Mrs. Seibert warned them, "You had better hustle up. My son, Dick, will give you more facts."

What Dick told them scared even an old-timer like Bill.

When Bill asked Dick, "What's the full name of the suspect?" Dick answered, with a very serious look, "Suspect? Hell, he's no suspect; he means business. He's got nitroglycerine with which he intends to make a bomb to blow up Roosevelt, and he don't mean maybe."

Bill had heard many stories like that from cranks and he

could tell a crank a mile off, but he immediately sensed that Dick was rational.

Dick continued, "His name is Christopher Clarence Cull. He's from Tulsa, Oklahoma. He deserted from the S.S. *Florida* at Para, Brazil, in December 1941. I was a crew member with him and we were quite friendly. He was at my house last night. He has nitroglycerine, nearly enough to blow up a battleship. He's a clever mechanic and knows exactly how to make a bomb. He hates Roosevelt and our form of government. He's desperate and really intends to carry out his threat."

Dick also told Morris that Cull bragged about beating the rap on a stabbing affray on a freight steamship on the high seas for which he was later arrested at Mobile, Alabama. He added, "Cull told me, 'I sure did cut that guy up.' "

During the time that Dick and Cull were shipmates, he heard Cull discussing the war and Hitler with the crew. Cull bragged, "Hitler is the greatest man in the world. I would like to get into Germany so I could get some special training and then I would sneak back into the States and do some sabotage jobs on airplane plants or on ships."

Dick informed Agent Morris that Cull hated Jews, Negroes, and Catholics, claiming that between them and women, they were the causes of all trouble on the face of the earth. Cull claimed that "when the war is over there is going to be a revolution in the United States and all Jews, Negroes, and Catholics, and aliens will be driven out of this country or slaughtered."

During discussions aboard ship, Dick said that Cull freely and frankly expressed himself and that he did not seem to care who was listening. Some of the crew of the S.S. *Florida,* who resented his wild statements, threatened to throw him overboard to the sharks. One of the deck hands remarked, "Cull ought to be boiled in oil." The members of the crew were so bitter against him that at Para, Brazil, Cull decided he had better make a getaway, and he stole the ship's work boat, starting out to row to a Spanish ship. He was seized by the harbor police and returned to his own ship, where he was locked up, not being released until the vessel got underway. It was dark at that time and he jumped overboard, swimming three miles to shore.

Cull had called at Dick's home in Bellmore the previous night and confided that he intended to make a bomb, adding, "I'm going to get close to that ————— Roosevelt and blow him to hell, and I'll go along with him."

Dick urged Cull not to do so. "I told him it was a crazy idea, that he could not possibly succeed, and that any sensible man with such ideas would not, under any conditions, brag about them even to his closest friend for fear of being betrayed and turned over to the police."

Cull cooled off after that, but later in the evening he mentioned going to Washington in a few days.

Agent Morris asked Dick if he thought Cull would mind taking his own life, and Dick replied, "No. He's the type of person that once he gets an idea into his head he'll carry it through to the end regardless of any circumstances." He added, "Cull said that in the event he could carry out his plans and he was killed, it would make his cause seem all the more vital to the American people and they would realize that there must be something wrong with our form of government or else a man would not give his own life to assassinate the President."

"Can you tell me where Cull is now?" Bill asked.

"He left my house about twelve-thirty last night. I think he may be located at one of the New York hotels," Dick replied, adding, "Don't let him know that my mother and I reported him. I'm afraid he might come back and kill us."

Bellmore is only about twenty-five miles from New York City. Several agents and New York City detectives immediately canvassed the hotels, especially flop houses around the Bowery.

Dick had described Cull as "about thirty years old, one

hundred and fifty pounds, five feet, six inches tall, with dark brown hair and blue eyes. He has a stub mustache, a gold-tipped front upper tooth, a small mole on the left cheek, and most of the time he has a sneer on his face."

We got the teletypes going and soon had agents in Mobile and Tulsa digging up information regarding Cull's reputation in Tulsa and ascertaining whether a sailor named Cull had been involved in a criminal case at Mobile. The agent at Mobile wired that Cull had been indicted for stabbing his shipmate, Ernest Lord, seven times, that Lord nearly died, that after the fight Cull was placed in irons aboard ship, that he was turned over to the authorities at Mobile, and that he had escaped. The report of the stabbing convinced me that we were dealing with a desperate character, and I telephoned to New York to have extra efforts made to pick up Cull.

Since Dick had informed the agents that Cull was going to Washington, we started a search for him there, and alerted all Secret Service agents and the White House police to keep a sharp lookout for him. Next, we got a wire from Tulsa that Cull had deserted his wife, that he had deserted from the United States Army, that he had been arrested for armed robbery at Tulsa and was declared insane, being committed to the Eastern Oklahoma Hospital for the Insane. That report also stated that he was suffering from delusions of persecution and that he claimed he was a seeker after truth and thought he would eventually be crucified. He had escaped from the mental institution after a month and had never been located.

These reports confirmed my conviction that Cull was too dangerous to be at large with a nitroglycerine bomb earmarked for President Roosevelt, so I phoned the New York office to put even more agents on his trail. A little later I got a report that they believed Cull had been located at a flop house, and that Agents Morris and others were waiting in a room directly opposite the one he occupied. Cull had left his room early in the day and Morris and Agent O'Shea were ready to grab him on his return.

They waited from three o'clock in the afternoon until two-thirty the next morning, when they heard a man tiptoeing along the corridor. He was carrying something about two feet long and two inches square in a newspaper. He placed the room key in the lock and just then Morris and O'Shea pinned his arms down. He kicked Morris in the stomach but he was quickly controlled. The newspaper contained a razor-sharp butcher knife with a blade sixteen inches long. In his inside pocket they found a needlepoint sharpened ice pick. Later Cull, for this was he, admitted that he got to thinking that perhaps Dick may have squealed on him to the Secret Service, and he had the knife and ice pick with which to stab agents if they tried to arrest him.

Morris and O'Shea slipped a pair of handcuffs on Cull and carefully searched him. In another inside coat pocket they found a paper containing formulae for the manufacture of nitroglycerine, black powder, and nitrocellulose. In his room they found some new tools—an emery stone, pliers, screw driver, ice pick, awls, a clamp, two butcher knives— an Army rifle and bayonet, and other material necessary for the manufacture of a bomb.

A clerk in the flop house informed the agents that when Cull left that morning about seven o'clock he had carried a black suitcase. After lengthy questioning, Cull admitted that he had engaged another room that day at the Star Hotel. In a search of that room, the agents found the suitcase, and hidden under several boxes in the back of a clothes closet, they found two bottles of nitroglycerine and a bottle of nitric acid, as well as two razor-sharp knives and some ammunition for the rifle.

The tools and chemicals in these rooms were confiscated and taken to police headquarters in New York City for examination by Captain James Pyke of the Bomb Squad. Captain Pyke was an outstanding expert on bombs, and in his offices he had one of the largest collections of home-made bombs in existence. He examined the contraband, tools, chemicals, and other material seized in Cull's two hotel rooms and advised me that a man with a little mechanical ability could easily make several powerful bombs from it in an hour or two.

After Cull was arrested, he was rushed to headquarters and questioned by Secret Service agents and Captain Pyke. He emphatically denied ever having made any threats against the President. He claimed that the chemicals were for testing questionable gold coins he had picked up in South America, this despite the formulae containing the exact proportions for the manufacture of nitroglycerine, found in his wallet. Cull was very evasive and defiant in all his statements to the agents. He was finally confronted with the formulae. Then he stated that there was no use in "boxing" with the officers any further, and that he would tell the truth.

He bragged: "My purpose was to kill that son-of-a-bitch Roosevelt. I want to destroy him in order that we can get a new Commander in Chief who will make peace with Germany and then go after the Japanese. I hate President Roosevelt. He was responsible for our entry into the war and the killing of a great many sailors in the North Atlantic."

Cull then wrote a statement in which he reiterated his hatred of the President and his desire to kill him. He proudly explained that he intended to kill the President by preparing three nitroglycerine bombs, strapping them about his waist, and, as detonating caps were difficult to obtain at that time, he intended to use dry cell batteries also strapped to his body. From the batteries he would be able to obtain a spark to ignite the bombs. He defiantly said, "I intended to put on an Army uniform, get close to the President's automobile, short the batteries, spark the nitroglycerine, and blow myself and the ———————— President to bits, and also kill any g.d. Secret Service agents or other people who were nearby."

Cull was sent to Bellevue Hospital in New York where

the psychiatrists found him to be insane. He was then committed to the Pilgrim State Hospital, West Brentwood, New York. However, as he still insisted that he intended to assassinate the President and as he would have little difficulty in escaping from Pilgrim State Hospital, we requested his transfer to the Matteawan State Hospital for the criminally insane at Beacon, New York.

A series of fifty-five of the most violent and shockingly obscene poison-pen letters ever sent to a President came to the White House postmarked from the Chicago area in 1944 and 1945. The first one made cold shivers run up and down my spine, and as they continued to arrive at the White House, the threats and insulting, sickening statements became worse and worse.

The criminal mind responsible for these letters displayed unusual cunning, as the words written in the letters and the addresses on the envelopes were always hand-printed. The guilty person had no intention of having his penmanship identified, so he cut out cartoons and printed matter from newspapers and magazines and pasted his arrangement of them on the stationery. He called Roosevelt and Churchill "World Criminals No. 1 and No. 2," and wrote, "Hang these War Gangsters who pushed the U.S. into England's war."

Some of the mildest statements in the first letter—the rest being too foul for repetition—included these:

I hope to God you have a heart attack to end your crooked career, because if not, I'm going to cut your guts out. . . .
To bad Zangara missed you when he killed Cermak, to bad.

The first letter had been mailed in Cicero; others that followed were from Evanston, South Chicago, and other Chicago suburbs. The fifth letter was in an envelope of a better grade of paper and in the upper left-hand corner, where the return address usually appears, we found some heavy black ink marks indicating that the writer had destroyed a printed name. He had scratched deeply and completely obliterated the name. Our laboratory in the Secret Service Protective Research Section at the White House examined the envelope and gave me a report that under the black scratches was the name "Bowman Dairy Company." That gave us a good lead, and we felt it probable that somebody employed by the dairy was responsible for the letters.

The personal records of the entire staff of a thousand employees of the dairy were examined. We found an eccentric German fellow who seemed a possible suspect, and we put an undercover man on his trail.

Meanwhile, every week or so, new letters in this series arrived at the White House, each one more shocking than the previous ones. A few were in envelopes with the Bowman Dairy return address crossed out with heavy scratches. The twenty-first letter said:

The people ought to take your family, the —————, put them in the Public Square and execute them.

The people should tear one foul limb from your deseased body every week until you die.

Before election you'll get a lead slug in your sick brain which will end the war in a jiffy.

The agents at Chicago were growing a little discouraged, but when the forty-ninth letter arrived at the White House, we were able to send them another good lead. The letter was in a Bowman Dairy envelope, with the return address heavily crossed out as usual, but on the back of the envelope another address had apparently been crossed out. The envelope did not have the usual stamps on it, as the writer had cut out from another envelope an oval embossed stamp. When our Protective Research Laboratory examined the back of that envelope, they found that the typewritten name "Avondale Public School" had been crossed out on the back. The Chicago office was notified immediately to check on the employees of the Avondale School. An examination of

Christopher Clarence Cull planned to assassinate President Roosevelt with a home-made nitroglycerine bomb

Joe Doldo, who "hated presidents" and threatened Roosevelt with the "Hand of Mistery"

President Truman, well guarded, during a New York City parade in 1945

On November 1, 1950, an attempt was made on President Truman's life by two Puerto Rican revolutionaries who tried to storm Blair House in Washington. Griselio Torresold was killed by police bullets at 'A' and Oscar Collazo was wounded at 'B'. Truman was waved back by Special Agents when he looked out of the window ('C')

all letters received up to that time showed that a one- and a two-cent stamp had been used on each envelope.

Agent Jim Burdette interviewed the Principal of the school, Miss Augusta Peterson. She was shocked but could not suggest any suspects. She said that about two years previously some envelopes and some one- and two-cent stamps had been stolen from a teacher's desk and a tough kid, who was later expelled, was thought to have stolen the stamps. The boy she named was located and was then living in another state a thousand miles away and could not, therefore, have mailed the letters in Chicago.

Agent Burdette showed Miss Peterson the envelope with the oval embossed stamp and immediately a puzzled expression showed on her intelligent face. "Oh, I have some envelopes with that kind of stamp," she said, and produced some from her own desk addressed to the Board of Education. The personal files of all teachers and other employees were checked, but no promising leads were obtained.

The fifty-fourth letter arrived at the White House and it also had the name of the Avondale Public School on the reverse side, heavily crossed out. Among other things, it said:

When Cermak got shot by Zangara, that bullet was meant for you, you ——————. You can't walk the streets like a man with a clear conscience for fear you will get a bullet in the head, which you so well deserve. You stay secluded now. Many a person would like to put a bullet through your sick brain. So would I. I'll get you soon.

Enclosed with the letter was a cartoon from a daily paper upon which was printed obscene remarks and the legend, "Roosevelt the Jew." Agents established that the cartoon had been cut from the Lake Geneva *Herald*. Some of the later letters were on the stationery of the Plaza Hotel, San Francisco, and a hotel in Albuquerque, New Mexico.

There were about seventy-five employees in the school, including teachers, engineers, janitors, and charwomen. We wanted to get specimens of their hand-printing to compare with the poison-pen letters, so, with the co-operation of Miss Peterson, we prepared a brief questionaire about their previous employment record which they were told was required information for the Board of Education.

The instructions accompanying the questionnaire included one which said: "Print your name and address on the bottom line."

It worked. The printing of the head janitor, Louis Sprenzel, was identical to the printing on the envelopes addressed to the President. We submitted the sample of hand-printing to a handwriting expert, who confirmed our conclusion but said that it would be necessary to secure a lot more of this printing before he could go into court and swear that the janitor had written the letters. In the meantime we had an undercover man watching Sprenzel day and night. A neatly-dressed, medium-sized, gray-haired man, he lived in a quiet manner, and was never seen to go to a mailbox; he went to a corner saloon every evening, had a few beers, and then went home.

We finally decided that the best method to get him to do some hand-printing samples without his getting suspicious of us would be to send a form letter to him to call at the Office of the Collector of Internal Revenue regarding his income-tax return for the previous year. With the help of an agent in the Chicago office of the Internal Revenue Intelligence Unit, we prepared a fake form for taxpayers to fill out, and in large print at the top of the form we specified: "All answers should be typewritten or printed for the convenience of examining clerks."

When Sprenzel appeared in answer to the letter, he was questioned briefly and then requested to fill out the questionnaire. He printed his answers. In our opinion his hand-printing tallied with that on the anonymous letters.

He was courteously dismissed and informed that he need not worry about his income-tax returns, as they were all in order. He seemed greatly relieved. The specimens of his hand-printing were rushed to a handwriting expert. He gave us a written opinion, supported by exhibits of enlarged specimens of the hand-printing on the fake tax form and enlarged portions of the poison-pen letters. The opinion stated without qualification that the anonymous letters had been hand-printed by Sprenzel. Agents proceeded to the school and brought him to the Chicago Secret Service office. Sprenzel strongly protested his innocence, but as piece after piece of convincing evidence was stuck under his nose, he wilted. We also showed him the letterheads of the Plaza Hotel, San Francisco, and the hotel at Albuquerque, and copies of his registration at both these hotels.

Sprenzel finally reluctantly made a full confession, asking, "Why did I do it?" with tears of self-pity rolling down his face unchecked.

With the nature of the vile letters to the White House in his mind and the feeling that he would personally like to punch this tear-stained face into pulp, Agent Burdette bluntly replied, "What's the use of asking me why you did it? Get on with your statement."

"But I had nothing against the President. I'm truly sorry," Sprenzel blubbered. "I don't know why I'd live until I'm fifty-five years old and then do such things. It must have been that I got a few too many beers in me and got excited."

Agents went out to Sprenzel's home with a search warrant, and after an intensive look found a copy of the Lake Geneva *Herald* from which the cartoon enclosed in one of the letters had been cut. They also found some Bowman Dairy envelopes and one Board of Education envelope with the oval stamp. In a suitcase we found a few sheets of stationery from the hotels at San Francisco and Albuquerque.

In the early days of the roaring twenties, Sprenzel had driven trucks of alcohol for the Capone syndicate. I was not sorry at having another of that gang on the way to the penitentiary.

Several employees at the Avondale school were interviewed and testified that they had heard Sprenzel violently denounce the President, calling him "Rosenfeld, the —— —— of a dictator!"

Sprenzel was interviewed again the next day, when he was in a cell in the marshal's office. He was in a highly emotional condition, continually crying and sobbing. He calmed down for a minute and whispered to Agent Burdette, "Oh—oh—oh, I'll lose my job and lose my home! I'll give you a thousand dollars if you'll get me out of this!"

Instead of getting him out of his trouble it only increased it, for Agent Burdette brought out the bribe offer in his testimony and the judge imposed a sentence of seven years in Leavenworth penitentiary.

While we were investigating many poison-pen letters and verbal threats against the life of the President from various parts of the country, we discovered a most serious case right on our front doorstep. Literally within the shadow of the Washington Monument and less than a mile from the White House were two expensive yachts, the *Sunshine* and the *Habana,* anchored in the Potomac River. One was owned by Edward de Rouchlac Blount and the other by his father, a highly respected gentleman of means, who had been a government attorney. Edward was employed in a responsible position in the Commerce Department. He was thirty years old, single, and lived aboard the *Sunshine,* valued at $75,000, where he threw many ritzy parties and entertained many socialites. I received a confidential tip that Edward had boldly threatened to kill "that s.o.b. Roosevelt, who has forced the country into war." The informant said that Edward de Rouchlac Blount was a great admirer of Hitler and that he was especially proud of his own little mustache, which was trimmed just like the one that decorated the mug of the Nazi dictator.

Knowing that President Roosevelt, while cruising on the yacht *Potomac,* frequently passed within a hundred feet of

the *Sunshine* and the *Habana,* I immediately passed the word
along to the *Potomac*'s captain that in future the two yachts
should be given a very wide berth. I also ordered a prompt
investigation to determine whether the information received
was well-founded.

Blount was placed under surveillance and agents were
directed to secure evidence regarding any threats that had
been uttered by him in the past. They diligently canvassed
the water front, yacht clubs, and taverns frequented by him.
Soon they found a loyal citizen who said, "Blount is praising
Hitler all the time and says he hates Roosevelt." From
another citizen they learned that Blount had a violent
temper and that about two years earlier he had nearly killed
a teenage boy on shore close to where his boat was anchored.
It seems that Blount was asleep in the cabin of the yacht and
some boys were singing popular songs on a dock nearby.
Blount came on deck with a rifle, cursed, and ordered the
youths to get the hell out of there. They felt that they had
a right to stay on public property and did not move, so
Blount aimed the rifle, fired, and slightly wounded one of
the boys. Another witness was located who said he heard
Blount brag that he intended to blast his way through the
front door of the White House and shoot the —————
President Roosevelt. Two other persons informed agents
that they were present when Blount shouted, "If he is elected
for a third term I'll kill him."

After securing this evidence, the agents boarded Blount's
yacht with a warrant and placed him under arrest. Then
they went below and searched the cabin. To their surprise
they found copies of two cablegrams sent to Hitler before
the United States entered World War Two, in which Blount
sent the dictator sincere wishes for a happy birthday. They
also found a formal acknowledgment of the cables from the
German Embassy in Washington, extending thanks for the
birthday greetings. In another part of the cabin they found
a big pile of newspapers and clippings in the German lan-

guage, together with some government reports which might be helpful to the Nazi government. Hidden in the stern of the yacht they discovered a rifle and a collection of fifteen revolvers.

The evidence was placed before the Honorable Edward M. Curran, United States Attorney for the District of Columbia. He was shocked by the conclusive evidence of Blount's brazen and disloyal actions. Curran and his assistant, Bernard Margolius, devoted their efforts very efficiently to securing a prompt indictment by the Federal Grand jury. Realizing that he would in all probability be convicted, Blount was advised by his attorney to enter a plea of guilty, and Judge Letts imposed a six-year sentence.

9

When the United States entered World War Two, our problems of protection and security for the President abruptly intensified, and changed.

As the war clouds had first gathered over Europe, we had all anticipated what might face us. But we did not know when and how it would strike. Around our house that Sunday, December 7, 1941, everything was peaceful and serene, as I imagine it was in most homes over America. Judith and I had attended early church and had taken a long ride in beautiful Rock Creek Park. Then we spent a happy hour in our yard, feeding our daily visitors, the gray squirrels, cardinals, and blue jays. About two o'clock we had just sat down to one of Judith's delicious dinners—roast pork, steaming hot mashed potatoes hidden under gravy, and hubbard squash—when the phone rang.

"Why don't they let us eat in peace!" I said disgustedly.

Judith came back from the phone with a disturbed look. "Hustle up. The White House operator said 'Get the Chief on the phone, quick!' "

It was Mike Reilly, Assistant Supervising Agent of the White House Detail. "Chief! The Japs have bombarded Pearl Harbor."

141

I was stunned to silence for a few seconds. Then I replied, "I'll be down as soon as my Lincoln will get there. In the meantime, telephone every agent in this district and all White House police to report for duty immediately. I'll have my auto radio tuned in so you can reach me while I'm en route."

The report of the sneak attack of the Japanese on Pearl Harbor raised my blood pressure, but I also had a satisfied feeling, because, anticipating our entry into the war, I had very definite plans for the Secret Service worked out and ready to be put into effect immediately.

By about three o'clock General Marshall and some highly disturbed and deeply worried Cabinet members—including Secretary Hull of the State Department; my chief, Secretary Morgenthau; Secretary of the Navy Knox; Secretary Ickes of the Interior Department; Attorney General Biddle; and Steve Early, Press Secretary—had arrived at the White House and were in conference with President Roosevelt.

F.D.R. was outwardly calm, but boiling mad. A big group of excited reporters were eagerly observing the Cabinet members as they hurriedly arrived, and were appealing to them for interviews. Radio stations had broadcast alarming reports regarding the sudden bombardment of Pearl Harbor and several hundred excited and troubled citizens had gathered on Pennsylvania Avenue and Lafayette Park in front of the White House.

My greatest fear was that a Nazi undercover agent or saboteur might be willing to sacrifice his own life if he could assassinate our President. I immediately decided to intensify to a high degree the protection extended to him.

The first command I issued was for the cancellation of all leave for Secret Service agents and White House police, and the number of agents on the White House Secret Service Detail assigned to protect the President was doubled. Secret Service agents quickly confiscated White House press credentials of all Italian, Japanese, and German correspondents, about twenty in all, including three taken from foreign newspapermen aboard a train bound for New York.

We stationed a White House police officer at the switch control panel of the White House. A hack inspector from the Washington police department was assigned to the gate at the White House to identify all cab drivers entering the grounds. All cabs and other vehicles were prohibited from entering the White House grounds except autos carrying official appointments, Cabinet members, secretaries to the President, and the President's physician. Only specially designated Western Union messengers were allowed to pass through the White House gates. Since the White House was not of fireproof construction, we detailed a squad of chemical warfare and incendiary bomb experts to twenty-four-hour duty. They also had on hand material to decontaminate areas or rooms affected by chemical warfare gases.

In accordance with previous plans, a company of carefully selected regular Army soldiers was immediately detailed to patrol outside the White House fence. This detail was our first line of defense. As a second line of defense we had our White House police inside the fence. They were a picked group of experienced police officers, who had won many championships in pistol matches. Next, and nearest to the President, we had our Secret Service agents of the White House Detail. These agents were young, athletic, specially-trained men, expert marksmen with a revolver or machine gun. They were ready at a second's notice to spring between the President and an attacker. They were my particular joy, for they were living testimony of the modernization program and the intensive training in the use of firearms which I put into effect when I first became Chief.

Colonel Edmund W. Starling, veteran Supervising Agent of the Secret Service White House Detail, was relieved of active supervisory duties and Assistant Supervising Agent Michael F. Reilly was promoted to Supervising Agent. The change constituted no reflection on Colonel Starling, whose twenty-nine years of splendid service were marked by achievements which were the pride of the Secret Service. However, the Colonel was sixty-four and in poor health, and I decided that the need for a young and very active man to head the Detail was urgent. So with his customary courtly grace, Colonel Starling stepped aside. I arranged for him to remain in an advisory capacity. Agent Thomas J. Qualters, an extremely efficient agent of the White House Detail, was promoted to Assistant Supervising Agent.

An important security measure was the radically changed design of the White House identification card, which was issued only to those persons on a carefully selected list. All previously issued White House identification cards were called in and declared invalid. The new cards were kept under the strict supervision of the Secret Service.

After those preliminary plans had been effected, I hurried across the street to my office in the Treasury Building, and was pleased to find my staff on duty and taking steps to effect other plans we had ready in a special file for use in an emergency. I sent teletype messages ordering all Secret Service field offices to function on a twenty-four-hour day, seven-days-a-week basis. I ordered a large detail of agents from several cities to proceed immediately to Washington for temporary assignment. Within three hours, Secret Service agents, along with other Treasury agents, were carrying out prearranged plans at various cities to seize for the Foreign Fund Control Division of the Treasury the assets of enemies located in the United States. They raided and seized such big establishments as the I. J. Farben Industries, the Bank of Naples, and Yamanaka's, the fashionable jewelry shop in New York City.

From the time of our entry into the war and for a period of four months thereafter not one Secret Service agent was able to take a single day off. Without exception, all of us worked Saturdays, Sundays, and holidays until I felt that the situation was under good control. On Pearl Harbor night

I had a large room in the Treasury Building converted into a dormitory for the use of the agents we were calling to Washington. We did that so that agents off duty would be in reserve for prompt action in the event of an air raid on Washington or other emergency. We borrowed blankets and cots from the Army. The Treasury Building was both office and home to these men for several months.

I also secured quarters in the basement of the Treasury Building for the company of regular Army soldiers we had detailed from Fort Myer to protect the White House. Inside of an hour, this company installed anti-aircraft guns on top of the Treasury Building so as to be in a position to intercept enemy airplanes attempting to bomb or strafe the White House. I drafted a detail of experienced firemen from the Washington City Fire Department, and they were stationed, with modern fire-fighting equipment, between the Treasury Building and the White House, so that they could protect these important buildings from fire resulting from incendiary bombs.

One of my little headaches was working out a complete "blackout" of the White House and the White House grounds. Flashlights equipped with blue bulbs were issued to the White House Secret Service Detail and White House police. The windows of the Executive Mansion and the White House Executive offices were completely covered with heavy black material. Pistol-grip flashlights with blue bulbs were placed at strategic positions on all floors of the White House, in rooms occupied by the President, and through the White House grounds.

We arranged for the use of a secluded railroad side track to enable us to move President Roosevelt from Washington, if necessary, in a secret, prompt, and safe manner. I placed an order for a new armor-plated auto and for the armoring of the touring car then in use by the President. An armored automobile with bulletproof glass, which we had seized from Scarface Al Capone, was pressed into service until the new car was to be delivered. President Roosevelt chuckled when I told him the auto had formerly been used to protect the notorious Capone from his gangster enemies.

Our greatest concern was of a sudden air attack. We had in mind the terrifying and destructive blitzes on London, which Hitler had been ordering almost continuously for over a year. I shall never forget the conference in my office the night the Japanese bombs fell on Pearl Harbor. We had before us a heavy file started two years earlier containing recommended plans to be put into effect immediately in event of war. Those in attendance with me were Assistant Chief Joseph E. Murphy, Assistant Supervisor of the White House Detail Thomas Qualters, Executive Aides Laurence E. Albert and Harry S. Neal, Supervising Agent Maurice Allen, and Charles S. Bell, Administrative Assistant to the Secretary of the Treasury. We decided to convert Treasury Vault No. 14 into a temporary air-raid shelter to house the President and the First Lady in the event of a sudden air raid on Washington, and to begin at once to build a permanent shelter.

About two A.M., I returned to the White House to make a further survey of the extra protection I had ordered put into effect. I was dead tired, but physical weariness could not count. I found the agents on the White House Detail "on their toes" and functioning in an excellent manner. The White House police had not been issued proper instructions by the Captain and I was shocked to find one police officer, the one on duty closest to the President's sleeping room, as his post was in the yard immediately below the President's window, snugly wrapped in a blanket and resting in an easy chair. He was so nearly asleep that I was not even challenged as I approached.

For once, I blew my top. I shook him, roaring, "Get out of that chair! Get out quick!"

I immediately ordered Captain Marcy, the officer in charge, to take that man off his post and put him at a post "furthest from the White House," and to get a good alert man placed under the President's room. I also ordered Captain Marcy to remove all chairs from all posts and to make half-hourly inspections.

When President Roosevelt announced he would deliver a message to Congress on the following day, I summoned to Washington an unprecedented number of experienced Secret Service agents from various cities so as to insure proper protection for him at the Capitol, the White House, or wherever he might be. On the trip from the White House to the Capitol and on the return we enlisted the valuable co-operation of a large detail of uniformed members and detectives in civilian clothes from the Washington Police Department, and also Army Intelligence investigators, in order to assure the best possible protection along the President's route. Street intersections were blocked off so as to avoid the necessity of reducing auto speed, since we realized that an enemy saboteur or a crank attempting to assassinate the President would face great difficulty if his car was proceeding at thirty miles an hour. All street manholes on the route were inspected for hidden bombs, and then sealed.

In his impressive address to Congress, the President declared the Pearl Harbor attack was "a date which will live in infamy." He asked Congress to declare war, and the declaration was passed with but one dissenting voice. I shall never forget the overwhelming roar of "ayes" in favor of the declaration.

After we returned from the Capitol, we made a careful survey of Treasury Vault No. 14 with the aid of Army Engineers, and discovered that the roof was not sufficiently strong for its use as an air-raid shelter. We, therefore, selected Treasury Vault No. 1 for that purpose, necessitating the removal of $7,000,000 worth of opium and other drugs, which had been stock-piled for war emergencies, from Vault No. 1 to Vault No. 14.

Three compartments in Vault No. 1 contained $700,000,-000 in silver dollars, and another compartment contained

$1,800,000,000 in gold certificates. A guard was placed on each compartment twenty-four hours a day. Executive Aide Larry Albert was designated to represent the Secret Service in supervising the extensive alterations to be made in Vault No. 1, such as two emergency exits which had to be drilled through the three-foot vault wall, a ventilating system, and the construction of a tunnel from the White House to the Treasury. The tunnel was 761 feet long, about 7 feet wide and 7 feet high, and of a zigzag design intended to lessen danger from concussion in the event of a direct or close bomb hit.

On December 8th, Albert delivered to Vault No. 1:

> 24 cases Poland Water
> 200 pounds of food
> 12 day beds
> 24 blankets, sheets, pillow cases, towels
> 12 first aid kits
> a portable toilet
> dishes
> tables and chairs

Another large vault was fixed up for use of a part of the Presidential staff. In addition to desks it was equipped with surgical tables, surgical instruments, drugs, crowbars, picks and shovels, plastic lighting fixtures, 12 telephone lines, an electric refrigerator, and 6 electric hot plates.

It was decided to build the best permanent bomb-proof shelter in the world, of concrete and steel, at the east end of the White House. Ground was broken on December 13th. Earth removed from the excavation was temporarily dumped on the grounds near the Washington Monument, and it soon made a miniature mountain.

The military protection of the White House, in the event of a direct attack, was outlined by Colonel Howell Estes of the Third Cavalry. He recommended that we have four antiaircraft batteries installed on the East and West porticoes of the White House. An emergency rescue detail was organized, consisting of one officer, three sergeants, and .five squads of eight soldiers for the rescue of persons buried in buildings during air raids. One rescue truck was assigned to the White House. It was equipped with twenty picks, twenty shovels, ten crowbars, four sledgehammers, one hundred feet of inch rope, two jennies, two blocks-and-tackles, four heavy jacks, twelve blocks of wood, twelve 2x8 planks, twelve 4x4 timbers, two ladders, four hooded lights (Coleman), six fire extinguishers, and four large saws.

The use of two-way radios was increased so as to form a complete means of quick communication between agents and offices in the Secret Service. Sets were already in some cars and were installed in others; stations were placed at various vantage points, including my private office and my automobile. Maintenance of this radio network was done by the White House Signal Detachment, a unit of the Signal Corps. This unit also handled cryptographic and other war communications to and from the President.

Practically living with a transmitter in my hand both in my office and in my automobile, I stood ready at all times promptly to countermand or revise any orders not in keeping with the highest protective standards. For my own satisfaction, I personally made frequent unannounced tours of inspection at the White House at various hours of the day or night.

We also built a heavier and much higher iron fence around the White House and installed an electronic signal system on it. This device, however, did not prove successful, as it was too sensitive, and many false alarms were set off by birds or small animals. We also tried out an electronic device, similar to those used at the entrances to prisons, to detect the presence of revolvers, stilettos, or other dangerous weapons on persons entering the White House grounds; but it was not considered practical. (The advance in electronics since then might make both these protective measures successful today.) With the help of the Army we also installed new and improved lookout booths for the military guards and the White House Police.

An armored speaking stand was specially built for the use of the President when he addressed public meetings. Gas masks were issued to the President, all White House servants and employees, and to Secret Service agents. The mask provided for the President was tied to his wheel chair so that it would be ready for immediate use at all times.

Two streets adjoining the White House, East Executive Avenue and West Executive Avenue, were closed to traffic.

In the middle of December, I was talking to President Roosevelt at the White House when he matter-of-factly said, "The Prime Minister—Churchill—is coming over for a series of conferences. There'll be plenty of work for your outfit, Frank. He will probably arrive around the first of the year."

The news sent me into a dither of preparations. Prime Minister Churchill's first visit to the United States during wartime would be anything but a picnic for me. I pulled in several Secret Service agents from other cities and made swift preparations to keep Britain's Prime Minister as safe as a baby in its mother's arms.

A week before Christmas I was driving down Connecticut Avenue one night with Judith, on a last-minute shopping trek, when my two-way radio crackled, "Copper calling Buffalo; Copper calling Buffalo. . . ." I seized the mike and replied, "Buffalo answering Copper."

"Buffalo" was my code name and "Copper" was the code name of the Supervising Agent of the White House Detail.

"Copper" informed me, in a kind of double talk which would baffle radio spies, that "the big fella" would hit the United States several days earlier than expected. So I replied, "I'll be at the White House in ten minutes to complete the plans for his protection."

"Oh—and I did *so* want you to help me choose that

Christmas present! Who'd be the wife of a Secret Service Chief is what I'd like to know!" Judith wailed with, I am bound to say, some justification.

After feeding her my current line, "We are at war, dear," I said good-bye and told her to be sure and get a taxi home and not to wait up, because I was bound to be late.

When I got to the White House I found Assistant Chief Joe Murphy and Assistant Supervising Agent of the White House Detail, Tommy Qualters, already there, revamping the original plans made for the Prime Minister's protection. Teletypes were sent out to the New York and Chicago offices ordering additional agents to report to Washington the next day. The Prime Minister and his party, which included Lord Leather, Minister of War Transport; Sir Dudley Pound, Lord of the Admiralty; Lord Beaverbrook, Minister of Supply; and many other high-ranking officials, were to arrive at Hampton Roads, Virginia, aboard H.M.S. *George V*. Mr. Churchill was flown from Hampton Roads to Washington, arriving at six-thirty P.M. on December 21st.

Of all the distinguished foreign visitors whom the Secret Service had to protect, I would easily place the late Sir Winston Churchill at the top of the list for personal popularity, but his earlier-than-expected arrival certainly added to the headaches of the Secret Service during the remarkable Christmas week of 1941.

Christmas Eve fell soberly upon the United States. The city of Washington was subdued and ominous. Outdoor decorations were few, for authorities had requested the people to display as little light as possible. At five P.M. on Christmas Eve the President and the Prime Minister participated in the ceremony of dedicating a community Christmas tree on the lawn south of the White House. For that occasion the White House grounds were opened to the public, and the two great statesmen appeared on the south portico of the White House where they greeted the people in serious messages broadcast to the world. The crowd of

L

some 28,000 people, which had assembled on the White House grounds for the double purpose of getting a glimpse of the two great men of the hour and witnessing the Christmas tree ceremony, replied to the Prime Minister's greeting in their own way: "Bravo, Winnie! At-a-boy! Hip-hip, hoo-oo-ray!"

There is always something basically thrilling about a full-throated roar from a mixed crowd, and it seemed as if the American people were voicing their admiration for the consummate bravery of the British people in their refusal to knuckle under or yield an inch to Hitler's savage onslaught. As the official program was ending, somebody in the front line of the crowd started the chorus of "Land of Hope and Glory," which is to England what "God Bless America" is to the United States.

It was a dramatic, moving spectacle. The President, with his imposing presence, stood beside Prime Minister Churchill, and his face was grave as the words, "God, who made thee mighty, make thee mightier yet," struck home. I saw tears fill his eyes.

My agents were standing very close to the two great leaders of their countries' destinies and I had an extra large detail of agents mingling with the crowds on the White House grounds. So for a brief moment I was reassured and let my thoughts have play while I listened to the singing crowd. I wondered why the world invariably lets its poets starve, when it is they alone who can express the thoughts that lie too deep for words that might come to the tongues of ordinary men and women.

Secret Service agents were up before dawn on that never-to-be-forgotten first Christmas of the war, preparing to protect President Roosevelt and Prime Minister Churchill while they attended morning service at the Foundry Methodist Church. The agents had surveyed the church for three days, and had worked throughout the night. I had many other agents on duty, as it was necessary to use every available man for this public appearance of the two world leaders on Christmas day. Agents had thoroughly searched every inch of the church the day before and were on guard from then until after the services were over. Before this, they were assigned to posts on the streets, in the cellar, in the choir loft, at the entrances, in the pews, and in the pastor's study. Entry to the church was by card only. The services were conducted by the pastor, Reverend Frederick Brown Harris (now Chaplain of the United States Senate), and the sermon was delivered by the Reverend Ze Barney Phillips, then the Chaplain of the United States Senate.

Two days after Christmas, I was proud to receive this letter from Dr. Harris:

Foundry Church, as you know, was virtually taken over by your Secret Service Agents for a week before Christmas in preparation for the National Christmas Service held there. . . . To adequately guard these two great leaders of world democracy, sitting together in the same church, their presence there having been announced beforehand, was a heavy burden and a grave responsibility indeed.

The Secret Service did it so well, so effectively and so courteously that as Pastor of the Church I want to express to you my admiration for that body of men. While they treated me with every consideration they allowed nothing to escape their vigilant eyes. From this personal association I have emerged with a very high estimate of the effectiveness of your organization.

That verbal bouquet sweetened my life for several days.

Judith and I had the real pleasure of entertaining as our Christmas guests two Scotland Yard Operatives, L. P. Thompson and J. F. Dudgeon, who came with the Prime Minister. We also invited a dozen of our old friends. That Christmas dinner will always loom out from the tapestry of my memory because of one incident in connection with the two Scotland Yard men.

With her usual sense of the appropriate, Judith had concentrated a great deal of effort on a most artistic seasonal decoration of our living room mantelpiece, a Christmas Crib, one which was calculated to excite a great deal of sincere admiration on the part of our guests. At almost the last moment, an appropriate touch in honor of our English guests suggested itself to what Judith tearfully called my "brutal mind," which was the placing of photos of King George and Queen Elizabeth (whom I had guarded during their 1939 visit to America) in the middle of the mantelpiece, flanked by a couple of small British flags.

"In the *middle* of all the animals of the Manger? And take away the Three Wise Men? Why, it spoils the whole scheme!" Judith protested. "Couldn't I place the photographs and flags on a little side table where they'd be bound to see them?"

I knew that the first thing to catch the eye of anyone entering our living room was certainly the mantelpiece, and I stood my ground for having the King and Queen and the flags where I wanted them. Judith consented to a last-minute transfer of the Christmas Crib from the mantelpiece to a table nearby. When we entered the living room, accompanied by our English guests, their spontaneous smiles and emphatic expressions of pleasure were more than sufficient to console Judith and to reward me.

"Make ourselves at home, Mrs. Wilson? How can we help it, with King George and Queen Elizabeth looking at us?" Agent Thompson exclaimed. That little attention promptly broke the traditional British ice and helped put our guests at ease.

Our Scotland Yard friends told me how "astounding" they considered our intensive security measures in regard to the President and Prime Minister's public appearances, both at the Christmas Tree Ceremony and when they attended church. Apparently, at that time at least, English protective methods were not nearly so rigorous as those we. employed. The Scotland Yard agents said that when they returned

home, they intended to adopt some of the methods they had
seen us use, in the future protection of the Royal Family
and the Prime Minister.

I am convinced that Prime Minister Churchill could have
made his mark in many other callings besides that of a
politician. As an author he is greatly admired, and his books
are deservedly successful; as a painter his work is far above
average; but in my opinion we lost a great actor when he
failed to put on greasepaint. His handling of a crowd was
superb and his popularity was instant and undoubted.
Around Washington he frequently gave the "V" for victory
sign which he made by holding up the first two fingers of his
right hand.

On the day after Christmas in 1941, when he went to the
Capitol to address Congress, I saw him amuse a big crowd
waiting outside to see him go in. After giving them the "V"
sign, he took off his famous black Homburg, put it on top
of his cane, held it high in the air, and then waved it. The
crowd gave a lusty cheer out of all proportion to its size, for
it was the full-throated sound of utterly spontaneous—not
merely polite—approbation. However, once inside the por-
tals of the Capitol, Winston Churchill became very much
the serious Prime Minister. I never heard a more impressive
speech, and it was easy to see that the members of Congress
were strongly drawn toward him.

After the luncheon in his honor, when he was ready to
leave for the White House, Churchill, like other Englishmen,
felt the need for exercise.

"I'll walk," he told me casually. "I'll meet you at the White
House."

I was a little startled, for I had very definite directives
from President Roosevelt regarding the safety of his distinguished guest while he was in America.

Very respectfully, I said, "Sir, President Roosevelt is
expecting you back and I am sure you would not like to keep
him waiting."

It worked, and the Prime Minister returned, safely protected in the armored automobile which we had placed at his disposal.

As well as being popular with the public, Mr. Churchill was undoubtedly popular with the White House press correspondents. Shortly after his arrival, during a press conference in the President's office, President Roosevelt talked briefly and then yielded to the Prime Minister. The room was packed with nearly two hundred reporters and only a few in the front row could see him, so he climbed spryly up on a chair and instantly made a big hit with the ladies and gentlemen of the press at the back of the room.

One of them yelled, "Attaboy, Winnie!" and he got a round of applause that brought a wide, bright smile to his cherubic face. Then, with his actor's sense of timing, he became very serious, and I think at the end of his remarks every correspondent present realized that we were in for a long, hard war.

The time of his visit coincided with the construction of our air-raid shelter and tunnel. Workmen were engaged on it twenty-four hours a day; the steam shovels and compressed air drills were filling the night with their hideous clamor and the echoes found their way into Mr. Churchill's room in the White House. He sent word that he could not sleep and would the workmen please let up a little? The boss of the job obliged me and went on a sixteen-hour shift during the remainder of Churchill's visit. On his next visit to the White House I told Churchill the tunnel was completed. "I'm glad that blasted racket is not going on any more," he observed.

As it turned out, the Prime Minister was the first official to use our new tunnel. He had an appointment with the British Ambassador, which he wanted kept secret from the vigilant press that tailed him everywhere he went. I took him from the White House through the underground tunnel to the Treasury Building, and then by car to the embassy on Massachusetts Avenue—with no reporters any the wiser.

Two days after Christmas I was called over to the White House and F.D.R. said with a smile, "The Prime Minister needs a rest and might go to Florida, if we can find a suitable place and it can be arranged so that nobody knows about it. Frank, see what you can do."

Churchill was not the sort of personality you could smuggle quietly into a big resort or hotel. He moved too fast; you couldn't keep him tied down to a suite.

I started shopping around and finally found a secluded house on the coast of Florida, about twenty miles south of Palm Beach, which belonged to Edward Stettinius, Jr., then Lend-Lease Director. After thorough investigation I decided that it was the ideal hideaway. It was isolated, curtained by palms and riotous tropical undergrowth.

There was a lot to do to cover that few days' vacation. We arranged for a private railroad car. We had the house emptied and a staff, made up of the Filipino boys in the Navy who served as part of the crew on the Presidential yacht, brought in. We installed our own wires and telephones, so that we did not have to go through local switchboards. Then we sent our celebrated charge to Florida with a full detail of agents, under the direction of Assistant Supervising Agent Tommy Qualters, several of whom were excellent swimmers.

Churchill's own retinue consisted of two male secretaries and the two Scotland Yard boys. It was fortunate, my agents told me, that it was an all-male party. The house and beach were completely surrounded by tropical growth—so that the residents could not be seen from any direction except the sea, and Churchill promptly took advantage of this privacy by indulging his delight in swimming nude. He did not need to worry: palms and eucalypti guarded his privacy. He plunged and gamboled. He came charging out of the surf with the uncertain movements of a landing craft to plop upon the sands and garb himself in a long cigar.

One afternoon, as he surveyed the surf, Mr. Churchill

mused to Agent Frank Burke, "Suppose a German submarine came up right in front of this cottage and started throwing shells at us. What would you do?"

Burke replied, "It won't happen, Mr. Prime Minister. You see that plane up there? That's a Coast Guard plane. It's keeping watch over you."

True, I had arranged for Coast Guard planes to patrol the coast continuously between Palm Beach and Fort Lauderdale. German subs had been operating in that district and had sunk boats that were headed for Europe with arms and ammunition, and I certainly did not want any German U-boat commander to run up his periscope and see the Right Honorable Winston Churchill splashing around off the starboard bow.

There were no subs or bulldozers to mar Churchill's Florida rest. He ended up staying an entire week, and returned to Washington looking pinker, cheerier, and more like Santa Claus than ever.

After our distinguished guest had returned to his own war-torn country in January, 1942, he took the time to write me a warm, appreciative note, thanking me and the members of the Secret Service "for all the trouble" we had taken looking after him on his visit. "There was no requirement, large or small," he noted, that our men had not proved ready to meet and even to anticipate. His thoughtful awareness of what our job had actually been made all the hard work seem well worth-while.

As I look back on it now, it seems almost incredible how many things were done, during those first few weeks following Pearl Harbor, to safeguard our President, our government, and our traditions.

The day before Christmas I received a visit from Archibald MacLeish, the Librarian of Congress. "Where would be the best place in the interests of safety to transfer the original Declaration of Independence and other priceless historical documents?" he asked me.

"Fort Knox, Kentucky, the government gold depository," was my recommendation, and I proceeded to make the necessary arrangements.

On Christmas day I assigned my Executive Aide, Harry E. Neal, to handle the transfer of these valuable documents. We decided to transport them from the Congressional Library to Union Station in an armored truck under guard of Secret Service agents. At the station the boxes were placed on a Baltimore and Ohio train leaving Washington at six-thirty P.M., December 26th. Three agents accompanied the shipment. They were met by Supervising Agent Lon Andrews at Louisville and a detail of agents to relay the boxes to Fort Knox in an Army truck.

I made arrangements with Mrs. Nellie Tayloe Ross, Director of the Bureau of the Mint, and her Deputy, Timothy J. Quirk, to have the time clock on the gold vaults at the depository set so that the vaults would be open to receive the shipment on Saturday, December 27th. The priceless documents were delivered to the Fort Knox depository and placed in Compartment No. 24 at 12:07 P.M.

A list of the documents comprising this unusual shipment will make the historic import of this transfer readily apparent:

Case 1   The Gutenberg Bible
               (St. Blasius-St. Paul copy—3 volumes)
Case 2   The Articles of Confederation
               (original, engrossed, and signed copy—1 roll)
Case 3   The Magna Carta
               (Lincoln Cathedral copy—1 parchment leaf in
                  frame)
           Abraham Lincoln's Second Inaugural Address
               (original autographed copy—1 volume)
           Abraham Lincoln's Gettysburg Address
               (first and second autographed drafts—1 volume)

Case 4   The Constitution of the United States
              (original, engrossed, and signed copy—five leaves)
          The Declaration of Independence
              (original, engrossed, and signed copy)

Only five people in Washington and two at the gold depository in Fort Knox were aware that these historic documents had been secretly transferred to what I considered the safest place in the United States.

At the time of the Pearl Harbor attack, there were several million dollars in United States money in Honolulu banks. To insure that the Japanese did not get their hands on it, we decided to destroy it. I assigned Art Grube, one of my finest agents, to proceed to Hawaii and carry out this mission. An observant man as well as a competent one, Art's report to me speaks for itself:

In San Francisco, I contacted John L. Schram, John F. Moran and Edward Barnes, who had been designated to cooperate on the mission, and we left San Francisco on a Clipper plane for Honolulu.

We made ourselves as comfortable as possible for sleep by lying on the floor of the plane. All curtains were drawn and the plane was blacked out for the trip to Honolulu where we arrived about 10 o'clock the following morning.

In the succeeding days we were engaged in acquiring all surplus American currency on the Island, including that stored in the vaults of the Yokohama Specie Bank, a Japanese institution which had been taken over by the Government. Also, inspection was made of various furnaces for use in the destruction of the surplus currency so as to avoid its falling into the hands of the Japanese in event of invasion. We found that several million dollars in circulation in Honolulu might be regarded as excess and should be destroyed. We decided to use the cremation facilities of the Oahu Crematory and seven big lots of American currency were destroyed.

The currency, five, ten, twenty and fifty dollar bills, was placed in mail sacks borrowed from the Post Office Department. It was conveyed in a large Military Police van with a Military Police escort from downtown Honolulu to the Oahu Crematory, which overlooks the newly-made graves of the soldiers and sailors who lost their lives in the attack on Pearl Harbor. During the destruction of the currency at the Crematory, it was surrounded by Military Police, a group of tall, good-looking young men all about six feet, under the immediate supervision of a rugged Irish sergeant who had been in the Army for twenty-nine years. They carried out their orders to exclude everyone with military exactness and it was necessary for us to rescue the Superintendent of the Crematory from the Military Police, who had halted him when he attempted to enter his own premises. The crematory had two incinerators, under the immediate supervision of a rather ghoulish individual who told us, "I don't care much for underground burials; instead, I like to burn 'em." He also told us that he often baked turkeys in the oven after a cremation. On one occasion while we were destroying the currency in one of his ovens he shoved a casket and body into the adjoining oven. The body was entirely consumed in an hour and a half, while to thoroughly burn the currency required more than double that time before the bills were reduced to ashes. He showed us how he disposed of the few remaining bones of an incinerated body. He placed the bones into a device similar to a coffee mill, operated by a hand crank, which ground the bones into a sandlike residue.

Another emergency wartime measure which fell into the lap of the Secret Service was to guard draft numbers.

General Lewis B. Hershey, Director of the Army Draft, asked the Secret Service to guard the boxes holding the draft capsules in which the serial numbers of the men who had registered for military service were kept. Agents were assigned to transport the boxes containing the draft numbers of the men who registered on February 16, 1942, for Selective Service. The boxes were taken from Selective Service Headquarters to the Treasury vaults for safekeeping until the official drawing, scheduled for March 17th, and lodged in a compartment in Vault No. 1 under a sealed lock bearing the initials of L. E. Albert, representing the Secret Service, and Major F. Davidson, representing the Army. Each of these men retained two of the only four keys to that compartment.

Two days later my telephone rang. It was Major Davidson, whose voice sounded harsh with nervous agitation. "Could I come over right away?" he asked sharply.

"Okay, Major. But what's the hurry? Anything wrong?"

"I've just received in the mail, anonymously, two of the official draft capsules."

The capsules contained numbers T-5498 and T-6430. A conference took place in my office among Larry Albert, Major F. Davidson, and myself. No finger of suspicion could be pointed at any employee of the Secret Service for the theft of the capsules, because they were given into the custody of the Secret Service in sealed boxes. Therefore, it was reasonable to assume that the two capsules sent to Major Davidson were removed from the lot before they were put in the sealed boxes. Since it was not known whether other capsules were missing, we decided it was necessary to count the entire lot. Major Davidson, accompanied by three of his Army associates, and Agents Larry Albert, Maurice Allen, and Harry Neal, went to Vault 1 and brought the boxes to a large compartment, which had been converted into an air-raid shelter and emergency quarters for the President.

There, they emptied the capsules onto the floor. The four Army officers and three Secret Service agents proceeded to count the capsules, which should have totaled seven thousand. When the count reached 6,700 everybody took a deep breath and the remaining pellets were counted very carefully by Majors Davidson and Noell. The count of the balance showed 298. With the two capsules received in the mail, the total of seven thousand was duly accounted for. All present breathed a sigh of relief. How the two capsules were stolen and why they were anonymously returned is still a mystery.

Early in the war, reports of new and tremendously powerful death-dealing weapons being secretly developed by the Nazis gave me great concern. The United States also was secretly working at high speed on a new and tremendously powerful weapon at the University of Chicago, Oak Ridge, and Los Alamos; but only a few scientists and top government officials had any idea of the power of that weapon as the work was "top secret." It was this terrible weapon, used at Hiroshima and Nagasaki, that finally brought World War Two to a quick end.

I talked to my nephew, Carroll L. Wilson, about my responsibility as Chief of the Secret Service for the protection of the President, and told him about my fears that President Roosevelt might be assassinated by new secret Nazi weapons, death-dealing rays, or other inventions which Hitler's scientists might develop. Carroll was Assistant Director, under Dr. Vannevar Bush, in the Office of Scientific Research and Development during World War Two. This organization had the overall responsibility for scientific research in connection with atomic energy and other vitally important scientific developments. Carroll was the first General Manager of the Atomic Energy Commission.

Carroll asked me, "Suppose, Uncle Frank, a Nazi saboteur contrived to secretly hide some radium or highly radioactive substance in a desk, or a room, or in an auto, or other place close to the President. How would you discover it before it seriously affected him?"

That possibility threw a real scare into me. "I don't know," I confessed, and added, "but perhaps you can tell me what to do."

"Well, I'll fix you up," he replied.

His confidence was reassuring. "Thanks, Carroll," I replied, "but please don't delay."

He immediately delivered to the White House a newly-developed instrument called the Geiger counter, instructed us regarding its use, and said, "You must have the agents protecting the President use this instrument daily."

The Geiger counter was designed to detect any radioactivity above normal and measure how strong it was. With the counter one can locate and measure radioactive substances even though the amount is too small to harm anyone. If the amount is large enough to affect persons in a room or a certain area, the counter will show this fact. In case some slick spy, or a silent saboteur, or a hater of our government, or of the President secretly hid some radioactive material where it would harm the President, the use of this gadget would enable Secret Service agents to locate the deadly substance promptly. We could then remove it or move the President before he could be seriously affected.

The Geiger counter was in a metal box about two feet by nine inches by nine inches, with registration dials on the front. It had just been perfected and was in daily use at Los Alamos, Oak Ridge, and other laboratories where secret work relating to the development of the atom bomb was being conducted and where radioactive material was in use. We began using the counter regularly at the White House. Once we had a scare when the dial which registered radioactivity jumped sharply and there was a buzz in the instrument. An expert was quickly called and he noticed a new wrist watch with a radium face being worn by the agent operating the instrument. He explained that the counter was so sensitive that it would even be affected by the slight amount of radium on the face of a watch.

Most of these sudden improved protection procedures were adopted without consultation with the President. However, it was deemed advisable to confer with him in reference to a few of them. F.D.R.'s gracious and prompt approval was a big satisfaction to me. He frequently expressed his deep appreciation of our efforts—and he never missed a chance to razz me about making him ride in the ancient, armored jalopy which had belonged to Public Enemy Number One.

10

A President traveled outside the United States for the first time in 1906 when Theodore Roosevelt, the first President to have formal Secret Service protection, made a trip to Panama, and his two White House Detail agents accompanied him. In 1918, when President Wilson attended the Versailles Peace Conference, a detail of ten agents accompanied him. By 1939, there were sixteen agents and two supervisors in the White House Detail—a number which was increased to thirty-seven at the time we entered World War Two. Part of this increase was due to the extra protection necessary on the President's trips, domestic and abroad. While President, F.D.R. made 400 trips and traveled 350,000 miles. Since then, our Presidents have roamed the world.

I did not go with F.D.R. when he went abroad, but I did accompany him on many of his domestic inspection tours during the war, when he visited Army and Navy bases and munition plants. I also attended him when he went into Mexico as the guest of President Avila Camacho. These trips were made by train and automobile. During the war we used an armored railroad car with bulletproof glass three

165

inches thick, which was constructed with the co-operation of the Association of American Railroads and the Pullman Company.

The Secret Service precautions were increased by thousands of soldiers guarding the route of the President's train. Every inch of railroad track was carefully inspected before the Presidential train traveled over them. Every switch along the route was spiked so that there would be no accident. The soldiers were ordered to keep crowds away from the train when it stopped. Loiterers were not allowed to linger near bridges or crossroads.

Before touring the war plants, we sent Secret Service agents ahead of us to inspect them. Every part of the factory which the President was to pass was inspected. Factory officials and managers were ordered not even to whisper about the proposed visit to their employees.

The President's auto would slowly drive through the main corridor of a factory. An employee would look up from his machine and shout, "There's the President!" The excited man, without thinking, would start running for the President's car with his hand outstretched. But before he got near the car an agent would jump in front of him, shake his hand, spin him around, and give him a powerful shove toward his machine. The employee would think he had shaken the hand of a big shot in the President's party and would be so elated that he would brag about it the rest of the day.

One of our security headaches when the President traveled was posed by his famous black Scotty dog, Fala. Fala was such a celebrity in his own right that he couldn't go for his necessary "walk" without someone recognizing him. And, being a star and enjoying the status, Fala compounded our problems by making a graceful scene if allowed. It was not actually the duty of the Secret Service to walk Fala; this responsibility supposedly rested with the President's valet, Prettyman, or one of F.D.R.'s secretaries. However, whenever the Presidential train stopped anywhere for more than a minute, Fala needed to be walked, and it often fell to one of the agents to perform this function. After we became painfully aware that there weren't that many other black Scotties with such kingly bearing in the United States, we made a point of walking him under cover of darkness only. We all got a kick out of the Fala debate between the candidate, Thomas Dewey, and the Boss, when Dewey supporters charged, during the campaign, that F.D.R. had accidentally left Fala on a Pacific island and commissioned an Army plane to fetch him—at an unmentionable cost to the taxpayers. None of us who had traveled with the Boss could believe he would leave Fala anywhere, although none of us doubted Fala would have enjoyed all that publicity.

I was present in the Statler Hotel in Washington when President Roosevelt, speaking before the International Brotherhood of Teamsters, castigated the Republicans in a nation-wide broadcast which was the highlight of the campaign. I will never forget the wild applause when he climaxed his address by ridiculing the widespread criticisms of the Republicans in relation to Fala.

With his charming smile and his hearty contagious chuckle President Roosevelt asserted that

The Republican leaders have not been content to make personal attacks upon me—or my wife—or my sons—they now include my little dog, Fala. Unlike the members of my family, Fala resents this. When he learned that the Republican fiction writers had concocted a story that I had left him behind on an Aleutian Island and had sent a destroyer back to find him—at a cost to the taxpayer of two or three or twenty million dollars—his Scotch soul was furious. He has not been the same dog since. I am accustomed to hearing malicious falsehoods about myself but I think I have a right to object to libelous statements about my dog.

The issue gave F.D.R. a chance for scathing rhetoric, and as a matter of public record, the charge was not true.

Through the wholehearted co-operation of the press and

M

radio, there was no advance notice or publicity relating to President Roosevelt's travels away from the White House. This procedure was a tremendously important safety factor. Reporters accompanied the President, but, by a gentleman's agreement with those of us who were responsible for his protection, they withheld all stories until he was safely home once more. This applied to weekend and holiday visits to Hyde Park as well as his trips to conferences at Casablanca, Yalta, Teheran, and to trips on which the President inspected Army bases and munition plants.

Before World War Two the American flag did not fly over the White House when the President was absent, therefore the presence or absence of the flag provided public notice as to whether he was traveling or in residence. During the war we saw to it that the flag flew every day.

F.D.R.'s willingness to allow me to keep his movements secret made my job infinitely easier. Like other men in the Presidency, I'm sure constant guard sometimes annoyed him, but, realist that he was, he understood the necessity. Whenever he left the White House, security measures had already been taken at points of departure and arrival; and the trip itself was kept secret.

In peacetime as well as war, I feel strongly that there should be no public announcements of a President's arrivals and departures. Criminal acts require some advance planning—to assemble the necessary equipment and to get to the place where the crime will be committed. If there is no advance publicity to establish where the intended victim will be, there is infinitely less chance of the crime's success.

Another point I felt very strongly about was the speed of the automobile in which the President rode. A slow, parade-paced car is an easy target. I routed the Presidential car in Washington and other cities where F.D.R. visited so that, if at all possible, it could maintain a minimum speed of about ten miles per hour. In Monterrey, Mexico, where we took F.D.R. to meet President Comacho, the official procession—over which I had no authority—crept through crowd-packed, rose-strewn streets at under five miles an hour. I was shocked at the procedure and gravely concerned for the President, since the crowds threatened to engulf the car.

When the President was on the road, the Secret Service agents with him surrounded his auto or railroad car whenever it stopped—even if only for seconds. All approaching persons were halted several feet away. With the official car moving at such a snail's pace, the agents stayed on foot, and ran alongside the car in an effort to keep the President separated from the pressing crowd. The dog-trot mileage for my agents that day under a hot April Mexican sun was over seven miles per man. And, while running, they had to keep their eyes on second- and third-story windows and balconies, snatch screaming Mexican children from beneath the wheels of the Presidential car, and ward off bouquets which hurtled toward the President at frequent intervals. It was a tremendous relief to me when we finally arrived at the reviewing stand, where a regiment of the Mexican Army was reviewed by both Presidents.

On December 20, 1942, I was in my office in the Treasury Building, solemnly looking out of the window at the White House, when Joe Murphy, Assistant Chief, entered. I didn't even notice. "Why so serious, Chief?" he asked. "Is the world coming to an end?"

"No, but the Secret Service has cause to be serious," was my reply.

I had just been advised that for the *first* time a President was to make an airplane flight and that the flight was to be across the Atlantic Ocean. I was wondering whether the clever espionage agents of Herr Hitler would obtain information about the proposed trip and plan to "get the President."

"We've got a big job ahead of us, Joe," I announced. I told him that the President was to attend a conference at

Casablanca starting January 14, 1943, and, furthermore, that he was to cross the Atlantic by air from South America to Africa.

President Roosevelt had flown as a campaigner before he became President, when he made the trip from Albany to Chicago to accept the Democratic nomination. But the Casablanca trip was the first time he flew as President.

I was glad to see Joe as concerned as I when I broke the news to him. He was a veteran of the Service and had over forty years of experience protecting Presidents from Teddy Roosevelt to Franklin D. Roosevelt. He had been to Europe on two occasions protecting President Wilson, and to South America three times protecting Presidents Hoover and Roosevelt.

"Well—this is the toughest job that the Secret Service has ever had," was his solemn reply. His usual smile and calm manner disappeared. "Why—it's only six weeks since our troops took over Morocco," he exclaimed. "I'll bet all of that area is infested with Nazi spies and sympathizers, who would kill Roosevelt if they had half a chance."

"I know," I told him, "and in spite of the large number of persons who must necessarily be informed regarding certain details in connection with the conference, we will have to see that everything is handled in such a confidential manner that Hitler's clever espionage agents will not get wind of it."

We discussed some phases of the job which required immediate attention. I had my secretary get Frank Masi, General Passenger Agent of the Atlantic Coast Line, on the phone, since most of the route to Miami, where the President would board a plane, was over his line.

"Frank, we have a little special business to take up with you."

Frank had handled secret railroad arrangements for many other Presidential movements. He was a quick thinker. "I'll be over any time to suit you, Chief."

"Well, come right along. Joe Murphy is here and we'll be looking for you in ten minutes."

Masi arrived promptly and we quickly got down to business.

"A very secret trip will be made to Miami early in January. From now on, Frank, we will call it 'Troop Movement Number Eight Seventy-seven.' Please start your plans at once. On this trip use Walter Brooks as conductor and the operating crews you wish to select, but leave it to the Secret Service to furnish the steward, waiters, and pullman porters."

That was unusual and seemed to surprise him, but he replied, "Okay."

I cautioned him, "Of course, you will go all the way to the destination and personally supervise all the railroad arrangements?"

"You can depend on that, Chief."

Just before Masi left, a message came through the radio on my desk.

"Dallas calling One."

The message came through clearly. I was surprised and pleased because it showed that a radio sending and receiving set we had just installed in a moving train to be used by the President for an experimental test was working successfully. "Dallas" was the code for the experimental train and "One" was my office. That was the first message to come through. I knew we could use this unique equipment to special advantage on the Eight Seventy-seven movement.

When Joe Murphy heard the message he exclaimed, "Well, I never thought we could sit in this office and talk to a person on a train going full speed five hundred miles away."

I then informed Masi, "We'll have an extra coach, our communication coach, in the set-up. It's a car we have chartered from the Baltimore and Ohio Railroad and that radio message you just heard came from it."

That was the first of a chain of conferences which was not to end until January 31st, when the return trip of Movement Eight Seventy-seven was completed.

During these day and night conferences of key men—including Joe Murphy, Frank Masi, Mike Reilly, Dan Moorman of the Baltimore and Ohio Railroad, and Dewey Long, transportation expert at the White House—a thousand and one seemingly minor details, but vitally important ones, were ironed out.

Planning the security of this trip could be likened to the caulking of a boat to prevent small but serious leaks. Trained espionage agents report minor details, which become the warp and woof used by their superiors in an attempt to weave a facsimile of their enemy's plan of operation. In a shooting war both sides play this game intensively, and absolute security about information as to future operations is the only effective antidote.

At that time Washington was the ideal place for wagging tongues to beat a secret into a froth of dangerous gossip. In that atmosphere, as Chief of the United States Secret Service, I had had one of the prize secrets of World War Two dumped into my lap: President Roosevelt and Prime Minister Churchill were to rendezvous at Casablanca in North Africa.

My responsibility in connection with the new historic "Unconditional Surrender Conference" was clear in my mind—too clear for personal comfort. The protection of the life of the President of the United States was my job, be he at home or abroad. I knew that the Secret Service would have to justify its name on this assignment, as secrecy of movement was the only adequate defensive weapon. If the slightest slip or leak occurred, I was certain that all the tentacles of the Axis espionage net would be grasping frantically for the complete details. Yet the secret relating to an important conference in a war zone in Africa had to be shared in whole or in part with some associates at Washington and with certain high officials of our allies. I silently thanked God that I had many trustworthy persons to assist us in the accomplishment of this vital task.

Between December 20th and January 8th, I sent agents to various points in Central and South America and Africa to make the necessary surveys, contacts, and advance arrangements. The operational deception necessary to screen the movement of a wartime President and Commander-in-Chief of the Armed Forces into a combat zone in Africa involved plain and fancy juggling of the truth. Such lies as were told bleached to pure white in the light of security necessities, but that did not make the telling of them any easier. Truth is a powerful weapon and it is easy to handle, but when you adopt deception as a weapon the user is in danger, due to its boomerang characteristics. The plan we adopted was simplicity itself. The cover would be preparations for a trip to Hyde Park, then the most routine travel movement of the President.

To illustrate a minor but important detail, let us take the case of Agent X, one of the agents selected to accompany the President on his important and hazardous journey.

Agent X was a married man and, of course, his wife, his neighbors, and his friends knew that he was assigned to the Secret Service White House Detail engaged in Presidential protection. Agent X had been thoroughly schooled in safeguarding secret information, but in this case his tongue was more effectively tied: he did not know his destination. He was merely advised that he had been selected for a trip. When Agent X departed from his home on this assignment he carried no baggage. An inconspicuous delivery truck picked up the baggage at X's home and delivered it, not to the White House but to a point where it was secretly placed aboard the Presidential train. The unitiated may think that such a ritual was a little absurd. Don't make that mistake. During the war, one of our major military surprises was jeopardized by the careless marking of a shipping crate.

My advance agents in the tropics must have been hot, but as the zero hour approached, the temperature in my office seemed to rise in sympathy with them. In the language of the G.I., I began to "sweat it out." On January 9th, President Roosevelt secretly left the White House at ten P.M. in an armored auto. In advance, and following his auto, were Secret Service autos filled with alert agents, heavily armed. I was in the head car driven by Secret Service Agent Frank Murray. I was nervous, but I tried not to show it.

We proceeded by an indirect route through a back road in Potomac Park to a secret railroad siding inside the new Bureau of Engraving and Printing Annex on Lower Fourteenth Street. We quickly put the President aboard the special armored Presidential railroad coach. This car was hidden in a brick addition to the Bureau, which had been constructed ostensibly for storage. It was guarded night and day by the Secret Service. The tracks were sunk, and the platform was level with the floor of the train, so that we could drive the President onto the platform to about five feet from the entrance to his railroad car. Hence a ramp, which otherwise we would have to use for President Roosevelt's wheelchair, was unnecessary.

A switch engine had backed onto the side track a few minutes before we arrived with the President. The train crew expected to pick up an empty freight car that had contained distinctive paper manufactured only by the Crane Manufacturing Company to be used in printing dollar bills.

The railroad crew was surprised to find Frank Masi and other top railroad officials present to issue other orders directing that they pick up the Presidential Special. In pursuance of the unusual and extraordinary precautions being taken, the engineer had not been advised where he was going. A specially selected engineer was in the engine cab and piloted the train north into Maryland and then it was switched to the main line of the R. F. & P., en route to Miami.

The regular Pullman porters, steward, and waiters, who were topnotchers and had accompanied the special Presidential train on previous trips, were not on duty. Filipino boys from the crew of the *Potomac*, the Presidential yacht, had been selected for this trip, as this would provide more secrecy. They did not know their destination nor how long a trip was to be made. I had asked Masi to have Pullman Conductor Walter Brooks, a veteran of forty years of service, on the train, as I had utmost confidence in him and regarded him as a deputy Secret Service agent. Walter was especially proud of his assignment on the Presidential train, as his grandfather, James J. Brooks, was a former Chief of the Secret Service; that made him also qualified by heredity.

Some very special equipment had been provided for the trip, such as the specially designed radio communication system which was in a converted baggage car. The equipment increased the degree of protection in this way: if an area toward which F.D.R.'s train was speeding was suddenly bombed by enemy planes, the train could be notified promptly and quickly stopped or diverted in another direction. If other emergencies developed, which might jeopardize his safety, a radio report to the train while it was in motion would warn the Secret Service agent in charge, so that appropriate action could be taken. Telephone lines tied in the communication coach with the Secret Service agents on duty in each coach of the train.

This equipment also made it possible for the President to be promptly and constantly in touch with officials in Washington and in all other areas. It consisted of two generators, which provided the power; four transmitters of which two were for code, one for code and voice, and the other one for voice only. It was provided with two sending and receiving positions, and with an extremely complicated attachment to automatically code and decode messages. It was a miniature but powerful Army Signal Corps radio station, and if it had been necessary, President Roosevelt could have broadcast to the country from the train and could have done so on short notice.

Several agents had been sent in advance to Casablanca, including Supervising Agent Reilly and Jim Rowley, who is now Chief of the Secret Service. Agent Behn was sent to Miami to arrange for the transfer of the party from the train to the Pan American Airways Airport and to make necessary protection arrangements for the take-off. Agent Anderson was sent to Trinidad to prepare for the stop at that point. Agent Peterson was sent to Belem, Brazil. Agent Deckard was sent to Bathurst, Gambia. Lieutenant Colonel Weller McCarthy was assigned by General Marshall to co-operate in the Army arrangements, and Commander J. Bardwell was assigned by Admiral King to co-operate in making arrangements in which the Navy had a part.

Agents Spaman, Fredericks, and Hipsley were assigned to accompany the President on the airplane. All three were good swimmers and trained in rescue work. Hipsley, an especially powerful swimmer, had won many trophies, and for years had been a Red Cross instructor in life saving. It was reassuring for me to know that in the event of a crash at sea, Hipsley would be most likely to reach a life raft, and I knew whom he would have in tow. F.D.R. was himself a good swimmer, but he would require assistance ditching at sea, and a person with knowhow in the water can make the difference between survival and death. Although I was especially concerned because of the President's physical disability, I would recommend this same sort of protection for any President on an overseas flight.

A second, follow-up plane, which accompanied the President's plane throughout the Casablanca trip, carried Agents Beary and Marshall. The agents on the two planes left with the President when he departed from Washington on January 9th, and were continuously with him until his return to the White House on January 31st.

The President arrived in Miami at one-thirty A.M., January 11th, the exact moment scheduled. Agent McDavid of the Miami office and Agent Behn of the White House Detail had quietly made the necessary advance arrangements with railroad officials, airport officials, and others at Miami and at the Pan American Airways Airport. On the arrival of the train, they split the party into two groups, transporting them to the airport in autos obtained ostensibly for another purpose. The President was taken from the train at a side track on a military reservation in the outskirts of the city.

I was relieved to know that the first leg of the trip had been successful, but I was worried about the next leg, more than I have ever worried in my life.

I had a right to be. The President was about to set a precedent by flying across the ocean and entering dangerous war zones on the continent of Africa. I was nervous for fear enemy agents might, despite our precautions, have learned of the trip, and that their best and biggest fleets of planes, battleships, and submarines would be hunting for the plane which was secretly and swiftly bearing the President over the Atlantic. I was worried about hurricanes, sleet storms, and other hazards that might suddenly show up and damage or wreck the plane. I was confident that the plane's pilots and crew were the very best-qualified for the important assignment, and that the plane and its equipment were in perfect shape, but, in spite of that, I thought of the many unexplained airplane crashes. I said prayers for the success of the trip, and although I could not discuss the trip with Judith or friends who asked what was bothering me, I asked them to say some special prayers for the success of a very important war project about which I might tell them later.

I knew that airplane travel was justified, because the vicious bites of the German U-boat wolf packs then operating in the Atlantic had fully demonstrated that it was extremely dangerous for any ship afloat on the Atlantic.

When President Roosevelt arrived at the airport on Biscayne Bay (now Dinner Key), just south of Miami, he saw two powerful, commodious, giant clippers, the *Dixie* and the *Atlantic*, the largest and safest ones available in the opinion of the civilian and military aeronautical experts on whose judgment it was necessary to depend. They were Boeing clippers, owned by the Pan American Airways, under charter to the Navy. They were powered by four Wright 1550 horsepower engines, and had a cruising range of 3,800 miles. Each plane's tanks could carry about 4,600 gallons of gasoline. These clippers had been flying munitions across the ocean. Now they had been hurriedly reconditioned and fixed up with special equipment for the safety and the comfort of the President.

The party was divided, and in the first plane, *Dixie Clipper*, were President Roosevelt, Harry Hopkins, Captain John McCrea, Admiral W. D. Leahy, Admiral Ross T. McIntire, three agents, and J. Prettyman, the President's valet.

In the second plane, *Atlantic Clipper*, were Colonel William Beasley, Captain George Durno, Captains Terry, Black, and Hoch, aides to the Admirals on the other clipper, and two agents. The Secret Service and General Harold C. George of the Air Force insisted that the clippers should carry special equipment, including gas masks, steel helmets, and the most modern life rafts, in the event of a forced landing.

Exactly at six-thirty A.M., on January 11th, the first clipper, the *Dixie*, took off. Biscayne Bay was almost like a mill pond, according to the telephone report I got from Agent McDavid. He said it was an impressive sight and that the pilot demonstrated great skill in his preliminary maneuvering before the huge flying boat lifted itself off the bosom of the bay.

The first day the clippers were in sight of each other and most of the time were around an altitude of eight thousand feet. The *Dixie Clipper* made a perfect landing in the harbor of Port-au-Spain, Trinidad, at four-forty P.M. It anchored

near the Hotel Macqueripe, which was under the control of
the United States Navy, and small power boats took the passengers to the hotel dock.

A little later, the President was escorted to the patio of
the hotel, from which a fine view of the shores of Venezuela
was enjoyed. He had cocktails and dinner with Admiral
Leahy, Harry Hopkins, Rear Admiral McIntire, Captain
McCrea, and Rear Admiral J. B. Oldendorf, who was in
command of the Trinidad Army Base. The grand old man of
the party, Admiral Leahy, became sick, and the President's
physician, Dr. McIntire, treated him, diagnosing influenza.
So, over the protest of the patient, he was sent to the hospital.
The President was distressed over the illness of Admiral
Leahy. Because the Admiral had been United States Ambassador to the puppet French government, set up by Hitler
in 1940 at Vichy, his valuable counsel at the conference
would be sorely missed.

On the next day, January 12th, the clippers took to the
air at five A.M. At noon, the *Atlantic Clipper* crossed the
Equator, and at that point the pilot put the big ship through
some fancy maneuvers to celebrate the crossing. There were
no fancy maneuvers of the *Dixie Clipper,* because the sole
objective of that flight was to land the President safely, as
soon as possible. That afternoon at two o'clock the planes
settled down in the Para River near Belem and the passengers were taken to the South Atlantic Station of the United
States Air Transport Command.

At four-thirty the *Dixie* took off for the 2,100-mile jump
from America to Africa. This was the most hazardous flight,
as it was the longest hop of the trip. It was headed for Bathurst, Gambia, on the western point of the coast of Africa.
The plane had a bad break, as it encountered some heavy
head winds. Its speed for a considerable period was only
slightly over one hundred miles an hour. It took nineteen
hours and fifteen minutes to reach Bathurst, and, on January 13th, at four-forty-five P.M., made a safe landing. I was

at the White House when a message came in that the President had safely arrived in Africa, and I was thrilled and thankful that my prayers for his safe crossing of the ocean had been answered.

The President was cheered on arrival by the sight of the United States Cruiser *Memphis* and the Destroyer *Somers* at anchor in the harbor. Captain H. G. McCownn, the Commander of the *Memphis,* and E. F. Lowder, British Navy Commandant at Bathurst, approached the *Dixie* in a power boat, and the President, McIntire, McCrea, and Hopkins were taken to the *Memphis,* where the President spent the evening in his cabin engaged on reports and other business, which caught up with him there.

Next day the President was met by General C. R. Smith, Chief of the Air Transport Command, who had just arrived from Algiers. They drove to Yundam Air Field, eighteen miles over a rough, crooked road. At the airport, the party found a four-motored C-54 plane awaiting them. The 1,540 miles to Casablanca took them over Dakar, and the plane flew low to give the President a good view. They flew about a thousand miles over the desolate Sahara Desert and crossed the Atlas Mountains, 13,000 feet high. At five that afternoon Captain Otis Bryan landed them at Mediounea Airport, twenty-five miles from Casablanca. The President was greeted by General Mark Clark, Colonel Elliott Roosevelt, and Supervising Agent Reilly. Some definite signs of recent fighting at the airport, such as bomb craters, were evident. Reilly hustled President Roosevelt from the airfield in an armored auto, which had no marks to identify it as conveying a person of importance. Prime Minister Churchill had already arrived at Casablanca.

Before the arrival of the heads of state, security arrangements had been perfected by the Secret Service, Scotland Yard, and Army officers. The area was completely surrounded by high barbed-wire fences and selected companies of troops guarded it. The Anfa Hotel and twelve villas were prepared for the conference and for housing the American and English groups. The security officers found dictographs hidden in some of the villas which were to be used by the conferees. They used Geiger counters to search for radioactive material. They were suspicious of everyone, especially servants and employees. In the surrounding country were many refugees of many nationalities, some of whom were believed to be Nazi spies or saboteurs. The place was full of wild stories which came to the attention of American and British Intelligence Officers, because some of the activities in preparation for the big conference could not help but attract the attention of inquisitive persons. One story went around that King Victor Emmanuel and Prince Umberto were seeking a separate peace for Italy, and that Roosevelt was to meet with the King and some of his Cabinet through an arrangement made by the Pope.

In order to avoid leaks, certain general instructions for the guidance of persons arriving for the conference were issued:

... The perimeter of this Camp is wired and strongly guarded, but it should be borne in mind that in the hotel and in each villa there are servants of whose affiliations and contacts we have slight knowledge.

Therefore, the safeguarding of secret information must depend on the common sense and care observed by each individual, whatever his rank.

Special attention should be paid to:

1. Secret waste and secret papers must never be left in an unoccupied room.

2. No reliance should be placed on locks and doors.

3. Many of the doors and walls are not soundproof.

4. While every effort has been made to assure the security of the telephone system, conversations in a loud voice may be overheard through windows and doors.

Security Officers will collect secret waste, in company with a representative of each department, and have it burned under proper safeguards.

Other safety measures were that the only food consumed during the conference consisted of Army rations, and bottled water was exclusively used when stronger liquids were not desired. Servants recruited for service were forced to remain within the camp during the entire period of the conference. Distinctive passes were furnished to every member of the party who might be required to leave or enter the gates to the camp. The gates were guarded by specially selected Military Police and Secret Service agents. Special antiaircraft batteries were placed in strategic positions and camouflaged. Special details equipped with powerful binoculars were placed on the tops of buildings in order to spot enemy aircraft.

The telephone system was efficiently supervised by the Army, and a detail from the Signal Corps, including some extremely efficient WACs, handled the various switchboards. Strict control was maintained over entry and egress to the villas occupied by the President and the Prime Minister. An air-raid detail was constantly on the alert. A swimming pool was converted into a first-class air-raid shelter, where President Roosevelt and Prime Minister Churchill could be rushed in event of an air raid. Churchill sneered when he was told about the air-raid shelter. Roosevelt only chuckled.

When President Roosevelt arrived in Casablanca, on January 14th at seven P.M., he was promptly joined at his villa by Churchill, Sir Dudley Pound, Sir Charles Portal, Sir Alan F. Brooke, and Vice Admiral Lord Louis Mountbatten. They were soon joined by the American delegates, including General Marshall, General Eisenhower, Admiral King, General Arnold, Harry Hopkins, Robert Murphy, and Averill Harriman. Colonel Elliott Roosevelt was also present.

They had cocktails and dinner and started the conference.

Eisenhower had to leave in two days to return to the battle-front in Tunisia, where he was in command and where the advance had been seriously slowed down by Hitler's forces. After the group left, President Roosevelt and Prime Minister Churchill conferred, and it was after three A.M. when Churchill left for his villa.

I was relieved that the President was safely at his destination. But my satisfaction that our arrangements had proved so successful thus far was quickly dispelled by thoughts of security leaks in Africa and the possibility of a blitz of Nazi planes over Casablanca, with some extra big blockbuster bombs or some new secret weapon to be used to kill the leaders of the United States and Great Britain. My concern was intensified when my Assistant Chief, Joe Murphy, who usually was as cool as a cucumber, suddenly spouted, "Say, Chief, you know Hitler in his desperation sent over two thousand planes in one night to blitz London? If he learns that Roosevelt and Churchill are having a rendezvous at Casablanca, he may organize another such desperate air raid in order to get the Boss and Winnie."

I tried not to think about it. But I could not help but recall the recent assassination in Africa of our good friend, Admiral Jean François Darlan, the French High Commissioner in Africa, which had taken place not far from Casablanca. His assassination demonstrated that dangerous and fanatical characters were circulating in that area. Darlan's co-operation had been expected in connection with the Casablanca Conference, especially in effecting the absolutely necessary reconciliation of the two very stubborn French factions, the Free French and the Fighting French. They had been at dagger's points ever since Hitler had conquered France. Darlan's death made the desired reconciliation much more difficult.

The Joint Chiefs of staff were meeting every day. I wished they would decide to cut that conference short and hustle back to the U.S.A. However, I was to remain on the anxious

N

seat and have the worry of the President on a foreign continent in a dangerous war zone for another ten days.

The President left his villa for the first time at four P.M. January 18th to inspect a guard mount of the Third Battalion, Thirtieth Infantry which was guarding the President's camp. The President was in a jeep and was accompanied by General George S. Patton, the commander in that area. The troops were startled when they saw the President, for while they knew that many "Brass Hats" were attending a conference, they did not know their Commander-in-Chief was present.

On January 21st, the President, with General Patton, inspected military forces and installations near Rabat and Port Lyautey, and lunched in the field on regular Army rations of boiled ham, sweet potatoes, beans, fruit, bread and butter, jam, and coffee. It was a ninety-mile trip. A big fleet of speedy fighter planes was patrolling the sky, protecting the entire area the President traversed from possible air raids. There were some 22,000 American soldiers in the immediate vicinity.

Just north of Rabat, the President boarded a jeep and inspected the Second Armored Division and the Third Infantry Division and stayed for dinner—again of Army rations.

A few miles further, he inspected the Ninth Division. He visited an American and a French cemetery, and wreaths were placed in honor of the gallant soldiers who had been killed in that area. A terrific rain storm spoiled the trip back to Casablanca. The Secret Service agents riding in the jeeps without raincoats were soaked to the skin, and because of a sharp drop in temperature they were also chilled.

The toughest and most vitally important immediate problem facing the allies at that time was to get the opposing French parties together. The forces of the Free French, led by General de Gaulle, and the Fighting French, led by General Giraud, were still in opposition. It was of tremendous importance to the cause of the allies to get them pulling as a team; hence Giraud and De Gaulle were urged to come to the conference. Satisfaction was expressed when General Giraud appeared on January 18th.

General de Gaulle was expected the next day, but instead he sent a disappointing communication to President Roosevelt saying he would go to Washington to confer with the President, if he so desired. De Gaulle was extremely sore because he had not been given advance notice of the landing of our troops in Africa and of the Casablanca Conference. He was not given that advance notice because we were afraid to trust the information in the hands of some of his associates. The conferees tried to figure out how to persuade De Gaulle to come to Casablanca. He had escaped from France when Hitler's armies conquered his country. As he was then in England, it was left to the British to produce him.

General de Gaulle finally appeared on January 22nd. That evening, a formal dinner was given by President Roosevelt for the Sultan of Morocco, Sidi Mohammed; the Crown Prince, a youngster of thirteen; and other members of the Sultan's staff. Because of the religious beliefs of the Mohammedan Sultan, no liquor was served. Others present were Winston Churchill; his son, Randolph; Harry Hopkins; Richard, his son; Robert Murphy of the State Department; General Patton; General Monges; Captain McCrea; and Colonel Elliott Roosevelt. The Sultan brought some fine presents: a gold dagger for the President, a gold tiara for Mrs. Roosevelt, and some gold bracelets for the ladies in the guests' families. It was the first and only formal dinner at Casablanca, and the American and English diners were attired in tuxedos. Shortly after that, Churchill and Roosevelt met with De Gaulle, but they couldn't melt the stubborn General.

On January 23rd, it was arranged that the conference would end on the 24th, even though a reconciliation had not been effected, and that a press conference would be held at the wind-up. Liaison between the quarters of General Giraud and the quarters of General de Gaulle was again established, and Murphy, Hopkins, Harriman, and Macmillan—who was in North Africa as British Minister—were sweating out their diplomatic endeavors to get the two Frenchmen into accord.

On the morning of January 24th, everyone was discouraged and some were getting desperate, especially the Secret Service, Scotland Yard, and others concerned with security. Every additional hour extending the conference increased the possibility of a leak and the possibility of a surprise move by the Nazis with some new terrific weapon which we felt Hitler might be saving for just such an occasion.

High noon Sunday was the time when the press and radio conference was finally set. Thirty war correspondents, radio reporters, and photographers had been flown in for the conference. No one wanted to hang around Casablanca any longer, even though the two French leaders could not be reconciled. About eleven o'clock, General Giraud was in conference with President Roosevelt. General de Gaulle and others arrived shortly thereafter. Finally Giraud was persuaded to become reconciled with De Gaulle and to work closely with him in the future.

General de Gaulle was not inclined to agree. Then President Roosevelt unleashed his great persuasive powers on the stubborn Frenchman and urged him, for the sake of his devoted countrymen, to change his mind. The President's fine command of the French language was a great asset. Harry Hopkins told me that Roosevelt seemed to hypnotize De Gaulle. After a tense period of silence the General rose to the occasion and agreed to co-operate. Smiles broke out all around.

It was just noon, time for the big press conference. The President and the Prime Minister were in the center and Giraud and De Gaulle were near them. The correspondents

and photographers were excited. A smart photographer
called out, "Let's have some action!" and asked for the two
French Generals to please shake hands. They acquiesced
without enthusiasm, but Roosevelt and Churchill were
tickled because the pictures proving the reconciliation would
soon be seen by French patriots of each of the two factions
that had been so bitter toward each other.

A few days after the return of the party to Washington, I
was told that Harry Hopkins had asked the photographer to
make the suggestion that the French Generals shake hands,
and I asked Harry if it were true.

He said, "I didn't initiate it, someone smarter than I did;
it was the Boss."

After the French leaders shook hands, the President announced that General de Gaulle and General Giraud had
been invited by the Prime Minister and him to the conference, and added:

I believe that all that could be said at this time is that the
Prime Minister and I were here in Africa and felt that it would be
an appropriate time for these two fine gentlemen to meet—one
Frenchman with another Frenchman. They have been in conference for two days and we have emphasized one common purpose,
the liberation of France. They are in accord on that. We hope
that, as a result of getting to know each other better under these
new conditions, we will have French armies, French navies and
French airmen who will participate with us in the ultimate liberation of France herself.

The harmonizing of the two opposing French factions
had been effected. It was an important factor in the final
success of the allies in World War Two.

The conference agreed upon plans for the early invasion
of Sicily as the next big military operation. President Roosevelt also announced that "unconditional surrender" would
be demanded of the axis powers. He suggested that the con-

ference be termed the "Unconditional Surrender Conference."

I saw General de Gaulle in Washington in August, 1945, when he was the guest of President Truman. He was brought directly from the airport to the White House, where some pictures were taken of him. While I watched him pose, I thought of the tough job Roosevelt and Churchill had had at the Casablanca conference trying to reconcile Giraud and De Gaulle and of the appropriate picture taken at that time of the two French Generals shaking hands. De Gaulle is the tallest man I ever saw in the White House. As I studied him, his countenance struck me as that of a very stubborn fellow, so I was not surprised at the difficulty they had with him at Casablanca.

After the press conference no time was lost in getting Roosevelt away from Casablanca. Inside of an hour he left, proceeding by auto to Marrakech, a trip of a hundred and fifty miles. Agents Rowley, Anderson, Deckard, and Willard had left Casablanca previously to make detailed advance arrangements for the return trip.

At eight the next morning the President left Marrakech by plane. Churchill, dressed in a fancy lounging robe, bedroom slippers, slouch hat, and smoking his usual long cigar, rode to the airport with him. Churchill was talking about the exquisite scenery and said he intended to do some painting that day.

The President's plane, *Dixie Clipper,* landed in the river at Natal, Brazil, on January 28th, making the 1,840-mile ocean hop in eleven hours and fifteen minutes. At Natal the party was met by Agent Peterson and taken aboard the U.S.S. *Humboldt.* During the afternoon the President went ashore, and in the company of President Vargas of Brazil made an inspection of United States and Brazilian shore installations.

On January 29th, the President motored to Panamarin Air Field, Air Transport Command, departing at six A.M.

in·a C-54 land plane and alighting at Waller Field, U.S. Army base at Trinidad, at four P.M., where he enjoyed a happy reunion with Admiral Leahy, who had recovered from his illness.

On January 30th, his sixty-first birthday, the President and the group who had left Miami with him boarded his *Dixie Clipper* at seven A.M. and departed for Miami. They had a special meal in honor of his birthday, including a birthday cake with candles. Signals were flown on the mast in code: "Happy Birthday to the Commander-in-Chief." The *Atlantic Clipper* crew and passengers sent a radio message in code to the *Dixie Clipper:* "Inform the President we will drink his health and happiness and wish him many happy returns on his birthday. That our Commander-in-Chief should for the first time celebrate his birthday in the vast freedom of the sky seems to us symbolic of the new day for which we are all fighting."

The *Dixie Clipper* settled down on Biscayne Bay, Miami, at four-thirty that afternoon. I received a telephone message from Agent McDavid at the airport that all was okay. My joyful relief was unbounded. They left Miami by the Atlantic Coastline Railroad at six P.M.

I was at the railroad siding at the Bureau of Engraving and Printing Annex in Washington. It was Sunday afternoon on January 31st, and I wanted to make sure that all was in readiness for the arrival of the President. It was the most satisfying feeling of my life.

Everyone in Washington and all over the country seemed elated over the success of the "Unconditional Surrender Conference," but I was elated over the safe return of the Commander-in-Chief. The Casablanca trip added up to a total mileage of 16,960, traveled by the President variously in train, seaplane, land plane, automobile, and jeep. The first flight of a President, compounded by having been made overseas and in wartime conditions—and it had been a success from the standpoint of security, as well as diplomacy.

I felt prouder of the Service at that moment than at any other time in my career.

I boarded the train before it came to a full stop and shook hands with the President, saying, "I wish you a happy and successful year, Mr. President. We were all sorry you didn't get back to Washington for your birthday." I added that I was particularly happy because of his safe journey and the success of the conference.

He was smiling, but looked tired. "The Secret Service did an excellent job from start to finish," was his cheerful answer. "The agents attended to everything along the route in a perfect manner." He added that he wished to thank everyone concerned, and he wished me to know that he appreciated what a big job the Secret Service had done.

I greeted Supervising Agent Reilly and his assistants, telling them how proud I was of them, of my satisfaction over their successful efforts, and that I appreciated their again upholding the Secret Service record in protecting the President.

Harry Hopkins smiled and shook hands with me, saying, "The Secret Service did a swell job, Frank. I'll bet that you were worried about the Boss all the time until we landed him at Miami."

"You said it, Harry," was my reply, "but I'm going to sleep soundly tonight, for we will have the Boss safely behind the White House fence."

It was a happy homecoming when the President got out of the car at the south door of the White House. He had a satisfied look and a twinkle in his eyes. I asked Dr. McIntire how the President had stood the trip, and he said he stood up under the strain in first-class shape and that he was a good flyer. I told him I hoped that would be his last wartime airplane trip, as such hazards should not be undertaken by the President unless absolutely necessary.

Actually, the Casablanca trip ushered in the air age for American Presidents. F.D.R. flew frequently after that, although not again overseas. Presidents since have flown as regularly as they once traveled in their private railroad cars.

On February 2nd, the President held a press and radio conference before the biggest group of correspondents that I had ever seen crowded into his office. That day and the next his report of the "Unconditional Surrender Conference" was fully covered in all the papers in the country and by the radio commentators. I was especially proud when, during the conference, he graciously referred to the splendid efforts of the Secret Service in connection with his protection and told the reporters some incidents relating to the activities of the agents. Several newspapers carried these comments:

Speaking of the protection for him during his stay in Morocco at the Casablanca Conferences, President Roosevelt said today that his Secret Service men thought there was little danger from the Moors, who comprise 90% of the population, but they felt that some of our French brethren, like some people in Washington, might be so concerned about political affairs that they might get excited. Two Secret Service men rode on the jeeps that carried him, the President said. When they saw Europeans in the crowd they cried "Look!" and pointed upward, or one of the Secret Service men pretended to fall from the jeep to distract attention of the onlookers. Failure of an onlooker to be distracted was regarded as a sign that he needed watching.

Looking back upon that dangerous and historic conference today, it makes me exceedingly proud to realize that the so-called "clever espionage agents of the enemy" were completely outwitted by the agents of the Secret Service, Scotland Yard, Office of Strategic Services, and British and American Intelligence Forces.

11

Just as he had asked me to "look after" his Vice-presidents before this duty was formally allotted to the Secret Service, F. D. R. also took the bull by the horns and set a precedent for the protection of all distinguished guests. Before Prime Minister Churchill's visit at Christmas in 1941, we had the responsibility of guarding his King and Queen, when they came to this country in 1939.

I was especially concerned (being of fighting Irish descent myself) about the bitterness that existed between Ireland and England at that time. We had plenty of wild Irish here, and one bomb tossed at the Royal couple during one of their public appearances in Washington or New York would put us out of business. A Scotland Yard man was due in Washington a few days ahead of the royal entourage to co-operate with me about security measures for their Majesties. Before that I went to Hyde Park with President Roosevelt, and he spent one entire morning driving me around his estate in his Ford auto, making detailed plans for the stationing of guards at strategic points on the estate and in the adjoining country. I was deeply impressed with the President's serious concern over the safety of the King and Queen, and pleasantly surprised at the extremely practical and pertinent suggestions he made about the protection of the royal couple.

By the time the Deputy Chief of Scotland Yard, Albert Canning, arrived, our plans were set. He proved most cooperative and, although many of our procedures seemed to astonish him, Mr. Canning gracefully yielded on every point. "I bow to your judgment."

When the British King and Queen arrived in Washington, they were met at Union Station by President and Mrs. Roosevelt, and the rulers of the two greatest democracies in the world paraded down Pennsylvania Avenue to the White House between crowds packed forty- to fifty-feet deep from the curb. These powerful rulers were protected by the largest Secret Service detail ever used on one assignment. Over half a million patriotic Americans of Irish, Scotch, English, Italian, German, or other descent were milling around in eager, friendly confusion, all straining to get a good look at the famous royal couple and our own President with the First Lady.

As Chief of the Secret Service, charged with the terrific responsibility for their safety, I was greatly worried by the knowledge that just before the King and Queen left England several bombs planted by unknown persons near Buckingham Palace had been exploded. My fear lay in my knowledge of the basic psychology of the haters of democracy. The opportunity to make a highly dramatic coup by the assassination with one bomb of two world leaders might prove too tempting to poisoned minds even to consider resistance. That there were desperate enemies of our country ready to go to any lengths was shockingly demonstrated a few months later at the New York World's Fair, when a powerful bomb, secretly planted there in an innocent-looking suitcase, exploded and blasted to pieces five New York City policemen. The assassins were never apprehended, although New York City offered a $25,000 reward, and some of the ablest detectives in the country concentrated their efforts over a very long period in order to solve the dastardly crime.

When the parade down Pennsylvania Avenue was at last over and the leading cars carrying the President and Mrs. Roosevelt and the King and Queen entered the White House grounds, the clanking shut of the iron gates was like music to my ears. I breathed the deepest sigh of relief that my lungs allowed. Besides the Secret Service agents who had been called in from all over the country, we had enlisted the able assistance of the police of the City of Washington, Intelligence agents of the Army and Navy, soldiers and sailors—and we secured the highest degree of efficient co-operation from them.

Queen Elizabeth was the most beautiful member of royalty I ever saw and just what you hoped a Queen would be, regal in manner but with great personal charm and a radiance about her face. You had only to take one look at her to know she was a Queen. Her graciousness was equal to her beauty. King George was also gracious to those about him, but his native shyness coupled with his slight speech difficulty made him the quieter, more withdrawn member of the couple. It was the Queen who greeted—and charmed—people.

Together I think they fulfilled everyone's idea of what royalty should be like. But I do not think I drew one easy breath the entire time their Majesties were in our country.

When the time came to arrange for their appearance in New York City, I met with Grover Whalen, Director of the New York World's Fair, and Police Commissioner Lewis J. Valentine to decide what should be done about showing our royal guests an enthusiastic reception. I was accompanied by Colonel Starling, Supervising Agent of the White House Secret Service Detail. Whalen wanted a big show with bands and pennants and a parade along Broadway in an open auto with ticker tape and drum majorettes. But I refused.

"Grover," I said, "that's all very well for you. But if anything should happen to the King and Queen, then Commissioner Valentine and I are going to be responsible." Over the strong protest of Whalen, I was backed up by the Police Commissioner. We agreed upon a fast motorcade up the West Side Highway and a well-guarded visit to the World's Fair.

The King and Queen were given a sumptuous luncheon at the Fair. My agents, Scotland Yard agents, and New York police officials lunched together in an adjoining room. When the meal was almost over, a Scotland Yard agent came running to the table where Agent Harry Neal was sitting with New York Police Commissioner Valentine and exclaimed, "Where's the King's hat? We can't find the King's hat!"

The Police Commissioner gathered his plain-clothes men around him and issued a curt order: "Get that hat!"

The head of the Scotland Yard detail announced to his agents, "His Majesty has lost his hat! We must retrieve it."

Harry Neal told the Secret Service agents, "On the ball, boys; the King's hat is gone!"

The search was on.

A Secret Service agent remembered that prior to the luncheon he had escorted the King to the rest room. He raced back to the scene, pushed open the rest-room door, and beheld a Negro porter doing a cakewalk with the King's felt Homburg perched rakishly on the side of his head and a group of porters expressing high approval.

"What are you doing with that hat?" the agent barked.

"Man, that ain't no hat," chuckled the dancer, "that am the King of England's chapeau!"

The agent quickly retrieved the hat, and turned it over to the Police Commissioner, who put in on his lap and said,

"This lid isn't going to get out of my sight until the King's ready to leave here!"

Two minutes later a waiter hurriedly brought the Commissioner's pie à la mode. Another waiter bumped his arm as he served it and sent an oozing scoop of chocolate ice cream straight onto the royal Homburg. The Commissioner quickly dumped out the ice cream and swabbed the hat furiously with his handkerchief. He looked up at the speechless aggregation of cops, Scotland Yard men and Secret Service agents and said in tones of cold steel, "Nobody saw anything happen to this hat!"

King George and Queen Elizabeth wound up their United States visit at Hyde Park, where they were entertained by President and Mrs. Roosevelt at a picnic and hotdog party. F. D. R. drove them to the railroad station. Just as the train was ready to leave, he found a book on the car seat which he had meant to give to the King, and he handed it to me and asked me to get it on board.

It was only about sixty seconds from the scheduled departure, so I sprinted over, not taking time to look at the book, hopped aboard, and delivered it, telling the King the President wished him to have it. Accepting it, the King's gracious smile of thanks disappeared as he noted the title, and a look of such startled sternness came over him that I was taken aback.

"Good Lord!" he said. "We can't let that ever happen!"

I glanced at the jacket to see what had perturbed him. The title of the book was *Bombs over London*. I was so surprised in turn that I could think of nothing more appropriate to say than, "Not on your life." And then I had to hop off the train, since it had started to roll.

Later, during the war, when the blitz of London was at its height with the Nazi bombs falling night after night, for many months, near Buckingham Palace as well as the rest of London, I often thought of that moment when I had handed the book to King George, and his shocked words, "We can't let that happen!"

After midnight I got a message from the detail of Secret Service agents that traveled with the royal party to the Canadian border reporting their safe arrival in Canada, and again I breathed a deep sigh of relief. Everything had run smoothly while the royal party was in this country and not a single untoward incident had occurred, but I was surely a happy fellow to see them safely off.

Shortly after the return of the King and Queen to England I received through the State Department autographed photos of the royal couple, appropriately framed and bearing the royal seal. I deeply appreciated this expression of their thanks for the efforts of the Secret Service to guard them. The smooth handling of the protection was also pleasing to my superiors.

Shortly after the royal party left, President Roosevelt wrote a very strong letter of appreciation to me and my boss, Secretary Morgenthau, expressed his approval of the excellent protection extended by the Secret Service to the King and Queen.

I was relieved that the President hadn't decided to take the British royal couple joyriding on his Hyde Park estate, for I certainly would have had to veto that. He was fond of driving his own auto. One day he took me for a spin around the estate in his Ford. As he went down a steep hill he stepped on the gas and took a curve on two wheels. I grabbed onto the door. He peered over at me and chuckled at the frightened look on my face.

"I scared hell out of Jim Farley when I took him down this hill," he laughed.

I noticed a gold St. Christopher medal on the dashboard and remarked, "I think that you need St. Chris to watch over you in your driving, Mr. President!"

He gave me his infectious laugh. "Do you think so? Miss

Le Hand [F. D. R.'s secretary, Margaret Le Hand] gave me that medal and I am glad to have it," he replied.

President Roosevelt's driving was always a worry to me. He often took his eyes off the road and his hand off the wheel in order to wave to people. When he drove past the golf course at Warm Springs, he would shout greetings to his friends and kid them about their bad shots. I tried to impress him with the importance of watching the roads, but it did very little good. Once I seriously considered putting a governor on his engine. Finally I decided to have agents cut off all the side roads and sent a pilot car a few hundred yards ahead and another behind when he went driving. But this simply provided him with a new game. He tried hard to ditch the pilots. Once he drove down to the railroad siding at Hyde Park, made a sharp turnabout, and tore back to his house far ahead of both the pilot drivers. When he got home, he grinned impishly at me and said, "I don't know what happened to your agents. They just disappeared!"

One of my pleasantest assignments was accompanying the President to Quebec in 1943 for a conference with Prime Minister Churchill. They were staying at the Citadel, an ancient fort with a commanding view of the beautiful St. Lawrence River, as guests of the Governor-General of Canada, the Earl of Athlone. I stayed at the Chateau Frontenac where I had pleasant memories of my previous visit to Quebec, for I had spent my honeymoon there in 1926.

"You are wanted at the Citadel as soon as possible. President Roosevelt would like to see you," was the telephone message that awaited me one noon at the Chateau.

I hustled up to the ancient fort and was delighted when the President, smiling brightly, said, "I am going to take a day off tomorrow and go fishing. The Prime Minister will be with me. Do you think you can find a good spot for us?"

I inwardly wished that all my assignments were so pleasant. "Certainly, Mr. President." I grinned.

I telephoned the Commissioner of the Canadian Bureau

of Fisheries, and when I told him that I had a confidential matter to discuss with him, he placed himself at my immediate disposal. In a few minutes he was in my hotel room. The Commissioner was a wonderful example of French-Canadian diplomacy and politeness, and when I said, "I must quickly find a spot within thirty miles of Quebec where I will be absolutely certain to get some game fish," he smiled all over.

"I cannot disclose the names of the two gentlemen who wish to fish, but they deserve the best fishing Quebec can provide," I told him, hoping that he would catch my meaning.

He did. He gave a deep chuckle. "Don't explain any further," he assured me. "I'll guarantee the gamest trout and plenty of them."

Aware that he knew the identity of the world-famous pair of fishermen, I looked at the spot on the map that he pointed out, saying, "We'll be proud to have the fishermen on this mountain lake."

I then told him that we did not have much time to spare, as it was then after noon and I would have to inspect the route to the lake to make sure that it was safe for a heavy armored car. I would also have to find a cottage or lodge where the fishermen could rest and have refreshments. And I would have to have a demonstration that the trout were biting.

When we arrived at the lake, the Commissioner produced tackle for Mike Reilly and me and we boarded a small power boat, which took us across the lake. Inside of five minutes I got a strike and it took another five minutes to land a three-pounder. A couple of minutes after that Mike got one even bigger. I was enthusiastic and wanted to fish longer, but I was also anxious to report back to the President, so we decided to hustle back to Quebec. Our Canadian host, who would not be gainsaid, insisted that we linger until his French-Canadian guide prepared a delicious fish dinner for us. He cooked some trout that he had caught earlier in the day and he packed in ice the two big ones we had landed.

F. D. R. was as delighted as a schoolboy being promised a treat when I told him of the grand day he had in store, and he smacked his lips when I added that the two pieces of evidence we had brought back were being saved for his breakfast the next morning. He and the Prime Minister had wonderful luck. The relaxation from strenuous conferences proved the finest of tonics for their tired minds.

Lord Beaverbrook ("The Beaver," as Britain's wartime Minister of Supply was called), who accompanied the Prime Minister in 1941, proved at the beginning to be an exceedingly difficult man to guard, primarily because he did not understand the function of the Secret Service and seemed to feel that the guard we had on him was more in the nature of spying—an invasion of privacy. He would turn around and see Secret Service men tailing his car, a sure sign, his Lordship thought, that something sinister was afoot. To test even his personal staff, he would tell one secretary a secret and then try to worm it out of another, to see if the first had betrayed it. My Secret Service agents, who were guarding him, never got an advance list of his appointments. They had to be prepared to move as he moved, unpredictably. One morning they started waiting for him to leave the Mayflower Hotel, where he was living, at eight o'clock. They were not informed until ten P.M. that he had been sick in bed all morning.

Coming for the first time as a visitor to the United States in a capacity that made him have to be guarded, and being entirely ignorant of the Secret Service, "The Beaver" was at first suspicious, thinking we did not entirely trust him. When he thoroughly grasped that our only interest in him was to keep him safe, he made a complete capitulation and treated the protection detail of Secret Service agents with great respect.

On one occasion, my Chief, Secretary of the Treasury

Morgenthau, invited "The Beaver" to his home for dinner.
One of our best agents, Quill Merrill, in charge of the detail,
put his Lordship in a State Department limousine, ordered
the chauffeur to head for Morgenthau's house, and then
followed in a Secret Service car. The chauffeur, in taking
Agent Merrill's instructions, said, "I've been to the Morgenthau home lots of times."

Beaverbrook alighted at the house and hurried up the
steps. The front door was opened by a surprised, kindly,
sweet-looking lady, who had lived in London a long time
and knew Beaverbrook well. She was Lady MacNeal.

"How perfectly charming of you to call so soon! I never
dreamed that you would answer so promptly. Come in,
come in, Lord Beaverbrook, and tell me all about what has
been happening to you since you came over. . . ."

The fact was that Lady MacNeal, who had been a good
friend of Beaverbrook's for years, had learned about "The
Beaver's" arrival and had written him a friendly note, extending an invitation to call at her home any time that he
had a few minutes to spare. On his part, Beaverbrook at
first assumed that she was a fellow guest also visiting Secretary Morgenthau, and they exchanged polite pleasantries for
several minutes before it suddenly dawned on him that
something was wrong. He must be in the wrong house! Getting out of the awkward situation with the suave grace of
the traditional Englishman of his kind, Lord Beaverbrook
took a hurried leave and left the house.

He then proceeded to give the chauffeur a thorough dress-
ing-down in language not fit to print.

"But, sir," the chauffeur apologized, "I was sure that was
Secretary Morgenthau's house. I've driven there many
times."

The fact was, Mr. Morgenthau had occupied the house—
a rented one—for three years, but had moved out just a fort-
night before, and Lady MacNeal had moved in. "The
Beaver" was late in arriving at the right house and Secretary

Morgenthau had been telephoning me to find out why my agents had not performed their duty by getting Lord Beaverbrook to dinner at his home on time. The Secretary was excited and angry. He bawled me out unmercifully. He ordered me to relieve Agent Merrill, the agent in charge of the Beaverbrook detail, and send him back at once to his post of duty in San Francisco. I knew that Merrill would be delighted to get back to his family in San Francisco, but I deliberately forgot about the order of the Secretary and, as he was an efficient agent, I kept him on the detail.

The next day I met Mrs. Morgenthau, one of the most charming ladies I ever knew, and she laughed about Lord Beaverbrook's having been delayed saying she was glad of it because her cook was a little inebriated that night and slow in getting the dinner prepared.

When "The Beaver" left Washington, he expressed his sincere gratitude to me for the efficient efforts of our Secret Service agents in protecting him. Although the agents all agreed that "The Beaver" might be described as a "little on the eccentric side," they were unanimous in voting him a "right guy." I voted that he was a real gentleman at all times.

Queen Wilhelmina of the Netherlands, while not beautiful and graceful like Britain's Queen Elizabeth, nonetheless shared her warmth of spirit and her thoughtfulness of others. The Dutch Queen was extremely prompt about all appointments and we quickly learned that whenever she was scheduled to make a little trip of any kind, we could count on her being ready several minutes ahead of time.

Her first visit to this country was in June of 1942, when she came over accompanied by her daughter, Princess Juliana (now the Queen), and Juliana's two daughters, Princess Beatrix and Princess Irene, and a half-dozen ladies-in-waiting and maids. They arrived for a summer vacation at a private estate, owned by John Bross Lloyd, at Lee, Massachusetts. I detailed one of the President's armored cars to be used for the trips the Queen made around the estate and in the Berkshires, and assigned agents round the clock.

One morning the royal party was scheduled to leave at ten-thirty to drive to another estate, thirty or forty miles away, where they were to be luncheon guests of a millionaire friend. At ten twenty-five the Queen and Princess Juliana and the little Princesses appeared in front of the house, ready to depart. One lady-in-waiting, who was also supposed to attend the luncheon, was missing. At precisely ten-thirty the Queen said, "We will proceed. We cannot keep these nice Secret Service gentlemen waiting!"

The hapless lady-in-waiting appeared forty-five seconds later. But the royal car was already rolling out of the gates and the tardy lady was left behind.

In abrupt contrast to the gracious thoughtfulness and consideration of the Queens of England and the Netherlands was the high-handed imperiousness of Madame Chiang Kai-Shek of China. She lived in New York City during part of World War Two, and we provided her with twenty-four-hour protection, which necessitated a detail of eight to ten agents, so that two or three were always present. A beautiful little woman, Madame, by nature, was dour and unfriendly. In all the months we served her, none of us ever heard her say thank you.

Accustomed to having her own way in everything, Madame did not appreciate our efforts in her behalf if they happened to cross her own whims or desires. In 1944, she leased a house in the Riverdale section of New York City, where she took up residence with her retinue of eight or ten maids and secretaries. Her detail of agents was waiting outside for her one snowy winter morning, to accompany her to an appointment in midtown New York, when she came out of her house, spied a troop of children with sleds taking belly-busters down a steep street, and decided she wanted to play, too. Without a word to her agents, who were responsible for her protection, she cried, "I want to do that," and ran to the children and demanded one of their sleds.

As anyone who knows anything about children is well aware, the demand to borrow their property is always resented. If it is made by one of their own age, it is often a fighting matter and always a subject of serious argument. When the request is from a peremptory adult, the resentment may be hidden under puzzled consent, and that happened in the case of the Madame. The children were not alone in being puzzled. So were my agents. It was an unprecedented predicament.

"What do you do when the first lady of China wants to take a belly-slam on the streets of New York?" asked one dubious agent, Sam Callaghan, of Agent Mitch Lipson.

"Search me," Lipson answered worriedly. "Our job as a Secret Service detail is to prevent her from attack, injury, or assassination."

"Doesn't this belly-slamming business come under 'injury?' " Sam asked, doubtfully.

"Not if she chooses to injure herself. I guess if she wants to take a belly-slam, the best thing is to block off the street and let her go to it."

The agents ran to the intersections at the foot of the hill and held up their arms to stop traffic.

Madame Chiang held the sled in her arms and started off at a sprint.

Bang! She slapped down the sled in a belly-whopper that made the juvenile audience giggle and cheer as the Number One Statewoman of the Far East came speeding down the hill with her legs in the air.

Just at that moment a taxicab came barreling along the snowy street toward the intersection at the bottom of the hill. The agent stationed there waved frantically for the cab to stop. But the driver, seeing only a man in plain clothes wig-wagging frantically at him, assumed he was just another over-eager passenger trying to flag a taxi. The cabby shook his head and tore on through the intersection, made a sharp turn, then slammed on his brakes with a screech as he saw Madame on her sled sailing straight toward him. The cab crunched to a halt; Madame let out a shriek—and passed within three inches of the wheels of the cab which might easily have crushed her to death. The cab driver stuck his head out, swore at the irresponsible little lady on her sled, then drove on, not realizing how close he had come to creating an international incident.

The Madame was hard on her agents in many ways, since she was utterly indifferent to the rules governing their conduct. On one occasion I had to remove an agent from her detail because of his failure to follow the regulations in the Secret Service manual. Madame's aide did not politely request but somewhat insolently demanded that the agent be restored to the detail. This I respectfully refused to do, explaining that the agent had violated important rules governing such details. Madame's aide then ordered me to discontinue the entire protection detail, which I also respectfully refused to do. He immediately telephoned to the White House and told Harry Hopkins to order me to discontinue the detail.

I could visualize the twinkle in Harry's eyes as he kidded the Chinese staff member along and finally said that unless he got a communication bearing the seal and signature of Generalissimo Chiang Kai-Shek himself, with adequate and explicit suggestions for the detail's discontinuance, the Secret Service would function as directed by its Chief, and that no member of the staff of any distinguished guest would be allowed to designate the agents to be assigned to their Secret Service detail. Hopkins then telephoned me, stating that President Roosevelt said not to permit the staff of the Madame to interfere in any manner with my conduct of the Secret Service.

At another time, when Madame was making a public appearance at the Waldorf Hotel in New York, an agent was handed a beautiful and extremely valuable fur coat (appraised at $50,000) with the instruction, "Hang on to this coat. The Madame prizes it highly." I was in New York and observed the agent carrying the coat. I ordered the agents on that detail not to carry that coat or any other article of wearing apparel again. An agent's arms must not be encumbered, as the agents should be free to spring quickly upon a potential assassin. An aide of the Madame became furious at my action, and I was again ordered to discontinue the detail at once. I respectfully refused to do so. Then the aide put through a phone call to the White House to have the detail discontinued. President Roosevelt again supported my action and ordered that under no conditions should the Secret Service allow any distinguished visitor under our protection to specify how such protection should be effected or to order its discontinuance.

Madame Chiang Kai-Shek is a beautiful and talented woman, but if I had to look after her safety again and had any choice I would say, "No, absolutely not!"

Despite the difficulties we had protecting her, however, I will say that Madame Chiang was very able and successful at shaping public opinion. She and Churchill were the two best visiting public speakers I heard during the entire war. After the return of Madame Chiang Kai-Shek to her native country, the Chinese government notified me that in appreciation of the efficient efforts of the Secret Service in protecting her, I had been awarded the Military Order of the Cloud and Banner. I was not allowed to accept it until I retired—and then Congress had to pass a bill before I could get my hands on it. But, at long last, I did get a "thank you" on behalf of Madame Chiang Kai-Shek.

The United States afforded a refuge to many who were forced to flee from their countries when Hitler's German military machine swept across Europe. Among those who came here were Crown Prince Olav of Norway; his attractive wife, Crown Princess Marthe; and their three beautiful children, the Princesses Ragnhild and Astrid, and the future King of Norway, Prince Harald. Arriving in the United States, the royal children, being very young, quickly adapted themselves to American life. By direction of the President, Secret Service agents were promptly assigned to protect the family.

Soon after her arrival, Crown Princess Marthe purchased a home about five miles from Washington. Prince Olav spent most of his time in Europe, but Princess Marthe did not return to Norway with the three children until May, 1945. We had the future King of Norway under our protection about four years. Many a night I dropped by unannounced and inspected their home to see if the agents of the protection detail were on the job. The future King was only about five years old when he arrived, and, of course, did not speak English. As most children do, however, he made quick headway with the new language and was sent to a school where he soon made friends with American boys.

One day, driving through Rock Creek Park, I spotted a Secret Service car near a playground. "So that's where my agents spend their time," I thought. I drove into the parking space and sat in the car. Within a few seconds I saw Prince Harald on a swing with two agents hovering close by, which gave me a satisfied feeling as I prepared to drive off. Just then the side door of my car opened and I heard an ominous voice ask, "Waiting for somebody?"

I looked over my shoulder into the businesslike countenance of one of my agents.

"Oh, it's you, Chief!" he sputtered. "I saw the car pull up and a man sitting there with his collar up—well, it looked suspicious."

We laughed and I walked over to where the Prince was playing. He had met a couple of kids in the park, kids with ragged clothing, and he was playing with them. Of course, they had no idea that he was a Prince.

"Hi, Chief! Want to swing with us?" cried Prince Harald. He stiffened, clicked his heels, and bowed.

"No thanks, Prince," I said.

The eyes of the two ragged kids popped. Half-frightened, they drifted away. I heard one kid say, "Hey, do you think that kid could be a real Prince? The man called him Prince."

"Naw," said the other boy. "Don't be a dope. Prince is a nickname. Some people even call their dogs Prince!"

After the war Prince Harald did not want to go back to Norway. I saw him the day before he sailed, and he said sadly, "I like all the boys here, Chief Wilson, and we have a lot of fun. I don't know any boys over there."

In recognition of the protection extended by the Secret Service to their royal family, the Norwegian government conferred on me the Order of St. Olaf.

For a democratic country we received a goodly share of attention from royalty throughout the war years. It was my observation—and short of belonging to their families, it could hardly have been a closer observation—that the more royal the personage, the greater the degree of appreciation for our free-and-easy, unaffected ways and manners.

12

Any person who is a head of state, and personifies government or authority, is the potential object of assassination plots—contemplated if not acted out. It may be hard to imagine, for instance, that anyone would want to take pot shots at such a homey dumpling of a lady as Queen Victoria, yet there are on record six attempts upon her life during her long reign. Europe has long been inured to the fact that all reigning monarchs are potential victims, but here in America that idea is so foreign to our democratic free way of life that it has been a hard and terrible lesson to learn. Yet, as Judge le Baron Colt stated in 1902, in his brilliant critique of our failure in Presidential protection following McKinley's death, the American liberties we so cherish do not include "the liberty of assassination."

Historically, America kept its head in the sand concerning this awful fact of political life, although every President has had enemies who would have liked to see him wiped out. Enemies plotted to assassinate George Washington, but alert Army intelligence officers discovered and squelched their plan. President John Adams was once accosted bodily, and received many threatening letters from his enemies. Here is a sample:

President Adams—

Myself and my family are ruined by the French. If you do not procure satisfaction for my losses, when a treaty is made with them, I am undone forever and you must be a villain to your country!!! Assassination shall be your lot, if *restitution* is lost to America through your means, or if ever you agree to a peace without it. The subsistence of thousands, who have lost their all, *depends upon it.*

> *A ruined merchant*
> *Alas! With ten children!!!*
> *Made beggars by the French*

Andrew Jackson had a very narrow escape from assassination. He attended the funeral service of a Congressman at the Capitol. After the sermon, President Jackson and his Cabinet members filed past the casket. As Jackson left and entered the rotunda of the Capitol, a man edged near him and held a pistol close to his chest. The man pulled the trigger and the cap exploded, but the charge failed to go off. Before anyone realized what was happening, the man jerked out another pistol and fired a second time. Again the cap exploded, but the charge failed to fire. President Jackson grabbed the attacker and aided in overpowering him. The two pistols were carefully examined by a small-arms expert of the Army. He found that they had been loaded properly in every respect and could not explain their failure. Experts figured that the chances of two successive misfires, under the circumstances, were 1 to 125,000. The potential assassin was Richard Lawrence. He intended to kill President Jackson because he said he was ruining the country. Physicians pronounced him insane and he was committed to an asylum, where he died in a few months.

President Jackson received many threatening letters. One of the letters was from Junius Brutus Booth, the father of John Wilkes Booth, the assassin of Abraham Lincoln. It read:

Brower's Hotel, Philadelphia
July 4, 1835

You dam'd old scoundrel if you don't sign the pardon of your fellow men, now under sentence of death, *De Ruiz* and *De Soto*, I will cut your throat whilst you are sleeping. I wrote to you repeated cautions; so look out or damn you I'll have you burnt at the stake in the city of Washington.

Your Master
Junius Brutus Booth

P.S. You Know Me! Look out!

President John Tyler had rocks thrown at him. Both the Roosevelts narrowly missed assassins' bullets.

During the hundred years in which we lost four Presidents by assassination, there were also three attacks upon a President, President-elect, and candidate for the Vice-presidency which failed, which brings us to the shocking record that there have been attempts upon the lives of one out of every five of our Presidents. And this does not include all the would-be assassins, whose evil plans are discovered well enough in advance so that they never have a chance to act.

In times of war, we have rallied round and shown some concern for our Presidents' safety. Lincoln had such a heavy guard in his public appearances during the Civil War that citizens complained they couldn't see into his carriage. In 1917, Congress was sufficiently chivalrous to authorize full protection for President Wilson and his family.

But in peacetimes, memory dims and rules relax. Following the Civil War, the detail guarding the President was curtailed, and Presidents after Lincoln moved about at will with little or no protection. Garfield was shot in the back and killed, in 1881, while walking to a train in a Baltimore and Potomac Railroad station in Washington. McKinley met the fatal bullet with his hand outstretched in greeting and a smile on his face.

Agent Jim Sloan, who was on the White House Detail when William Howard Taft was President, told me about a man who appeared one night in 1910 demanding a personal audience with the President. He was ushered into Jim's office at the gate of the White House.

"What's troubling you, brother?" Jim asked.

"I've got to see the President."

That was a familiar beginning to hundreds of similar stories Sloan and other agents had heard. The man proceeded to tell an incoherent story about enemy spies on his trail, saying he had to warn the President.

Sloan sympathized with him and then asked the man about a bulge in his overcoat pocket.

"In my 'business' you have to be prepared for anything. I'm Charlie, the gunman," said the man, placing a revolver on Sloan's desk.

Jim picked up the gun and dropped it in a desk drawer. Charlie sneered at Sloan disdainfully. "Now, you don't think I'm that dumb, do you?" he exclaimed, reaching into his coat again. And out came another revolver.

Jim grabbed it and put it in the desk. Then he waited for Charlie to make the next move. "You're pretty smart," said Jim.

"You bet I am. I've outwitted all these foreign agents after me." Then Charlie pulled out another revolver.

Dropping the third one in the desk drawer, Sloan shook his head in amazement. "I'll tell you something, Charlie," Sloan observed. "The President is not here today. But why don't you and I take a little ride and talk this whole thing over."

Charlie readily agreed, and Jim drove him directly to Gallinger Hospital, where he was detained for observation. He was pronounced insane, given first-class medical treatment, and he eventually recovered.

With the exception of Oscar Callazo, the Puerto Rican who stated he and his friend, Griselio Torresola, were both demonstrating in behalf of Puerto Rican nationalism when they tried to kill President Truman, our assassins and would-be assassins have, in the main, been loners, not identified with any organized group.

The closest the White House and its incumbent came to the scare of an "organized attack" occurred during Teddy Roosevelt's administration when, to the horror of the Secret Service detail on guard, six black-hand prints were discovered mysteriously smeared on a side door of the White House one afternoon. At this time the infamous Mafia had extorted money from its victims through the Black Hand Society, which went around leaving that warning imprint on the front door of the intended victim. The agents who found the six black hands on the White House door reported immediately to the President.

An investigation was made, and the culprits were found in short order: the White House Black Hand Society was made up of Quentin Roosevelt, the President's ten-year-old son, and five of his young pals who had been allowed to come to the White House to play.

It is natural that all Presidents chafe, as men, at the "necessary thorn," as T. R. called it, of the White House Detail. At some time or other, every guarded President has indulged in a normal, healthy desire to "shake" his detail.

F.D.R. never did it to me, although before I became Chief, during his first term, he gave Colonel Starling something of a chase from his Presidential yacht. While under my jurisdiction, Truman once slipped out of the White House and went to his own bank to conduct personal business, but his agents caught up with him there before he had finished.

Teddy Roosevelt gave his guards a run for their money (this was before he narrowly missed death at the hands of an assassin, which occurred when he was campaigning for another term on the Bull Moose ticket in 1912). Once he

decided to take his sons and go for a camping trip in Rock
Creek Park. Confident that he had successfully shaken his
guards, T. R. spent a blissfully "free" night camping out,
although the agents were actually present at a discreet dis-
tance. Next day, at the White House, T.R. couldn't resist
needling the agents about having given them the slip. They
told him they had been there. When he demanded proof, they
told him at precisely what time he had started his supper
fire and what his supper menu had been.

The assassin is usually not trying to kill another "person."
He is plotting to destroy a symbol of authority or government by which he feels persecuted. Often, there is so much
chance involved in which official dies and which one lives
that it is chilling to contemplate. For many assassins, the
victim could be one prominent leader or, just as well, another. Oswald, you will recall, had once tried to get General
Walker and had talked of killing Richard Nixon. Zangara
was aiming at F.D.R. when he fatally wounded Mayor
Cermak. Czolgosz killed McKinley, but, from his testimony,
it might just as easily have been someone else in a position
of authority.

When I interviewed Zangara in Miami, he bluntly admitted, "As a man, I like Roosevelt. As a President, I want
to kill him. In Italy, ten years ago, I want to kill the King,
Victor Emmanuel, but I can't get near enough to him."

I sized up Zangara as a crafty, crazy, deluded character
who had a hate for all rulers and all governments. He gloated
over his sinister crime, and reveled in the international publicity it had accorded him. The fact that he was soon to die in
the electric chair seemed to have no meaning for him. He
had won his day of glory and he was enjoying it.

A bomb, addressed to President Roosevelt, was discovered in the White House mail a few days after Zangara
had failed to kill him. It was made from shotgun shells and
this note, scrawled in large, bold letters, was attached to it:

Dear Roosevelt:

I want to congratulate you for escape gunman Zangara.

Yours,
Paul Altroni

P.S. I am Paul Altroni of Italy.
   I will go home in July.

The same day the Chief of Police at Watertown, New York, received this letter scrawled in the same large, bold letters:

Chief,

I am second guy who hate presidents' and other officer's of the nations, and hated millionaires. I am Italian Calabrese and friend of Joe Zangara. I am mad. I will kill all officers of this city when they are on duty at midnight. I killed denver millionair. My friend Joe Zangara missed Roosevelt. I take his place to get rid of him. I stay out at midnight and rest at hotel because my friend is held.

that's all.

I am costumer at Factory St. barber shop and he's my friend too I come there every Saturday to shave.

Paul Altroni of Italy.

Secret Service agents, post office inspectors, and Watertown police snapped into action, as it was clear that other treacherous hands belonging to haters of our President were reaching out to harm him. It was feared that those hands belonged to a close associate of Zangara. The case baffled these experienced investigators. Two weeks later, a strange angle was brought to this perplexing case. A letter was mailed in Watertown addressed to the Blair Laboratories, Lynchburg, Virginia. The writing was similar to the previous letters. It was originally addressed in pencil, then traced over in pen and ink. This letter read:

P

Sirs:

Will you delivery this to the President. I give you $500 if you will. Please will you. I warn you.

Enclosed with that letter, drawn in pencil across a sheet of paper, was the outline of a human hand. On the bottom of this sheet was a crude drawing of a pair of balance scales and the signature "Hand of Mistery." Another sheet of paper was enclosed and read:

Honor President Franklin D. Roosevelt. I am coming to Washington to visit you and this is the first time I'm going to be there. I am mad. Your going to be murdered by this hand. I will be there.

Hand of Mistery.

Mail clerks in the Watertown post office, who had been alerted to watch for suspicious letters, intercepted another letter addressed to President Roosevelt on June 14th. It contained a counter check of the Northern New York Trust Company of Watertown made out for two million dollars payable to bearer and signed "Sergeant M. Burns, U.S.A. and England." On the back of the check was this message:

My cousin in England will see the Chamberlain and get the bonds and send them to you by private mail.

Also in the envelope was a Seaboard Air Line timetable folded in a most peculiar manner. Agents ascertained where such timetables were distributed in Watertown, one of which was the Jefferson County National Bank. Bank officials and personnel in the other offices promised that a close watch would be kept over persons picking up timetables or other travel literature.

On June 20th, an assistant cashier observed a poorly dressed young man taking some of the travel literature. Approaching the young man, he asked, "Are you going traveling?"

The young man paled and he replied, in a swift, hurried, alarmed fashion, "I didn't do nothing. I no harm anybody." The words were jerked rather than said.

The assistant cashier called the police, who identified the young man as Joseph Doldo, a resident of Watertown. He coolly denied any connection with the letters and bombs. Then an officer casually handed Doldo a Seaboard Air Line timetable similar to the one enclosed in the last letter to President Roosevelt and told Doldo to place it in an envelope. He quickly folded the timetable in exactly the same *unusual* manner in which the timetable enclosed in President Roosevelt's letter was folded. He was then shown this other timetable and told that the writing on the letter was his hand. The denouement instantly and dramatically took place.

Throwing back his head, Doldo startled the officers by shouting, "I, Joe Doldo, done do it! I hate Presidents!"

Then he stood up, holding his right hand high above his head, and yelled, "The Hand of Mistery will done more! The Hand ain't sorry!"

At that moment the unrepentant Hand of Mistery was seized by the strong hand of the law and steel handcuffs were quickly snapped on his wrists.

Doldo had been born in Watertown in 1911. He attended school until he was sixteen years of age and had completed only four grades. He worked at odd jobs and was regarded as a lazy, cunning fellow, who would never amount to much. He lived with his father and uncle. His mother had died when he was four years old. The father and uncle knew of our investigation in Watertown and, although they found out that Joe had written the letters and sent the bombs, they failed to report it to the authorities. Such failure to co-operate with the government was the defiant procedure of members of, or persons influenced by, the Mafia. They claimed that they "beat hell out of Joe and told him to stop his foolishness." A month later Doldo pleaded guilty before a judge of the United States District Court and was sentenced to sixteen years in the Federal penitentiary.

Assassins, upon interrogation, usually have a "cause," albeit most of these causes are obscure to other people. Zangara claimed that he wanted to "get even with the Capitalists" because he had stomach trouble. John Schrank, who almost finished Teddy Roosevelt, claimed that he considered Roosevelt responsible for McKinley's death and that he was avenging McKinley at the request of that poor President's ghost. Czolgosz, McKinley's assassin, considered that he "done my duty" because the President was the "enemy of the working class." Charles Guiteau, who shot Garfield, had a massive display of "reasons" set up in the form of declarations and proclamations, which were relatively untranslatable to anyone else.

Assassins also share a common ambition to take their own place in history. They are, to a man, unrepentant about their murders and pleased with the celebrity their crime brings them. Emotionally, they seldom have close, normal ties with others. They suffer from a sense of persecution and feel apart from society and hostile to it. Upon medical examination, most assassins qualify as paranoid.

Since such personalities are always with us, the problem of protecting a President from their assaults lies primarily in eliminating the chances of such people getting close to the President.

In November of 1944, I was startled when a teletype message from our Detroit office notified me that a dangerous hater of governments was in Washington for the avowed purpose of assassinating President Roosevelt, and that he carried a .38 caliber revolver. It also stated that he had sent a letter to his wife from Washington saying, "I have been hanging around the White House waiting for a shot at Roosevelt." He informed his wife that he had stolen a rifle from an Army truck on guard near the White House. The teletype gave a complete description of him.

I immediately assigned six agents to the case, and the men on the White House Detail and the White House police were warned to be especially alert. In about two hours Agent Jim Stringfellow, one of the cleverest agents of our Service, found that the potential assassin was registered at the Congress Hotel. With the permission of the manager, Jim searched his room and found a loaded revolver in an elk leather holster and ten extra shells in his suitcase. The manager described the fellow's conduct as rather unusual, in that he refused to talk to any other guests of the hotel.

Stringfellow and two other agents waited at the hotel for this man to return, while other agents searched for him at other places. In a few minutes two Washington police officers appeared and made inquiry of the hotel manager as to whether he was registered. They said that he had been arrested for violating a pedestrian control (crossing the street against a red light), that he fought arrest, violently attacked an officer, and was in the Municipal hospital for observation. The sigh of relief that I breathed when I learned that this potential assassin was in the hospital in safe custody was heartfelt.

We located an aunt of his who informed us, "Will called on me after his arrival in Washington and bluntly told me that he was in the city for the express purpose of killing the President."

"Why did you not co-operate with the government by reporting the matter at once to the police or the Secret Service?" she was asked.

"Well, I knew Will was cracked, so naturally I didn't take him seriously," she replied in all sincerity.

It certainly would aid law enforcement officers in their always difficult work of protecting the public if the public would give even a minimum of co-operation to them instead of adopting either an indifferent or, as is sometimes the case, a frankly hostile attitude toward the efforts of these officers.

What President Roosevelt had escaped was brought home very vividly when Will was interrogated.

"For three years electric currents have been going through my body and just recently they have been getting stronger and more frequent."

From that statement the agents interviewing him knew practically his whole story, since they had heard many similar ones; but they encouraged him to continue, not only because they had to get a complete and exhaustive statement down to the last detail but because they knew the therapeutic value of giving the man a hearing.

"President Roosevelt and nobody else is responsible and I came to Washington to kill him if he would not hear me and stop the currents that are slowly killing me. Would you like to be killed by electric currents going through your body all day and all night—would you?" he demanded to know, his voice rising to a shrill crescendo.

"I certainly would not," soothed one of the agents.

"I made a survey of the neighborhood hoping that Roosevelt would leave the White House and I could get a good shot at him. I hung around Lafayette Park on Sunday thinking he might go to St. John's Church across the street from the White House."

Will continued, "At ten o'clock on Friday night I was in the neighborhood and approached the State Department Building from the north. I went between the building and the White House, coming out on West Executive Avenue, in the restricted section adjoining the White House. There I saw an Army truck with two machine guns and a 30-30 rifle. No one was in or near the truck. I picked up the rifle and put it under my overcoat and started to leave West Executive Avenue by the south entrance. I saw a White House policeman at the entrance so I turned around and went in the other direction."

When he got to that point, Will suddenly stopped talking

as if tired of the subject, a condition of mental illness that often calls for a recess.

"And then what happened, Will? Did you get cold feet?" prompted the agent.

"No, the electric currents started bothering me, so I hid the rifle in a flower box at the back of the State Department building. A little later I was stopped by a White House policeman who asked why I was in the restricted area, and I told him I was just looking around.

"He took me to the Pennsylvania Avenue end of West Executive Avenue and said, 'Don't ever come back here again.' I was tired and went back to the hotel."

"Do you know that you might have been shot for being in that restricted area adjoining the White House and for stealing the rifle?" the agent asked him.

"That's just what I wanted, someone to shoot me to save me from having to do it myself," the poor fellow replied.

Upon his arrival in Washington, Will had called on a Congressman who had given him a pass to the Senate galleries where he had heard Senator Henrik Shipstead of Minnesota make a long speech.

"While I heard the Senator speaking on the floor of Congress, the electric currents started and I was going to shoot him, but when they stopped I didn't," he explained.

I have often wondered if Senator Shipstead shivered when he realized how very thin was the dividing line between life and death for him that day.

Our agents confirmed that Will had stolen the rifle from the Army truck, which had been left temporarily unguarded, and that the next day it was found in the flower box. The soldiers concerned were severely disciplined for their serious lapse of duty. It always seemed to me that the Almighty One protects such unfortunate persons and that perhaps Will or one of the soldiers was saved from a sudden death in this instance. If Will had been detected taking the rifle, he might have become excited and fired it at the soldiers and possibly have killed one of them, or he might have been killed.

Will was then sent to a mental hospital for treatment.

The most effective weapon that we had in apprehending and diverting assassins from F.D.R. lay, I felt, in our Protective Research Section, where a constant, running file, with an elaborate "tickler" system for keeping in touch with all the cranks and crackpots over the country, was in operation. By its use, we not only kept many dangerous people under surveillance, but we were able to stop many from coming into Washington to make an attempt upon the life of the President. In the conclusions of the Warren Commission, the Commission finds that the Protective Research Section is somewhat obsolescent for current use and needs updating in terms of equipment and manpower. I wholeheartedly agree. The system which we established in 1940, for President Roosevelt, can hardly handle the amount of crank mail and threats that reach the White House in 1965. Nothing would please and reassure me more about our security efforts today than to see the Protective Research Section adequately expanded to meet today's needs. Although it did not catch in its net the tracks left by President Kennedy's assassin, Lee Harvey Oswald, the files of the division did succeed in averting an earlier tragedy, when Kennedy was President-elect in 1960.

While the Kennedys were in Palm Beach, the Protective Research Section received a report from New Hampshire that a crank was on his way to Florida to "blow up the President." This desperate character, Richard Pavlick, had obtained seven sticks of dynamite and secreted them in his automobile. He headed South when he read in the newspapers that the Kennedys planned to be in Palm Beach. There, he systematically photographed the entrances to the Kennedy home and to the church they attended. His plan was to wait until he saw the President-elect leave home for Sunday Mass, then throw his own auto into high gear, smash the Kennedy car, and detonate the dynamite. Before our report came through to Palm Beach, he had actually once parked his car outside the Kennedy home and seen the President-elect and his wife come out, then changed his mind, according to his later confession, because "I looked at Mrs. Kennedy and I did not want to kill her."

Upon receiving the report regarding Pavlick's activities, the Secret Service Agents on duty at Palm Beach made a hasty and intense search, and he was captured before he made a second attempt to carry out his diabolical plan. He was declared insane and committed to a Federal hospital.

13

My biggest headache in providing Presidential protection occurred at those times when public parades or large public gatherings at the Capitol, such as an inaugural, were going to take place; they always presented unusual hazards. Immediately after President Roosevelt was elected for his fourth term, in 1944, we began preparations for the inaugural.

Congress organized a Committee of Senators and Representatives to make the necessary arrangements for conducting the important ceremony at the Capitol, and made $25,000 available for grandstands and other expenses. Some enthusiastic Congressman predicted that it would be the most impressive spectacle ever carried out at the Capitol. Colonel Edwin Halsey, Secretary to the Committee, and David Lynn, Architect of the Capitol, who would have the responsibility for the erection of the grandstands, and were anxious to award contracts promptly, called at the White House to discuss the inaugural plans with President Roosevelt. To their surprise he indicated that in deference to war conditions, with thousands of American boys in the armed forces and a tremendous number on the battlefronts on distant continents, it would be highly inappropriate to make a gala affair out of the event or to spend $25,000 for grand-

224

stands and other expenses. It was his desire to have an impressive but austere inauguration. He also indicated that he wished it to be held at the White House, and said that the expense could be kept to around $2,500. The Committee acquiesced to the wishes of the President, and the plans for conducting a spectacular inaugural at the Capitol were promptly dropped.

From "behind the scenes" on Capitol Hill, word reached us that some Congressmen strongly protested against the disregard of the long-standing tradition (about one hundred and forty years) that the President be inaugurated at the Capitol. A radio station reporter alleged that a rumor was being slyly spread that the change from the Capitol to the White House was due to the President's deteriorating health and that he would never again be able to leave the White House. That rumor was proved ridiculous when, a few days later, he journeyed to Hyde Park. Some other asinine, sinister, and ugly stories were spread about his failure to go to the Capitol to be sworn in as President.

The decision not to have the inaugural exercises at the Capitol was a great relief to me. I did not have to worry about the hazards in relation to potential assassins and cranks on trips through crowded streets between the White House and the Capitol and at the inauguration ceremony.

President Roosevelt appointed a committee to arrange for the inauguration at the White House. He selected his Military Aide, General "Pa" Watson, as Chairman, and Steve Early, his Press Secretary, as Vice-chairman. I was named as a committee member, and others included Colonel Edwin Halsey, Secretary of the Senate; Joseph Davies, State Department; Stanley Woodward, State Department; and William Hassett, White House Secretary. General Watson's diplomacy and efficiency as chairman contributed highly to the effectiveness of the committee, although caustic comments were made by Senator McKellar of Tennessee and others "on the Hill," because the President had failed to appoint any members of Congress to his committee.

For his previous inaugurals the President had attended a religious service at St. John's Episcopal Church on Lafayette Square, directly across from the White House, before proceeding to the Capitol. On this occasion the religious service was conducted in the East Room of the White House, and two hundred friends were invited.

The following prayer was led by Reverend John G. Magee of St. John's Church:

O LORD our Governor, whose glory is in all the world; we commend this nation to Thy merciful care, that being guided by Thy Providence, we may dwell secure in Thy peace. Grant to Thy servant, Franklin, THE PRESIDENT OF THE UNITED STATES, and to all in authority, wisdom and strength to know and to do Thy will. Fill them with the love of truth and righteousness; and make them ever mindful of their calling to serve this people in Thy fear; through Jesus Christ our Lord, who liveth and reigneth with Thee and the HOLY GHOST, one GOD, world without end. Amen.

At this solemn part of the service a brief, unexpected interruption occurred. Seated in the front row were Her Royal Highness, the Crown Princess Marthe of Norway; His Royal Highness, the Crown Prince Olav of Norway; and their children, Princess Ragnhild, Princess Astrid, and my little friend Prince Harald. Suddenly, as the prayer was drawing to its sober close, the future King of Norway slipped off his chair and with a loud bang fell flat on the floor. The eyes of all in the room were turned toward the unlucky boy. His father, registering a look of utter disgust, quickly picked him up and sat him back on his chair with such force that I thought the chair would break. After the service was concluded, Mrs. Roosevelt went over and patted the little boy on the back and in return she got a broad smile from him. His father still looked mad enough to bite a nail in two. Boys quickly forget embarrassing situations and when I talked with Prince Harald later in the day he was once again carefree and happy.

The night before the inaugural, Washington had had a surprise snowfall, and there was a beautiful white carpet on the White House grounds on the morning of Inaugural Day, January 20, 1945. But by noon it had turned to slush. Members of Congress, distinguished guests, and enthusiastic citizens determined to see for the first time the inauguration of a President of the United States for his fourth term had to wade through slush up to their ankles.

Sharp at noon the United States Marine Band indicated the appearance of the President on the South Portico with "Hail to the Chief." He was accompanied by his eldest son, Colonel James Roosevelt. His other sons, John, Elliott, and Franklin, were on the battlefronts on distant continents. Close to the President were Secret Service agents Howard Anderson, James Healy, and Charlie Fredericks. Thirteen of the President's grandchildren were present. In the front row were fifty wounded war veterans from Walter Reed Hospital. Some were on crutches, others in wheel chairs. In spite of their disabilities, they were smiling and enjoying a real thrill. As the President stood on the South Portico and greeted thousands in his snow-covered back yard, he was lustily cheered by the happy but chilly audience.

The opening prayer was offered by Bishop Angus Dun. Then former Vice-president Wallace administered the oath of office to Vice-president-elect Harry S. Truman.

Chief Justice Harlan Fiske Stone administered the oath of office to the President. In a strong voice, clear as a bell, President Roosevelt solemnly repeated the oath.

Then the President delivered his inaugural address. It was an impressive, but short address, only five hundred and forty words. The benediction was pronounced by the Right Reverend John A. Ryan, and the Marine Band closed the ceremony with "The Star-Spangled Banner." The historic event had lasted only thirteen minutes.

As the President did not leave the White House, his protection was a comparatively easy assignment for the Secret Service. However, we were concerned about the possibility of his catching cold, as he was the only man I saw that day who was not wearing a heavy overcoat. Most of the ladies were decked out in fur coats, very appropriate for that cold day.

Fred Othman, columnist for the Washington *Times Herald,* in his article covering the inauguration, took a friendly rap at my activities that day:

Chief Frank Wilson of the Secret Service stamped through the slush keeping an eye upon dozens of his assistants and puffing one of the foulest smelling cigars yet.

Two days later the President departed for the famous Yalta Conference. He took with him several of the fourth inaugural gold medals, which he presented to some prominent persons including King Ibn Saud of Saudi Arabia, King Farouk of Egypt, Marshal Stalin, and Prime Minister Churchill. Before he left Washington, he took the time to sign the following letter to General Watson:

The White House
Washington

January 22, 1945

Dear Pa:

I want to send you this personal note to thank you, and through you, all the members of the Inaugural Committee, who carried out so efficiently the tremendous job of arrangements for the Inauguration. Everything went off very well and I know how hard everybody worked to make it a great success.

Will you be good enough to thank, on my behalf, everyone who participated? I am indeed grateful.

With every good wish to all,

Always sincerely,

/s/F.D.R.

All of us around the White House were given a sudden shock when word came on February 20th, less than a month later, that our sincere friend and inspiring associate for so many years, General "Pa" Watson, had gone to his eternal reward. He had accompanied President Roosevelt to the Yalta Conference and died aboard the U.S.S. *Quincy* on the return trip.

I was at our secret railway siding at the Bureau of Engraving and Printing on February 28th when President Roosevelt returned from the Yalta Conference. Aboard the train was the body of "Pa" Watson, his devoted and dedicated friend and valued advisor over many years. The sudden death of his old friend had deeply affected the President. He seemed downhearted, and the usual pep he showed on his return from previous trips was not apparent. He acted tired, listless, and weary, and the deep lines in his thin, pale face showed that he had been through a severe and long ordeal.

General Watson was laid to rest in the Arlington National Cemetery with full military honors. The President was present. It was a sad day for all of us.

Thursday afternoon, April 12, 1945, a message came through from Warm Springs: "The President had a sudden attack. Condition serious." I rushed over to the White House. In a few minutes the sad news arrived, telling us that President Roosevelt had suffered a fatal cerebral hemorrhage. Mere words can't describe the sadness and the shock experienced by the folks in the White House—executives, clerks, servants, and friends. I will never forget the tears which were shed nor will I ever forget the effect of that sad report on me. My heart started to pound and I had to sit down to compose myself.

Steve Early, the ranking executive in the White House, had the job of breaking the news to Mrs. Roosevelt. She was making a speech at the Sulgrave Club and Early telephoned for her to return to the White House, where he told her the news. Mrs. Roosevelt was shocked and surprised. She had known her husband was not in the best of health, but she had not anticipated anything like this. I went in to express my sympathy, and she was already getting ready to fly to Warm Springs to bring back the President's body.

After he had located Mrs. Roosevelt, Steve Early put in a call for Vice-president Harry Truman, who was at the Capitol. I sent two agents to escort Truman from his office in the Senate to the White House. Within a few minutes he arrived, and Early gave him the distressing news. Soon Secretary of State Edward Stettinius and Les Biffle, Secretary of the Senate, joined Mr. Truman. We sent a Secret Service auto to the Truman apartment to rush Mrs. Truman and their daughter, Margaret, to the White House. Chief Justice Harlan Fiske Stone arrived to swear in the new President.

The simple and very brief swearing-in ceremony took place in the Cabinet Room. Cabinet members and others then stepped forward to shake the hand of the new President and utter a few appropriate words. I was about the last person in the room to shake his hand.

"God bless you, protect and guide you," were my serious words addressed to the new President.

He soberly replied, "Thank you, Frank, I do need His help."

My mind carried me back forty-four years to Buffalo in 1901, after President McKinley had been assassinated. As a thirteen-year-old boy, I had stood on the steps of the Ansley Wilcox home on Delaware Avenue when another Vice-president, Theodore Roosevelt, arrived in Buffalo, entered the home, and in a very few minutes emerged as our twenty-seventh President. That was a solemn and important event in our history that was indelibly impressed upon my young mind. This present solemn and important event in the history of our country was permanently impressed upon my now mature mind. I wondered what effect it would have on World War Two, on the future of our country, and on the future of the world.

I could not wonder or muse too long about the future. I had important work to do immediately. As the entire White House Detail of agents was at Warm Springs, I selected a new group of Secret Service agents to function as the White

House Secret Service Detail protecting President Truman. I had already made a survey of the Truman apartment on Connecticut Avenue, in case protection was needed, and had this survey on file. Now, I hurried out to the apartment house and assigned agents and guards at strategic points in and around the building, in order to assure proper temporary protection of the President, the First Lady, and their daughter.

The next day we moved the Truman family into Blair House across from the White House, and I assigned a large detail of agents and White House police to guard them. President Truman insisted that Mrs. Roosevelt take as long to move as she needed, and it was actually nearly a month before the Trumans took residence at the White House.

That same day, Saturday, I accompanied President Truman, Cabinet members, and other officials to the Washington Union Station, where the body of President Roosevelt was to arrive from Warm Springs. The remains were solemnly placed on a caisson drawn by six black horses and a military detail escorted it up Pennsylvania Avenue, crowded with thousands of sorrowful, mourning citizens, to the White House, where the remains rested in the East Room. An impressive memorial prayer service was conducted at four P.M. in the East Room by Bishop Angus Dun. It was a depressing contrast to the occasion, only eighty-four days before, when the President and a happy, carefree group attended the East Room prayer service before the fourth inaugural. That evening a special train bearing the body, Mrs. Roosevelt and the family, President Truman and his family, Cabinet members, and 277 officials left Washington. We arrived at Hyde Park on Sunday morning. President Roosevelt was laid to rest in the beautiful rose garden of the Roosevelt estate that day.

R

14

There was one immediate advantage for the Secret Service when President Truman took office. He had, at that time, no grandchildren, so I was able to release the thirty agents who had been assigned to the Roosevelt "Diaper Detail" for other duties. We put a detail on Mrs. Truman, and it took five agents per week to cover Margaret, on a twenty-four-hour-a-day basis. An animated, friendly young lady, Margaret took the protection measures in her stride. But fun-loving, high-spirited girls, such as Margaret Truman or President Johnson's daughters, pose special security problems. They like to be on the move, at parties and in public places, and their protection varies according to the occasion and number of people present. Depending on what sort of social function Margaret Truman chose to attend, I sent one, two, and sometimes three agents along with her.

The protection technique for President Truman was in many respects similar to the procedure we followed in relalation to President Roosevelt. For example, the advance preparations for trips around the country and abroad were about the same as for F.D.R.'s trips. In other respects, however, the protection procedure was entirely different. President Truman was an able-bodied person, full of life, and naturally wished to move around when the spirit moved him. He went for early morning strolls around Washington or other places, and, of course, the Secret Service had to extend direct protection to him at such times. He made unexpected visits to the Capitol to enjoy the company of his former associates "on the Hill." As a general thing, he co-operated wholeheartedly with the White House Detail and he expressed deep appreciation for the activities of the Secret Service.

It took us all a while to adjust to the new order. F.D.R. was so warmhearted in his dealings with those close to him that everyone in the White House adored him. There was no nervousness around "The Boss." Everyone knew his job and everything ran like clockwork, with an overall esprit de corps which I never had the pleasure of seeing before or since. With "The Boss" gone and a new man in his place, the atmosphere around the White House for the first few weeks was uneasy. People didn't know what was going to happen. Then the shake-down gradually took place and President Truman brought in his own people. They, also, were an able lot. But they were a different type than those with whom "The Boss" had been surrounded. President Truman had a hearty, friendly, brusque manner, without the nuances or persuasive charm of F.D.R. Truman was a politician from his toes to his head. But those of us who stayed around long enough had the pleasure of watching him grow enormously in his job.

Truman did a considerable amount of flying from the time he took office. I supplied the detail of agents, and the commanding general of the Air Force, who was equally as concerned as I for the safety of the President and the reputation of the Air Force, provided the best of equipment and pilots.

It was not until the night before V-E Day (May 7, 1945) that the Trumans actually took up residence in the White

House. Mrs. Roosevelt had accepted the President's thoughtful offer of "all the time you need," and had made frequent trips from the White House to Hyde Park and back, gradually dismantling the accumulation of a dozen years. I saw her several times before she finally left, and, with her usual graciousness she thanked me for the care the Service had taken of her husband during those years. Anna Roosevelt, also, gave me the feeling that what we had done had been greatly appreciated, both for the protection of her father and the watch we had kept over the grandchildren.

Victory in Europe brought unconditional surrender of the Nazis and unbounded happiness to the citizens of this country and our allies. For the Service, it meant a letdown of the wartime concern and tension about Nazi saboteurs, and we modified some of our protection procedures. We were all convinced that the final conquest of our enemy in the Pacific theater of war and the unconditional surrender of Japan was fast approaching.

At San Francisco, soon afterward, an historic conference of nations was convened to promote the extremely constructive objectives of permanent peace. The conference was addressed by President Truman on June 25th. He was surrounded by a large detail of Secret Service agents. On that day the United Nations Charter was approved and signed by the duly authorized conferees. The protection of the Charter was assigned to Secret Service agents, who guarded it until it was submitted to the United States Senate for approval.

The famous Potsdam Peace Conference was hurriedly scheduled, and I immediately sent to Germany an advance detail of fifteen experienced agents under the command of James Rowley, now Chief of the Secret Service, to assure the adequate protection of President Truman. They made checks on all the places where the President would be, especially the house assigned to him; then they awaited his arrival and stayed during the entire proceedings.

The President left Washington on July 6th, accompanied by the Assistant Chief of the Service and a dozen agents, and boarded the U.S.S. *Augusta* at Norfolk. It was during this conference that Churchill was voted out of power in England. He was replaced, at Potsdam, before the conference was concluded, by Clement Attlee.

At the conclusion of the conference President Truman stopped in England to pay a quick visit to King George VI. The President visited the King on the British battleship *Renown;* and the King returned the visit aboard the President's *Augusta*. President Truman returned to the White House on August 7th.

The previous day, August 6th, an atomic bomb—the most horrible, devilish, and powerful weapon of war yet used—was dropped by one of our airplanes on the Japanese city of Hiroshima. Thousands of unarmed, aged, and defenseless persons were killed. On August 9th, a similar disaster befell the city of Nagasaki, killing thousands more. The terrible damage to these two Japanese cities and especially the tremendous loss of life of the young and the old brought a prompt and full realization to the Japanese government that further resistance would be useless. V-J Day, victory in Japan, promptly resulted on September 2, 1945.

President Truman, surrounded by members of his Cabinet, former Secretary of State Cordell Hull, and a few officials, released to the White House press and radio correspondents the announcement of unconditional surrender by the Japanese government. Never before had I seen such a mad rush of White House correspondents, as the day that conference closed, and they raced to get the wonderful report to their papers and to the citizens of the world.

Soon after the news release a tremendous crowd of Washingtonians, wild with enthusiasm, milled around the White House, up and down Pennsylvania Avenue, and through Lafayette Park across from the White House. Thousands were screaming, shouting, dancing, laughing, and crying with joy. Their carefree happiness and their heartfelt joy seemed unbounded. They cheered and cheered and yelled and yelled and whistled and whistled until I thought my ear drums would burst. The unbridled din would almost die out and then another spontaneous blast would erupt. It was a delightful contrast to the solemn, the sad, and the worried citizens whom I had seen gathered outside the White House on Pearl Harbor Day.

I put out a call for extra agents from around the city, whose normal duty was that of counterfeit money investigators. I also called in an extra detail of White House police officers. Then we hastily set up a loud speaker on the North Portico of the White House, and President Truman appeared, flanked by agents, to greet the happy mob. Although we had the extra men out, we felt that with the war over we could let down security to some extent, and we allowed the tremendous crowds to pour onto the White House grounds. The agents beside the President were trained to observe the crowd and never look at him.

President Truman received some poison-pen letters and threats, but nothing compared to the volume drawn by F.D.R. There was much less evidence of hate for Truman, but when it finally did crop out—in the one attempt on President Truman's life—the agents and the White House police were not found lacking.

It was on the afternoon of November 1, 1950. While the White House was being remodeled, the Trumans had moved back to Blair House across the street temporarily. Lunch was over and the President was taking a nap in a bedroom on the second floor. A normal detail was on duty to protect him: two agents and White House police outside Blair House, and one agent, armed with a submachine gun, just inside the door.

At one-thirty, two Puerto Rican fanatics, Torresola and Collazo, suddenly appeared on Pennsylvania Avenue, blasting away at the guards in a desperate effort to rush Blair House and get through to the President.

Truman was awakened by the shots and stepped to the window. The agents waved him back. In the fierce gun battle being waged below, White House Police Officer Leslie Coffelt was killed by a bullet from the gun of one of the invaders, and Officers Donald T. Birdzell and Joseph H. Downs were seriously wounded. A shot fired by one of our sharpshooters pierced the head of Torresola, and he fell dead at the front door of Blair House. Another bullet hit Collazo in the head as, in his endeavor to reach the President, he rushed up the Blair House steps. He toppled over, unconscious. If Collazo had been able to get through the front door of Blair House, he was doomed, as an agent armed with a machine gun was inside only ten feet from the door and he was prepared to mow him down.

Our Secret Service marksmanship program, and the perseverance of the agents in faithfully following the required practice on the pistol range, paid a tremendous dividend that day.

Collazo recovered and was convicted in Federal court in Washington, D.C., for the murder of Leslie Coffelt. Judge Alan Goldsborough imposed the sentence of death in the electric chair, which President Truman later commuted to life imprisonment. When the Judge imposed the death sentence, Collazo, true to the assassin type, jumped up and defiantly exclaimed that he was a martyr to his "cause":

I know the American government has got the power to kill me! But it can't kill the ideals I die for; I am not pleading for my life, I'm pleading for my cause. You'll never kill my ideals!

The President showed no great concern about this attempt on his life. He did, however, take a deep personal interest in the men who had so ably defended him, and saw to it that the widow of Officer Coffelt was provided with a pension and a job with the government. A posthumous medal was presented to her in memory of her husband's bravery.

With the war over and a new administration well in hand, I decided it was time to retire. When I stepped down as Chief, at the end of 1946, my superior, Secretary of the Treasury John Snyder, issued this statement to the press:

> Chief Wilson had a major role in the investigation of evasion of income taxes at Chicago which resulted in the conviction of Scarface Al Capone and other Public Enemies. He participated in the Lindbergh kidnapping case, helping to devise the strategy that resulted ultimately in the conviction of the slayer, Bruno Richard Hauptmann.
>
> During his tenure as Chief the annual losses to the public from counterfeiting dropped from figures in excess of a million dollars to around $30,000.
>
> Mr. Wilson's long and distinguished career with the department has contributed greatly to enforcement, not only of those laws within the jurisdiction of the Treasury, but to the cause of law enforcement generally.

Another kind of recognition in which I took great pride was when the International Association of Chiefs of Police elected me a life member at their 53rd Annual Conference in Mexico City in 1946. I knew my policeman father would have been proud, too, if he had been alive.

In the United States the local police and Federal Law-enforcement officers bring the government closer to the American people than any other public agencies, and if the present world tensions should result in another war, the citizen will see from his window, there on the street corner, at his post, on his beat, or in a squad car, the police officer who represents the majesty, the dignity, the might, and the power of the government. He stands there in peace as a protector of life, of right, and of property; and he will be there in time of war as the people's staunch defender.

Upon retirement, I had intended to take a long rest, get a

boat, and resume my long neglected activity in sailboat races. My plans to take it easy and have some fun sailing did not materialize. Within a week after I left the Secret Service, I was invited to lunch with David Lilienthal, who a few days earlier had been appointed by President Truman to be the first Chairman of the Atomic Energy Commission. He wanted to put me to work immediately.

The A.E.C. was just being organized. They had a position as Director of Security and had me tagged for the job. It was a high honor, a heavy responsibility, and a tremendously interesting assignment. I was intrigued with the possibilities and agreed to consider the appointment. Before making important decisions involving my future I always talk them over with my partner, Judith. So I told Chairman Lilienthal that I wished to have twenty-four hours to consider the appointment.

Judith said, "What—take another heavy responsibility and have to travel most of the time?" She also pointed out that I was tired from the high pressure of the war years and needed and deserved a long rest. The conference with Judith resulted in a compromise.

I advised Chairman Lilienthal that I could not accept his offer, but would accept a temporary assignment as Consultant on Security on a dollar-a-year basis so as to help him get the Security Division organized.

I visited the plants at Oak Ridge, Tennessee; Los Alamos, New Mexico; Hanford, Washington; and other Atomic Energy Commission installations; and made surveys and recommendations for the improvement of plant protection. I also recruited some of my friends from the Secret Service to work for the Atomic Energy Commission. We set up a complete program based on the surveys, and put it into operation. I am proud to report that, although there have been some breakthroughs in personnel, the Atomic Energy Commission has suffered no breakthroughs on plant security.

After eighteen months, which had seen the program go

into effect, I was considering my temporary assignment completed and was ready for that long-awaited rest, when I got a telephone call from Stuart Symington, then Secretary of the Air Force, urging me to come to the Pentagon for lunch to talk over a grave matter.

After lunch Secretary Symington said that his friend John Snyder, Secretary of the Treasury, had recommended me as just the man he needed to conduct a special assignment for the Air Force. At that time Symington was in a very embarrassing position, as a Congressional Committee had exposed corruption in the Air Force. The press and radio were featuring the story and the publicity was very unfavorable to the Air Force. An Air Force General, Benny Myers, was involved in illegal awards of contracts. Mr. Symington wished me to make an investigation and submit recommendations to prevent such corruption in the future, so I agreed to help him for three months on a dollar-a-year basis.

I couldn't complete my assignment in three months. But at the end of four months I was able to submit a lengthy report to Secretary Symington. My job was not to investigate the unfortunate General Myers, but to survey the case and set up recommendations for avoiding such scandalous behavior in the future.

Bribery and influence-peddling are, like assassination, always with us in government. Anyone who has the ear of the President or who touches the Federal purse strings is in a peculiarly vulnerable position. As a public servant, with a salary paid by taxpayers, the government and military personnel have an obligation to the public, which includes a right to know their private affairs and dealings. As Herbert Hoover once aptly commented, "People in public office should have glass pockets."

But pressures are always at work on them. For the naïve, they can build up almost without the official's becoming aware of his own complicity. First there is the friendly bottle of whiskey at Christmas. Perhaps next year it is a case.

Then a fur coat for one's wife. . . . The schemers work gradually and shrewdly, worming their way under a man's skin, breaking his morale by the inch, until he suddenly wakes up to find himself trapped.

My feeling in studying the Benny Myers bribery case was that the crux of the problem of keeping bribery down in government was not to expect inhuman virtue of our public servants but to protect them from the pressures of temptation.

Government contracts, I found, were awarded according to the size of the appropriation. The largest expenditures required the most number of people to pass on them. If a million dollars were involved, for instance, it would take the agreement of a committee to give a contract. But small sums could be awarded by individuals. With such temptation before them, it is small wonder that the weak are apt to fall.

First of all I recommended that no contract of any size should be awarded as the province of an individual but only by committee. Then I suggested regulations which would make the official less subject to bribery, such as, no hobnobbing with contractors after office hours. The government could also protect itself by requiring all officials to submit a net worth statement when they are hired, then check it regularly. A check should also be made on the manner of living of people awarding contracts. Bribes invariably show up in new houses, cars, furs, gambling, and race-track expenditures—since the money is accepted in the first place to be selfishly enjoyed. It is not difficult, as I learned in my income-tax case days, to spot the person who is living over his reputed income.

My assignment was over when I turned in my survey and recommendations to Secretary Symington. As to what, if any, of my suggestions were put into effect, I have no idea. General Myers was found guilty of accepting a bribe from Air Force contractors and sentenced to the penitentiary. He was also court-martialed and kicked out of the Air Force in disgrace.

F.D.R. was fortunate in that he had such a high degree of confidence in himself that he was able to select the most able and loyal men—and hold them around him. Truman did not have such good luck. Loyal to his old friends, he stuck by some of his appointees who were themselves the victims of influence-peddling. Eisenhower had his Sherman Adams; Johnson, his Jenkins (while it might be possible for a perverted person to fulfill a government job capably, the security problem lies in his liability to blackmail). President Kennedy, like F.D.R., had the capacity for surrounding himself with top-level, dedicated men, and there was no scandal attached to his brief administration.

15

America will never live down the Kennedy assassination any more than we have been able to live down the assassination of President Lincoln. What we must realize is that within any crowd there may be fanatics who are willing to sacrifice their own lives for whatever their causes may be. They are always there, capable of assassination. It is up to us to protect our Presidents, by every means at our command, from these people.

Next to our democratic dislike for highly organized protection, the main roadblock in the way of adequate security for our Presidents stems from their role as political as well as national leaders. The President is the head of state, but he is also a party leader and a candidate for re-election. To court voters, it is politically advisable for him to be "in touch" and accessible to the mass of the people.

How, we all asked ourselves, could we have allowed our President to be killed, when experienced agents and police were aware that an expert marksman, equipped with a rifle with a telescopic sight, could pick him off in a moving open auto?

It happened because our Presidents traditionally have

243

been willing to face that hazard. They face that hazard because they want to be re-elected or have someone from their party succeed them. They feel that the closer they can get to the voters, the better their chances. Hence, they willingly parade in front of millions of voters, and the more open the conveyance the better they like it.

Indeed, they not only persist in parading in open cars, inviting the sniper's bullets, but on occasion they mingle with crowds, shaking hands with anyone who appears to be friendly but who just as well might be another Czolgosz, concealing an assassin's pistol in a bandaged hand.

President Kennedy, himself, knew full well the risks he took. The morning of November 22nd, he had remarked to Kenneth O'Donnell, "If anybody really wanted to shoot the President of the United States it was not a very difficult job —all one had to do was to get on a high building someday with a telescopic rifle and there was nothing anybody could do to defend against such an attempt."

Kennedy was perfectly aware that his life was in jeopardy, that there was massive hate at work against him, just as there had been against F.D.R. The difference, I feel, lay in the men's attitude toward death. F.D.R. was very aware of death. Kennedy was not only very young, with a young man's illusions of immortality, but he had come near death in his war experiences and in his serious illnesses, and by this time, I think, he almost felt he led a charmed life. He didn't seem to take death very seriously. At least not seriously enough to listen to the advice of his security men over that of his political advisors.

The Texas trip of President Kennedy was a "political show." It was aimed to make friends and influence voters in a politically doubtful state. In that state there existed some extremely bitter opposition to his party and some intense hate against certain top members of his administration, especially in Dallas. That climate of hate was fomented by vitriolic publicity in some local papers and in various other ways. For instance, a full-page rabid outburst appeared in a Dallas newspaper on the morning of November 22nd, and a short time before that day a top member of the administration, Adlai Stevenson, was struck at and brazenly insulted in Dallas.

It was that deep-seated, devilish hate which poisoned the weak mind of Oswald and influenced him to purchase a rifle under an assumed name. The motive back of that purchase was a sinister one. The disordered mind of the owner of the rifle recognized an opportunity—the publicized political parade in Dallas—to spring into action. Such minds often make uncannily logical, vicious, and at the same time intelligent plans; and always try to execute them at an unexpected moment.

Hate was the *indirect cause* of the assassination of our President. The political parade, with President Kennedy in an open auto seeking to influence voters, presented the opportunity for the assassination, and it was the *direct* cause of the terrible tragedy in Dallas.

President Kennedy had requested that agents not ride on the platform at the rear of the Presidential car. Therefore, there was no agent close enough to him to act immediately— as the agent did who was riding with Vice-president Johnson —immediately upon the sound of the first bullet. Agent Rufus Youngblood covered the Vice-president with his own body, shoving him onto the floor of the car at the instant he heard the first shot. There was no agent close enough to the President to perform such immediate service for him. By the time Agent Clinton Hill had crawled aboard the Presidential car, from his position on the running board of the follow-up car, the second, and fatal, shot had been fired.

As long as our Presidents and their political strategists insist on such hazardous and unnecessary exposures to crackpots, to haters of our government and others anxious to assassinate our Presidents, additional ways should be developed and adopted to reduce this hazard.

It may be advisable to have helicopters slowly patrolling parade routes, manned by the best of sharpshooters, with their crews using binoculars to scan the occupants of windows, people in the crowds, and those on roof tops. Building managers along the parade route should be given instructions to have all windows closed and roofs cleared of spectators. On special occasions, when members of the armed forces are on duty along the parade route, they should not stand in the customary position facing the President, but should have their backs to him in order to face and detect potential assassins in the crowd and fight them off.

Because the Secret Service is still woefully short of manpower, consideration should be given to securing assistance from Federal law-enforcement units and Defense Department investigators located in areas scheduled for Presidential parades. They could assist Secret Service and local police in checking all buildings, hotels, grandstands, and stores along parade routes, and in contacting managers of buildings to keep them on the lookout for suspicious persons. The additional manpower thus provided would permit agents with binoculars to be stationed on buildings along the parade route, so as to keep the roofs clear and to observe all persons in windows or on balconies on the opposite side of the street.

Without a doubt, the best method to reduce the hazard of Presidential assassination in political parades drastically would be to have him ride in a bullet-proof auto. I am doubtful that any President would consent to this, but certainly some form of modified bullet-proof car might be used. I am sure an auto manufacturer or the Defense Department could build a shell of bullet-proof glass to protect the President on all sides but the front. He could still wave greetings to the voters and others, but a large part of the President's body would be protected from bullets. In an emergency, to protect him from the front, we could have a steel curtain in the floor of the auto which, upon the pressing of a button by a Secret Service agent, would spring up in front of the President.

I recommend the return to the old-fashioned running boards on autos carrying the President. Autos so equipped were used during the ten years I was Chief of the Secret Service. Such running boards would permit three agents to be stationed on each side of the auto during a parade, so as to protect the President and, if necessary, to stop bullets or deflect bombs intended to kill our President. Agents on running boards at Dallas might not have saved the President from the first bullet but might have saved him from the second one, which was fatal.

The White House should not announce that the President is to appear in a parade or at a theater, or banquet, or reception, or arrive at or depart from an airport a long period in advance. This allows conspirators or potential assassins to have plenty of time to "case the job" and lay plans to slaughter the President when he appears. It was the advance notice of the public appearance of Presidents Lincoln, Garfield, McKinley, and Kennedy which gave the assassins the opportunity to kill them. Withholding advance publicity may not be practical when the President is to attend a dinner to raise funds for the next election campaign, where the attendance is influenced by advance notice of his presence, but it would be practical when he is to attend a theater, visit an airport, appear at a mass meeting, or before some other large group. It would be especially helpful if no advance notice were given to any public appearance of the President. For instance, I was at a church service recently and nine hundred were in the congregation. They were surprised when President and Mrs. Johnson were ushered to a front pew. Because there was no notice in advance, no hater had an opportunity to plot to assassinate our President that day.

With the co-operation of the press and radio, all of President Roosevelt's arrivals and departures were kept secret during the war years, and I would advise the same procedure for Presidents in peacetime. President Kennedy's goings and comings, on the contrary, were always public knowledge.

I feel especially that there should never be a public announcement when a President arrives at or departs from an airport. No matter how intensive the advance security measures are, there is always the chance that some crank might develop diabolical plans, work out original methods, or obtain some new death-dealing weapon, and take advantage of an opportunity, when excited crowds are milling around, to murder our President.

In an address before the convention of the International Association of Chiefs of Police at Cleveland in 1942, I predicted that serious crimes would be committed in or with airplanes. Since privately-owned airplanes are not uncommon, it would even be possible to assassinate the President in the air.

Selection of parade routes away from high buildings and congested sections, such as I insisted upon in New York City in 1939 for the King and Queen of England, is another simple way of minimizing the risks.

Kennedy's assassin, Oswald, purchased his rifle with telescopic sight under an assumed name from a mail-order house. If a report of the sale had been made to the police and they had investigated his previous activities, Oswald probably would have been under observation on November 22nd, instead of in a high window on the parade route. Legislation should be passed to forbid or control the mail-order sale of rifles and other firearms to unauthorized persons. Over the counter, retail sales should also be controlled. Sales should not be made to minors or persons with criminal records. A record of all mail-order or retail sales should be promptly furnished to the chief of police or to the sheriff. Suspicious purchases should then be reported to the Secret Service.

Obviously our present Federal laws are defective, as there is no provision for Federal punishment of haters of government who kill or attempt to murder our Chief Executive.

Because no Federal crime had been committed, the Federal agencies stood helplessly by in Dallas as the local police committed their blunders.

With the assassination of President McKinley by Czolgosz fresh in mind, Judge Colt recommended, in 1902, that the killing of a President should be made a Federal crime. That recommendation has been made several times since then, and most recently in the report of the Warren Commission. After sixty-three years, it is high time that Congress followed this recommendation.

"There is no conceivable crime so atrocious as the senseless murder of the chosen ruler of a free people," was Judge Colt's statement at that time. He added: "Such crimes rise infinitely higher than crimes against the individual. They are a blot upon free institutions, a strain upon the flag. They lower the standing of our fine country, in the opinion of mankind."

This was wise counsel then and is even more so today, when a world, still poisoned with hate and distrust, leans very heavily upon the United States to solve its vital problems.

As the Warren Commission report indicates, the Secret Service needs more manpower, more physical equipment (especially electronic equipment in the Protective Research Section), and more money. I would add that, while in some branches of government it is wise to be specific about expenditures, an appropriation of the Secret Service should not have too many specifications about how the money should be spent. "Mr. Congressman" does not have the experience or know what must be done or what the best methods to pursue in Presidential protection are.

I also agree wholeheartedly that there should be better procedures for anticipating threats against the President. I always worked very hard to get the co-operation of local police departments and make them aware of their part in our national protection procedures. I think conferences among the Army, Air Force, and Navy Intelligence, the F.B.I., the C.I.A., and the Directors of police departments of our larger cities and the Secret Service could produce improved procedures. The Service should have more men out in the field who work closely with the local police and with the agents of the F.B.I. Not for some years has the so-called jealousy between the two agencies existed, but the very nature of their separate and complex machinery has kept them from co-operating to the fullest. I do think that with the criticism of the Warren Commission to spur them, they will in the future endeavor to work more nearly hand in hand.

Last, but perhaps most important, our Presidents must themselves recognize and avoid potential hazards, by parading in an open auto only on extremely exceptional and important occasions. On such occasions it would be appropriate for the President to wear a bulletproof vest and to have a steel helmet available for quick use in an emergency. The Presidential car should also be modified so that the agent in the front seat can put his body between the President and an assassin in seconds. I also feel, as I did about President Roosevelt, that the fewer occasions a President drives a car, the safer he is, although it's only human nature for any man who can drive to want to take the wheel once in a while.

Reports are that President Johnson is very co-operative with the Secret Service. He had an awful shock in Dallas and he's not going to forget it for the rest of his life. He learned, as those of us who work in security have always known, that the assassin is always with us. He always has been with us. And he always will be with us—till kingdom come.

It is the responsibility not only of the Secret Service but of all America to keep the assassin away from the President of the United States, the man who is the most powerful human influence for peace in the world today.

INDEX